Parental Custody after Separation or Divorce

Europäische Hochschulschriften Recht

European University Studies in Law

Publications Universitaires Européennes de Droit

Band/Volume 6224

Shuang Wang

Parental Custody after Separation or Divorce

A Comparison Between German and Chinese Law

PETER LANG

Bibliografische Information der Deutschen Nationalbibliothek
Die Deutsche Nationalbibliothek verzeichnet diese Publikation in der Deutschen Nationalbibliografie; detaillierte bibliografische Daten sind im Internet über http://dnb.d-nb.de abrufbar.

Library of Congress Cataloging in Publication Data
A CIP catalog record for this book has been applied for at the Library of Congress.

Zugl.: Passau, Univ., Diss.,2020

D739
ISSN 0531-7312
ISBN 978-3-631-83837-2 (Print)
E-ISBN 978-3-631-84202-7 (E-PDF)
E-ISBN 978-3-631-84203-4 (EPUB)
E-ISBN 978-3-631-84204-1 (MOBI)
DOI 10.3726/b17848

Peter Lang – Berlin · Bern · Bruxelles · New York · Oxford · Warszawa · Wien

This publication has been peer reviewed.

www.peterlang.com

This book is dedicated to my grandparents

Acknowledgements

There are several people to be particularly acknowledged here for their contribution in the completion of my dissertation in which all the cited literature, laws and regulations are before 30 September 2019.

First and foremost, I would like to thank my supervisor Prof. Dr. Wolfgang Hau who provided me the opportunity to pursue my doctoral study in Passau University. Without his guidance and encouragement, this thesis could not be completed. In addition, my gratitude goes to Prof. Dr. Dennis Solomon who is the second supervisor of my thesis and Prof. Dr. Nina Dethloff from University of Bonn who sent her works and articles in family law to me.

My thanks and appreciation go to all the other people who helped me in any respect during the completion of the dissertation, especially Prof. Dr. Florian Eichel who allowed the chance to co-lead the seminar in the winter semester 2016/2017, Ms. Sabine Cichon who is always kind, patient and helpful, and Mr. Andreas Bernrieder who generously provides help and shares knowledge with me.

Furthermore, I sincerely thank *Chinese Scholarship Council* for having funded my research work for two years. It is really hoped that this dissertation could slightly contribute to improvement of the legislation regarding parental custody after divorce or separation of parents and to promotion of rights of the children born out of wedlock in China.

Finally, I would like to show my eternal thankfulness to my parents Ms. Huaqin Zhang and Mr. Jiuda Wang for their unconditional love and support, and I thank my husband Mr. Longhui Shi who has made available his support in a number of ways.

Contents

List of Abbreviations

AmtsG	District Court (Amtsgericht)
Anm.	Comment (Anmerkung)
AnwBl.	Journal for Lawyers (Anwaltsblatt)
a.F	Older version (alte Fassung)
BayObL	Bavarian Supreme Court (Bayerisches Oberstes Landgericht)
BGB	German Civil Code (Bürgerliches Gesetzbuch)
BGBl.	Federal Law Gazette (Bundesgesetzblatt)
BGH	Federal Court of Justice (Bundesgerichtshof)
BGHZ	Official Collection of Civil Law Decisions of Federal Court of Justice (Entscheidungen des Bundesgerichtshofs in Zivilsachen)
BR	German Federal Council (Bundesrat)
BR-Drucks	Printed Documents of German Federal Council (Drucksachen des Deutschen Bundesrates)
BT	German Parliament (Bundestag)
BT-Drucks	Printed Documents of German Parliament (Drucksachen des Deutschen Bundestages)
BVerfG	German Federal Constitutional Court (Bundesverfassungsgericht)
BVerfGE	Official Collection of Decisions of German Federal Constitutional Court (Entscheidung des Bundesverfassungsgerichts)
BVerwG	German Federal Administrative Court (Bundesverwaltungsgericht)
bzw.	Or rather (beziehungsweise)
CRC	Convention on the Rights of the Child
DFGT	German Family Court Committee (Deutscher Familiengerichtstag)
DRiZ	German Judges' Journal (Deutsche Richterzeitung)
ECHR	European Convention on Human Rights (Europäische Menschenrechtskonvention)

ECtHR	European Court for Human Rights (Europäischer Gerichtshof für Menschenrechte)
EheRG	The First Act of Marriage and Family Law (Erstes Gesetz zur Reform des Ehe- und Familienrechts)
etc.	Et cetera
FamFG	Act on Proceedings Concerning Family Matters and Matters of Non-contentious Jurisdiction (Gesetz über das Verfahren in Familiensachen und Angelegenheiten der freiwilligen Gerichtsbarkeit)
FamRZ	Journal of Family Law (Zeitschrift für das gesamte Familienrecht)
f.	The following page (folgende Seite)
ff.	The following pages (fortfolgende Seiten)
FGG	Act on Matters of Non-contentious Jurisdiction (Gesetz über die Angelegenheiten der freiwilligen Gerichtsbarkeit)
FGG-ReformG	Reform Law of Act on Matters of Non-contentious Jurisdiction (Gesetz zur Reform des Verfahrens in Familiensachen und in den Angelegenheiten der freiwilligen Gerichtsbarkeit)
Fn.	Footnote (Fußnote)
FPR	Journal of Family, Partnership, Law (Zeitschrift Familien, Partnerschaft, Recht)
FuR	Journal of Family and Law (Familie und Recht)
GleichberG	Law of the Equal Rights Between Men and Women in the Field of Civil Law (Gesetz über die Gleichberechtigung von Mann und Frau auf dem Gebiet des bürgerlichen Rechts)
GG	German Basic Law (Grundgesetz)
GPGL 1987	General Principles of Chinese Civil Law (Allgemeine Prinzipien des chinesischen bürgerlichen Gesetzes)
GRGL 2017	General Rules of Chinese Civil Law (Allgemeine Vorschriften des chinesischen bürgerlichen Gesetzes)
JWG	Youth Welfare Law (Jugendwohlfahrtsgesetz)
JZ	Journal of Jurists (Juristenzeitung)

LG	Regional Court (Landgericht)
KindRG	Reform of Parents and Child Act (Gesetz zur Reform des Kindschaftsrechts)
KJHG	Law of Child and Youth Welfare (Kinder- und Jugendhilfegesetz)
KICK	Act of Further Development of Welfare of the Child and Youth (Gesetz zur Weiterentwicklung der Kinder- und Jugendhilfe)
KKG	Act of Cooperation and Information in Protection of the Child (Gesetz zur Kooperation und Information im Kinderschutz)
NeheSorgRG	Reform of Act of Parental Custody of the Unmarried Parents (Gesetz zur Reform der elterlichen Sorge nicht miteinander verheirateter Eltern)
NJW	New Juristic Weekly (Neue Juristische Wochenschrift)
NJW-RR.	Case Report in Civil Law of NJW (Neue Juristische Wochenschrift-Rechtsprechung Report Zivilrecht)
No.	Number
Nr.	Number (Nummer)
NZFam	New Journal for Family Law (Neue Zeitschrift für Familienrecht)
OLG	Higher Regional Court (Oberlandesgericht)
P.	Page(s)
PStG	Act on Civil Status (Personenstandsgesetz)
RGBl.	Imperial Law Gazette (Reichsgesetzblatt)
Rn.	Recital (Randnummer)
Rz.	Point (Randziffer)
S.	Page(s) (Seite(n))
SGB VIII	Book VIII of Code of Social Law (Sozialgesetzbuch VIII)
SorgRG	Reform of Parental Custody Act (Gesetz zur Neuregelung des Rechts der elterlichen Sorge)
StGB	German Criminal Law (Strafgesetzbuch)

STIKO	German Standing Vaccination Committee (Deutsche Ständige Impfkommission)
v.	of (von)
ZfJ	Journal of the Youth's Right and Welfare (Zeitschrift für Jugendrecht und Jugendwohlfahrt)
ZKJ	Journal of Parents-children Relationship and Youth's Welfare Law (Zeitschrift für Kindschaftsrecht und Jugendhilfe)
ZPO	German Code of Civil Procedure (Zivilprozessordnung)
ZRP	Journal of Legal Politics (Zeitschrift für Rechtspolitik)

1 Introduction

1.1 Research Background

The legal term 'parental custody' (elterliche Sorge[1]) in the German legal system, deriving from parental authority (elterliche Gewalt), describes the rights and obligations that parents have towards their children. Although it is presumed as a guiding principle that parents exercise parental custody jointly after separation or divorce, parental custody generally must be reallocated after separation or divorce, which might exert important influence upon the child. Therefore, it is of significance to study parental custody after separation or divorce which concerns mainly care of the person and property, determination of habitual residence and is closely related to contact right.

Different from the traditional legislation in family issues which focused on marriage and divorce, current legislation in Germany has come to highlight the relationship between parents and children (parentage),[2] which has been witnessed by legislative reforms carried out to revise rules on parental custody during the past half century. From the *Reform of Parental Custody Act* (*SorgRG*) in 1979, *Reform of Parents and Child Act* (*KindRG*) in 1998 to the *Reform of Act of Parental Custody of the Unmarried Parents* (*NeheSorgRG*) in 2013, focus of reforms has been shifted from equality between parents in the right to exercise parental custody to redistribution of parental custody following separation or divorce. In addition, influenced by the value of equality and freedom, diversity of living and family forms has been legally acknowledged[3], which poses challenge to the traditional kinship that used to be established by blood. Therefore, parental custody under multiple parenthood has also become an object of reform. However, although rights of the biological but not the legal father have been promoted by the *Law to Promote Rights of the Biological but not the Legal Father* in 2013, the corresponding rights of the child have been ignored by the legislature.

1 The German legal term 'elterliche Sorge' used to be translated into 'parental care' (*Gottwald/Schwab/Büttner*, Family & succession law in Germany, 2001, P. 79) and is now translated into 'parental responsibilities' (*Schwab/Gottwald/Lettmaier*, Family and succession law in Germany, 2017, P. 86 Rn. 191).

2 *Schwab*, Familie und Staat, FamRZ 2007, 1 (3).

3 *Dethloff*, Familienrecht in Europa - Quo vadis? NJW 1–2/2018, 23 (28).

In the Chinese legal system, rules on parental custody are mainly provided for in the *Marriage Law* which, as a specialised and separate law under guidance of the *General Rules of Civil Law* (hereinafter referred to as *GRCL 2017*), functions as the family law in Book 4 of the German Civil Code (hereinafter referred to as *BGB*). Parents are both legal guardians according to the *GRCL 2017* and legal custodians who keep on exercising parental custody after separation or divorce according to the *Marriage Law*. Compared with the historical legal development in the field of parental custody in Germany, there have been no significant reforms in China in the past few decades. Even in the draft of the Book of Family Law of the Chinese Civil Code (the 2nd review on 25 June 2019), there are seldom reform provisions on parental custody.

It is understandable that there are significant differences between the Chinese and German law on parental custody after separation or divorce due to different history, culture and political systems. However, what is certain is that legislatures of these two states need to respond to changes brought about by social, technical and medical developments to traditional family structures and family law systems.[4] Therefore, the thesis, after a comprehensive study of the historical legal development and current applicable rules on parental custody after separation or divorce, intends to explore the potential legal reforms in this field for the two legal systems.

1.2 Current Research Status

Each important legal reform on parental custody was pushed forward by not only the research of scholars but also court decisions in judicial practice. Even before the legal term 'parental authority' was replaced by 'parental custody', there had been an introduction to the distribution of parental authority in the event of dissolution of marriage or permanent separation of parents in 'Die Verteilung der elterlichen Gewalt bei Auflösung der Elternehe und bei dauerndem Getrenntleben' of *Treitz* in 1974. Thereafter, *Horst* in 'Gemeinsames Sorgerecht nach Scheidung' and *Ballof* in 'Alleinerziehung und gemeinsame elterliche Sorge nach Trennung und Scheidung' argued for joint parental custody after divorce or separation, which along with decisions of *BVerfG* promoted the *KindRG* in 1998.

4 *Helms*, Rechtliche, biologische und soziale Elternschaft - Herausforderungen durch neue Familienformen, NJW-Beil 2016, 49; *Brokamp*, Die Verrechtlichung der Eltern-Kind-Beziehung in hundert Jahren *BGB*, P. 257; *Rummel*, Die Freiheit, die Reform des Kindschaftsrechts und das 'ganz normale Chaos der Liebe', ZfJ 1997, 202 (208).

Following decisions of the *ECtHR* in 2009 and of the *BVerfG* in 2010 on the right of the unmarried father to joint parental custody, works and essays on parental custody of the child born out of wedlock emerged in large numbers. For instance, 'Die Entwicklung des Sorgerechts der Mütter nichtehelichen Kinder in Deutschland vom Inkrafttreten des *BGB* bis heute' of *Berg* in 2012[5], '*Reformbedarf im nichtehelichen Eltern-Kind-Verhältnis*' of *Coster-Waltjen*, *Lipp* and *Schumann* in 2012[6] and 'Gleichberechtigung und Sorgerecht' of *Rist* in 2012[7]. After the *NeheSorgRG* came into force in 2013, *Heiß* and *Castellanos* present joint parental custody and the best interests of the child under this new law in their book '*Gemeinsame Sorge und Kindeswohl nach neuem Recht*'[8]. Despite great breakthrough in legislation on transfer of sole parental custody to joint parental custody to a child born out of wedlock, the *NeheSorgRG* was also criticised for the description in § 1626a II 2 *BGB* which might lead to negative evaluation criterion of the best interests of the child and the corresponding summary procedure according to § 155a *FamFG*.[9]

In the past five years, focus of research has moved to the switching model (hereinafter referred to as Wechselmodell) which, as an alternative caring model, is much more often practised now than before and to the rights of the biological but not the legal father which have been strengthened by the *Law to Promote Rights of the biological but not the legal Father* in 2013. In the book '*Wechselmodell: Psychologie-Recht-Praxis*',[10] *Sünderhauf* gives an introduction on the definition and application requirements of this new model to exercise parental custody and analyses a number of cases where the Wechselmodell was applied. Furthermore, she provides a suggestion on how to modify the related provisions.

---

5 *Berg*, Die Entwicklung des Sorgerechts der Mütter nichtehelicher Kinder in Deutschland vom Inkrafttreten des *BGB* bis heute 2012, Dekan Fachbereich Rechtspflege, 2012, S. 46–48.

6 *Coester-Waltjen, Lipp, Schumann*, Reformbedarf im nichtehelichen Eltern-Kind-Verhältnis, 10. Göttinger Workshop zum Familienrecht 2011, Universitätsverlag Göttingen 2012.

7 *Rist*, Gleichberechtigung und Sorgerecht - Die Stärkung der Rechte der Väter uneheliche Kinder durch den Entwurf zur Reform des Sorgerechts nicht miteinander verheirateter Eltern, in Jura Studium & Examen, Ausgabe 4, 2012.

8 *Heiß/Castellanos*, Gemeinsame Sorge und Kindeswohl nach neuem Recht, 1. Auflage, Nomos 2013.

9 In citation of the legal provisions in German law, '§', 'Roman numerals' and 'Arabic numerals' refer to 'section', 'subsection' and 'item', respectively.

10 *Sünderhauf*, Springer VS, Wiesbaden 2013.

As to the rights of the biological but not the legal father, *Plettenberg* calls for a double legal fatherhood in her work 'Vater Vater Mutter Kind' in 2016[11], which has brought us to think about the feasibility of expanding of legal paternity and the problems associated with it.

Amongst all the research results on parental custody, there are several works which are from a perspective of legal comparison, for instance, 'Das gemeinsame Sorgerecht nach Scheidung in Kalifornien und Deutschland' of *Pätzhorn* in 2000[12] and 'Das Personensorgerecht für Kinder nicht verheirateter Eltern in Deutschland und Italien' of *Feßmann* in 2000[13] and 'Das taiwanesische Sorgerecht der Eltern nach der Ehescheidung im Vergleich mit dem deutschen Recht' of *Won*[14]. Therefore, this thesis intends to make a short comparison on parental custody after separation or divorce between German and Chinese law to fill a research loophole in comparative legal study.

1.3 Structure of the Thesis

The first part (from Chapters two to six) introduces the legal status concerning parental custody after separation or divorce in Germany by first presenting the historical legal development and actual applicable laws in the second chapter. The following third chapter deals with certain basic legal terms related to parental custody, including care of person, joint and sole parental custody, the principle of the best interests of the child, etc. The fourth and fifth chapters as key parts of the thesis illustrate, respectively, how parental custody towards the children born in wedlock and out of wedlock is exercised after separation or divorce. In these two chapters, not only the new rules but also the case-law has been studied. As the child born in wedlock and out of wedlock enjoy the same parental custody, the fifth chapter only focuses on certain aspects which exist exclusively for the child born out of wedlock, for instance transfer from sole parental custody to joint parental custody according to § 1626a *BGB* and rights of the biological but not the legal father. The sixth chapter studies roles of public

11 *Plettenberg*, Vater, Vater, Mutter, Kind - Ein Plädoyer für die rechtliche Mehrvaterschaft, Mohr Siebeck Verlag, Tübingen 2016.

12 *Pätzhorn*, Das gemeinsame Sorgerecht der Eltern nach Scheidung in Kalifornien und Deutschland Ein Rechtsvergleich, EMF Bürotechnik GmbH, 2000.

13 *Feßmann*, Das Personensorgerecht für Kinder nicht verheirateter Eltern in Deutschland und Italien, Dissertation, Regensburg 2000.

14 *Won*, Das taiwanesische Sorgerecht der Eltern nach der Ehescheidung im Vergleich mit dem deutschen Recht, Köln 2001.

authorities, inter alia the family court and the *Youth Welfare Office*, in handling issues of parental custody after separation or divorce. The second part on parental custody after separation or divorce in Chinese law also begins with the research on historical development of legal rules, followed by an analysis of how parental custody is exercised according to applicable rules. At the end of this thesis, the author first tries to make a short comparison between the Chinese and German legal system in parental custody and then explores relevant legal reform in Germany and presents legal advice on how to promote legislation on parental custody after separation or divorce in China.

2 Historical Development of the Legal Concept 'Parental Custody'

2.1 Before the Implementation of the *BGB*

2.1.1 Ancient Roman Law (753 B.C.-A.D. 476)

As in modern times, the cornerstone of ancient Roman society was the family (*familia*), a closely knit unit of children and wife under the father's authority (*pater familias*). Free men in Roman society can be divided into two types according to their positions as member of a family group. Those subordinated to paternal power or authority (*patria potestas*[15]) were called *alieni iuris*, while those free from paternal authority were called *sui iuris*.[16] The oldest male member of the family enjoyed the most rights a Roman citizen could possess.[17] Although generally determined by kinship, *patria potestas* over children was not always due to relationship by blood, but the authority was acquired by means of adoption.[18]

Originally in the periods of the Roman Kingdom and Roman Republic, the power of the *pater familias* over his children was theoretically almost unlimited.[19] The ancient Roman Republic laws, influenced by the concept of *patria potestas*, granted the father the right to dispose any rights or property of his children. The father had control of their life and death (*ius vitae necisque*), including the right to beat them or sell them into slavery.[20] Furthermore, he could marry off or forbid the marriage or divorce of his children, as well as give them away

15 Originally, the paternal authority that *pater familias* had towards both his children and wife were called *manus*. Later, *manus* was only used for the paternal authority that *pater familias* had to his wife, while *patria potestas* referred to the paternal authority for the children and grandchildren. See *Meder*, Rechtsgeschichte, P. 41.

16 *Manthe*, Geschichte des römischen Rechts, P. 29; *Frier, McGinn*, A Casebook on Roman Family Law, P. 19; *Mousourakis*, Roman law and the origins of the civil law traditions, P. 88–89.

17 Besides, the paterfamilias also had authority over his wife if she had been married to him by virtue of a *cum manu* marriage, his grandchildren, slaves or other individuals who are dependent on him.

18 *Manthe*, Geschichte des römischen Rechts, P. 48; *Frier, McGinn*, A Casebook on Roman Family Law, P. 191.

19 *Mousourakis*, Roman law and the origins of the civil law traditions, P. 89.

20 *Manthe*, Geschichte des römischen Rechts, P. 28; *Borkowski*, Textbook on Roman Law, P. 115.

for adoption or emancipate them.[21] However, the paternal authority should not violate the social morals, which had priority over the legal regulations.[22]

As Roman society evolved over the course of time, the power of the *pater familias* over his dependents considerably decreased. The *pater familias* was not allowed to kill his dependents, sell them as slaves or dispose of them according to his own will.[23] Instead, the head of a family became responsible for his dependents. The obligations included support to his children and provision of a bridal dowry (*dos*) when the daughter entered marriage.[24]

The *patria potestas* came to an end in many ways, such as upon death of the *pater familias*, or when a *capitis deminutio* (for instance, loss of citizenship) changed his status. Furthermore, the *pater familias* lost control over a daughter immediately falling under her husband's authority when she entered marriage *cum manu*. The *patria potestas* also terminated when the *pater familias* gave his child to another for adoption (*in adoptione*) or when he released such child from his paternal power by means of emancipation (*emancipatio*).[25]

2.1.2 From the Early Modern Era to the End of 19th Century

The concept of *patria potestas* in the ancient Rome was absorbed by the Common Law (*ius commune*)[26] which also emphasised paternal authority and patriarchal structure of the family.[27] However, a significant change in the Modern Era is that a child could get rid of the paternal authority by establishing its own household.[28]

During the Early Modern Era[29], a child should show enough obedience to its father. According to the *Schwabenspiegel* (around the year 1275), the father had the right to sell their children in case of emergency.[30] In addition, he could decide when his children were freed from the paternal authority by means of

21 *Meder*, Rechtsgeschichte, P. 42.

22 *Manthe*, Geschichte des römischen Rechts, P. 14; *Meder*, Rechtsgeschichte, P. 42.

23 *Kaser, Knütel, Lohsser*, Römisches Privatrecht, P. 365.

24 *Mousourakis*, Roman law and the origins of the civil law traditions, P. 102–104.

25 *Manthe*, Geschichte des römischen Rechts, P. 48; *Honsell*, Römisches Recht, P. 183–184.

26 The *ius commune* is commonly thought of as a combination of canon law and Roman law which formed the basis of a common system of legal thought in Western Europe from the rediscovery and reception of Justinian's Digest in the 12th and 13th centuries.

27 *Schwab*, Familienrecht, P. 278 Rn. 635.

28 *Manthe*, Geschichte des römischen Rechts, P. 100.

29 It usually refers to the period from the Late Middle Ages (middle of 13th century to end of 15th century) to the end of 18th century in the European history.

30 *Muscheler*, Familienrecht, P. 315 Rn. 509.

entering into marriage and establishing their own households.[31] If the child did not comply with the rules stipulated by the state or the church, the *pater familias* should take liability. The state had control to the education of children received at home, especially the education related to religion.

In the Age of Enlightenment (A.D. 1650-A.D. 1700), duty of the parents to care for the child, replacing the exclusive and absolute rights over the child, emerged as the fundament principle of the relationship between parents and children. In addition, human rights of the child were emphasised. Therefore, rights of parents arising out of parental authority should be exercised to help the child to become an independent person.[32] The child could even file a lawsuit against its parents provided that competent state authorities granted approval, which was regulated in the *General Law of Prussian States* (*Allgemeines Landrecht für die Preußischen Staaten*) of the year 1794.[33]

It was not until the 19th century that the children having reached the age of majority could be freed from the parental authority automatically and without the consent of their fathers, which was provided in the *French Civil Code* of 1804 and the *BGB* of 1900[34]. In spite of the positive change in the child-parent relationship, the legislation related to parental custody in this period was greatly influenced by restoration of the traditional thoughts on the family, under which the family as an intimate unit consisted of family members should be free from legal conflicts and state control. In addition, the authority of the husband and father which was crucial for the integrity and coherence of the whole family should not be challenged.[35]

2.2 Milestone Reforms to the Laws on Parental Custody Since the *BGB* of 1900

Reform of laws in the field of family law, in particular on the matter 'parental custody' since the implementation of the *BGB* of 1900, has been influenced by the rise of feminism demanding equality between mothers and fathers on exercise of parental custody, awareness of personality development of the child and

31 *Schwab*, Familienrecht, P. 278 Rn. 635.

32 *Muscheler*, Familienrecht, P. 316 Rn. 509; *Schwab*, Familienrecht, P. 279 Rn. 637.

33 *Schwab*, Familienrecht, P. 279 Rn. 637.

34 Originally, both of them chose the age of twenty-one as the age of majority at the beginning, but in 1975 the *BGB* adopted eighteen as the age of majority.

35 *Schwab*, Familienrecht, P. 280 Rn. 639.

promotion of its legal status.[36] In addition, a fundamental shift in understanding of the parent-child relationship[37] has also witnessed the historical legal development on parental custody. Furthermore, evolution of legislation on parental custody is characterised by intervention of state authorities which fulfil their constitutional mission from Article 6 II 2 *GG*.

It is only from the year of 1957 that the Book 4 of the *BGB* has been fundamentally modified in the Federal Republic of Germany.[38] A great many reforms on parental custody have been further conducted, the most important ones of which are introduced as follows:

2.2.1 The *BGB* of 1900

The *BGB* of 1900 tried to find a balance between the patriarchal and more individualised family structure, but male and paternal authority still dominated. The term 'parental authority' used in the *BGB* of 1900 was derived from the *patria potestas* in the Roman law.[39]

According to the *BGB* of 1900, the minor child under the age of 21 should be subject to parental authority (§ 1626 a.F *BGB* of 1900[40]). Generally, it was the father who exercised parental authority under which he had the right and obligation to care for the person and property of the child (§ 1627 a.F *BGB* of 1900), represented the child (§ 1630 a.F *BGB* of 1900) and had the right to use the property of the child (§ 1649 a.F *BGB* of 1900), while the mother only had right and obligation to care for the person of the child during the marriage (§ 1634 a.F *BGB* of 1900). However, the mother could exercise parental authority if the father was unable or prevented from exercising it because of his death or own fault (§§ 1684 and 1685 a.F *BGB* of 1900).[41]

§ 1635 a.F *BGB* of 1900 specified clearly how parental authority was reallocated between parents after divorce. Accordingly, the parent whose fault had solely led to the divorce should be deprived of the right to parental authority.

---

36 *Boele-Woelki/Ferrand/González Beilfuss*, Principles of European family law regarding parental responsibilities, P. 13.

37 *Harris-Short, Miles, Rob*, Family Law, P. 577.

38 *Dethloff*, Familienrecht, § 1 Rn. 39.

39 *Peschel-Gutzeit*, Die geschichtliche Entwicklung der Vaterstellung im deutschen Recht seit 1900, FPR 2005, 167.

40 § 1626 a.F *BGB* of 1900: The child is under parental authority as long as it is minor (Das Kind steht, solange es minderjährig ist, unter elterlicher Gewalt).

41 § 1684 a.F, § 1685 a.F, RGBl 1896, 195.

However, if both parents should be blamed for the divorce, the gender and the age of their joint children should play the key role in redistribution of the parental custody (§ 1635 II a.F *BGB* of 1900).[42]

Although gaining a good reputation for its innovation and contribution to the legislation in civil aspects all over the world, the *BGB* of 1900 retained the father's patriarchal position in a family and did not try to eliminate the discrimination to the mother who was unequally treated on the matter of parental authority.

2.2.2 Law of the Equal Rights Between Men and Women

The *Law of the Equal Rights Between Men and Women in the Field of Civil Law*[43] which came into force on 1 July 1958 aimed at transferring the fundamental right per Article 3 II[44] of the *German Basic Law* (hereinafter also referred to as *GG*) to the civil law, especially to the family law. Compared with § 1627 of the *BGB* of 1900, it was emphasised that not only the father but also the mother should be entitled to parental authority (§ 1626 I a.F *BGB*). Although parents were required to reach an agreement in exercising parental authority to ensure the best interests of the child, it at the same time provided for that the father retained the right to make the final decision if a mutual consent was not in sight after opinions of the mother being taken into consideration (§ 1628 I a.F *BGB*). However, the right of the father to make a final decision was considered to be against the *GG* and therefore was declared void by the *BVerfG* one year after the implementation of this law.[45]

Furthermore, amendment was made in this law to allocation of parental authority after divorce. According to § 74 IV of *Marriage Act* in 1946[46], if divorce was caused solely or mainly by one parent's fault, she or he would be generally deprived of the right to exercise parental custody. The *Law of Equal Rights*

42 § 1635 II a.F *BGB* of 1900: if both parents should be blamed for the divorce, the mother has the parental authority over the daughters and also the sons under the age of 6 while the father has the parental authority over sons older than six years.

43 BGBl. I 1957, 609: *Gesetz über die Gleichberechtigung von Mann und Frau auf dem Gebiet des bürgerlichen Rechts* (short for *GleichberG*).

44 Article 3 II *GG*: Men and women shall have equal rights. The state shall promote the actual implementation of equal rights for women and men and take steps to eliminate disadvantages that now exist.

45 *BVerfG*, Urteil v. 29.7.1959 -1 BvR 205/58 -, juris Rn. 26 = *BVerfGE* 10, 59 = NJW 1959, 1483.

46 The *Marriage Act* (*Ehegesetz*) came into force on 1 March 1946.

Between Men and Women in the Field of Civil Law considered the parent whose fault had solely led to the divorce not suitable to take care of the child, unless significant circumstances showed that the child should not be put under custody of the other parent who was not to be blamed for the divorce (§ 1626 III 2 a.F *BGB*).[47] However, if neither of the parents led to the divorce, the child should be cared for by the parent who could better guarantee the best interests of the child.

2.2.3 First Reform Law on Marriage and Family of 14 June 1976

One of the most important contributions of the *First Reform Law on Marriage and Family*[48] effective on 1 July 1977 is the adoption of the principle of disruption as a criterion to grant divorce (§ 1565 I *BGB*). According to this Act, the court should decide *ex officio* on the matter with respect to parental custody of the minor child in divorce proceedings (§ 623 I 1 and § 621 I 1 a.F *ZPO* of 1977).[49] However, parents who lived separately not merely temporarily should apply to the family court for the decision concerning exercise of parental custody if they could not agree on it (§ 1672 a.F *BGB*).[50] In case of divorce, the court should determine which parent was entitled to parental authority (§ 1671 I a.F *BGB*) which could generally be transferred to only one parent (§ 1671 IV a.F *BGB*). Agreement made by parents on the parental custody after divorce could be amended by the court if it was necessary for the best interests of the child (§ 1671 II and III a.F *BGB*).[51]

2.2.4 Reform of Parental Custody Act of 18 July 1979

In the *Reform of Parental Custody Act*[52] which was promulgated on 18 July 1979, it was emphasised that to care for the child was not only a right, but also an obligation for the parents (§ 1626 I 1 a.F *BGB*).[53] To adapt this new concept, the terminology 'parental authority' (Elterliche Gewalt) indicating that the child

---

47 *Balloff*, Alleinerziehung und gemeinsame elterliche Sorge nach Trennung und Scheidung - Eine theoretische und empirische Vergleichsstudie, P. 194.

48 BGBl. I 1976, 1421: *Erstes Gesetz zur Reform des Ehe- und Familienrechts* (short for 1. *EheRG*).

49 *MüKo/Hinz* (1992), § 1671 Rn. 6.

50 BGBl. I 1976, 1432.

51 Ibid.

52 BGBl. I 1979, 1061: *Gesetz zur Neuregelung des Rechts der elterlichen Sorge* (short for *SorgRG*).

53 Ibid: the father and the mother have the right and the obligation to care for the child.

should be subordinated to the parents was changed to 'parental custody' (Elterliche Sorge). Furthermore, right of the father to make the final decision on the matters related to parental custody was removed. Thereby the absolute equality between mothers and fathers to exercise joint parental custody was finally realised. If parents could not agree on matters of parental custody which were significant for the child, the family court could upon application of either parent transfer the power to make the decision to one parent if it was consistent to the best interests of the child (§ 1628 I a.F *BGB*).[54]

However, joint parental custody after divorce was still not favoured by legislature having insisted that that collapse of marriage[55] should inevitably lead to a judicial arrangement of parental custody[56] in which one parent was awarded the sole parental custody (§ 1671 I a.F *BGB*)[57] so that more conflicts between parents on parental custody would be avoided.[58]

2.2.5 Reform of Parents and Child Act of 1 July 1998

2.2.5.1 Background of the Reform

Although it was already expressed by experts in legislative hearing of the *Reform of Parental Custody Act* that joint parental custody after divorce should be legally acknowledged on the condition that both parents were capable and willing to care for the child who was emotionally equally connected to both of the parents,[59] legal presumption of the sole parental custody after divorce still dominated (§ 1671 IV 1 a.F *BGB* from 1979 to 1998).[60] The exclusion of joint parental custody was criticised not only by scholars[61] but also some district courts[62]. However, it was not until 3 November 1982 that the *BVerfG* declared that § 1671

54 BGBl. I 1979, 1061.

55 *BT-Drucks.* 8/2788, 61.

56 *BT-Drucks.* 8/2788, 40.

57 BGBl. I 1979, 1061.

58 *BT-Drucks.* 8/2788, 41.

59 *Deutscher Bundestag*, Zur Sache: Themen parlamentarischer Beratung, 1/78, Elterliches Sorgerecht, Bonn 1978.

60 § 1671 IV 1 a.F from 1979 to 1998: the parental custody can only be transferred to one parent.

61 *Luthin*, Gemeinsames Sorgerecht nach Scheidung, S. 23; *Schwab*, Handbuch des Scheidungsrechts, 1977, Rn. 187.

62 *LG Mannheim*, Beschluss v. 11.12.1970 - 4 b T 15/70, FamRZ 1971, 185; *LG Wiesbaden*, Beschluss v. 8.9.1976 - 4 T 173/76 -, juris Rn. 18 = FamRZ 1977, 60.

IV 1 a.F *BGB*, which excluded joint parental custody after separation or divorce of parents, violated the constitutional right of parents in Article 6 II 1 *GG* if they were willing and capable to exercise parental custody jointly, which was also in the best interests of the child.[63] Unlike the lawmakers of 1979, who believed a family collapsed with divorce of parents[64], the *BVerfG* distinguished between marriage and family and insisted that the joint responsibilities of both parents after divorce should continue.

Despite this decision of the *BVerfG*, the joint parental custody was still not accepted legislatively with the explanation from the *Ministry of Justice* that the authority could not supervise the exercise or change of the joint parental custody, and only the sole parental custody could guarantee the child a stable living environment after divorce of parents; and the parents could raise the child by concluding a mutual agreement, which seemed to be the same as exercising parental custody jointly.[65]

Moreover, it was also frequently criticised that § 1634 a.F in *Reform of Parental Custody Act* focused only on the right of the parent who was not entitled to parental custody to request contact with the child, while interests of the child had been ignored.[66]

In face of the critics from all sides[67], further reform was inevitably required, which lead to entry into force of *Reform of Parents and Children Act* on 1 July 1998.

---

63 *BVerfG*, Urteil v. 3.11.1982 - 1 BvL 25/80, 1 BvL 38/80, 1 BvL 40/80, 1 BvL 12/81 -, juris Rn. 19 = *BVerfGE* 61, 358 = FamRZ 1982, 1179 = NJW 1983, 101.

64 *Kirsten-Pia*, Das Recht der elterlichen Sorge nach Trennung und Scheidung, Luchterhand 1993, P. 70; *Eckert-Schirmer*, Gemeinsames Sorgerecht nach Scheidung: Leitbild oder soziale Realität? FuR 1996, P. 206.

65 *BVerfG*, Urteil v. 3.11.1982 - 1 BvL 25/80, 1 BvL 38/80, 1 BvL 40/80, 1 BvL 12/81 -, juris Rn. 41 = *BVerfGE* 61, 358 = FamRZ 1982, 1179 = NJW 1983, 101.

66 *BT-Drucks.* 13/4899, 68 ff.

67 *Luthin*, Gemeinsames Sorgerecht nach der Scheidung, 1987, P. 65; *OLG Hamburg*, Beschluss v. 13.8.1985 - 12 UF 8/85 S, FamRZ 1985, 1284; *OLG Karlsruhe*, Beschluss v. 8.10.1986 - 2 UF 40/86, FamRZ 1987, 89; *Balloff*, Alleinerziehung und gemeinsame elterliche Sorge nach Trennung und Scheidung - Eine theoretische und empirische Vergleichsstudie (Teil A). P. 295.

2.2.5.2 *Main Content of the Reform*

In the *Reform of Parents and Child Act*[68], both the rights of the child and the best interests of the child have been promoted. Not only the legal term 'illegitimate child' but also provisions indicating discrimination between the child born in wedlock and out of wedlock were eliminated by this reform.[69] However, the most significant change in the field of parental custody brought by this Act is that joint parental custody after separation and divorce of the parents has been legally acknowledged. The lawmakers in 1979 insisted the child whose parents got married should only live with one parent[70], while the lawmakers in 1998 proposed joint parental custody as a general rule for the child after the divorce of the parents[71], which had already been affirmed in the decision made by the *BVerfG* on 3 November 1982.[72] The reason why it took such a long time to legalise joint parental custody might lie in the control of growing divorce rate.[73] Since the effectiveness of this Act, the family court shall not make decisions on the matters regarding parental custody in divorce cases *ex officio*, unless one of the parents submits such an application.

The Act also enabled the unmarried father to have access to parental custody towards the child born out of wedlock on the condition that the mother who had not got married granted the consent (§ 1672 a.F *BGB*). Concerning the right of contact, the Act acknowledged the right of the child to have contact to either of the parents (§ 1684 I 1 *BGB*). In addition, it emphasised that it is no more only the right, but also an obligation of the parents to have contact with their child (§ 1684 I 2 *BGB*).

---

68 BGBl. I 1998, 2942: *Das Gesetz zur Reform des Kindschaftsrechts* (Kindschaftsrechtsreformgesetz, short for *KindRG*).

69 *BT-Drucks.* 13/4899, 1.

70 *BT-Drucks.* 8/2788, 40.

71 *BT-Drucks.* 8/2788, 61.

72 *BVerfG*, Urteil v. 3.11.1982 - 1 BvL 25/80, 1 BvL 38/80, 1 BvL 40/80, 1 BvL 12/81 -, juris Rn. 30 = *BVerfGE* 61, 358 = FamRZ 1982, 1179 = NJW 1983, 101.

73 *Kirsten-Pia*, Das Recht der elterlichen Sorge nach Trennung und Scheidung, P. 73.

2.2.6 Reform of Act of Parental Custody of the Unmarried Parents of 19 May 2013

2.2.6.1 Background of the Reform

As the number of children born out of wedlock increased[74], more disputes over child care between the unmarried parents arose, among which there were a number of cases where the father who did not marry the mother but lived together with her and the joint child for a long time claimed the joint parental custody after the separation with the mother. However, such claims were generally dismissed by the court if the mother did not consent to the application of the father according to § 1626a II a.F *BGB*. However, deprivation of the right of the father to care for the child with whom he had lived together for a long period and could get along very well might be detrimental to the best interests of the child who had established a social family connection with the father. Although the *BVerfG* made a judgement on 29 January 2003[75] where the sole parental custody of the mother after the separation or divorce was found in accordance to the *GG* and did not injure the right to respect for the family life of fathers whose children were born out of wedlock, it further noted that the legislature should keep the development of legal practice under observation and be obliged to revise the legislation to provide fathers with the adequate possibility of obtaining the right to exercise parental custody.

In addition, the decision of the *European Court of Human Rights* (hereinafter referred to as *ECtHR*) on 3 December 2009[76] pushed the reform of the

74 See statistic in Appendix 3.1.

75 *BVerfG*, Urteil v. 29.01.2003 - 1 BvL 20/99, juris Rn. 47: the *BVerfG* found that § 1626a *BGB* was unconstitutional only because it lacked a transitional period for unmarried couples with children who were unable to make a joint declaration before *KindRG* entered into force in July 1998. In order to resolve the above-mentioned constitutional flaws, the German legislature introduced Article 224 (2) (a) of the *Introductory Act to the Civil Code* (*Einführungsgesetz in das Bürgerliche Gesetzbuch*) on 31 December 2003, according to which a court may substitute the mother' s consent to joint parental custody if the unmarried couple have a child born out of wedlock, have lived together with the child and were separated before 1 July 1998, provided that joint parental custody would serve the best interests of the child.

76 *ECtHR*, Case of Zaunegger v. Germany, Judgement on 3 March 2010, Application no. 22028/04.

rules on parental custody of the children born out of wedlock in Germany.[77] It was criticised by the *ECtHR* that the application of the father of a child born out of wedlock for joint parental custody without consent of the mother should not be unexceptionally dismissed by the court and the joint parental custody towards the child born out of wedlock with the biological father against the will of the mother might not be detrimental to the best interests of the child. Finally, *BVerfG* declared in its decision on 21 July 2010 that §§ 1626a, 1672 I a.F *BGB* violated the *GG*.[78] Afterwards, more and more scholars and practitioners called for the reform because the existing laws could not offer an optimal solution to the increasing controversies on parental custody of the child born out of wedlock.[79]

2.2.6.2 Main Content of the Reform

The *Reform of Act of Parental Custody of the Unmarried Parents*[80] has made amendments not only to substantive law but also to procedural law.[81] Since the entry into force of this Act, another door has been opened for parents to have contact to the joint parental custody for their children born out of wedlock. They can, besides by concluding a marriage or submitting a declaration for joint parental custody, apply to the family court for the transfer of partial or whole parental custody (§ 1626a I 3 *BGB*). In addition, according to § 1671 II *BGB*, the father can apply to the family court for the transfer of partial or whole parental custody to him alone if the mother is entitled to the sole parental custody in § 1626a III *BGB*. When deciding such a transfer, the court will not take objection of the mother as the most crucial element into consideration, but only decide according to the best interests of the child. In the aspect of procedure law, this reform tried to facilitate the transfer of the joint parental custody to an

---

77 *Huber/Antomo*, Die Neuregelung der elterlichen Sorge nicht miteinander verheirateter Eltern, FamRZ 2012, 1257 (1258); *Raumer*, Wozu braucht man Deutschland einen *EGMR* - wenn es ein *BVerfG* hat? AnwBl. 2011, 195–198.

78 *BVerfG*, Beschluss v. 21.7.2010 - 1 BvR 420/09 -, juris Rn. 46 = *BVerfGE* 127, 132 = NJW 2010, 3008 = FamRZ 2010, 1403 = FPR 2010, 465.

79 *Lambrecht*, Neuregelung der Sorge für nicht verheiratete Eltern, DRiZ 2010, 318; *Altrogge*, Diskriminierung eines nichtehelichen Vaters mangels gesetzlicher Regelung zur gerichtlichen Prüfung eines gemeinsamen Sorgerechts? FamFR 2010, 73 ff.

80 BGBl. I 2013, 795: *Gesetz zur Reform der elterlichen Sorge nicht miteinander verheirateter Eltern.*

81 The main changes are shown in § 1626a I 3, § 1671 II *BGB* and § 155a of Act on Proceedings Concerning Family Matters and in Matters of Non-Contentious Jurisdiction (*FamFG*).

unmarried parent in § 1626a II *BGB* by having introduced the summary procedure in § 155a *FamFG*.

2.3 Current Applicable Laws

2.3.1 Domestic Laws

2.3.1.1 Basic Law (GG)

The *GG*[82] providing guiding principles for legislation and judicature exerts significant influence on development of family law. Although it is not explicitly provided for in the *GG* that the child has the right to demand parental custody from its parents, the *GG* acknowledges the natural right of parents to care for and raise their children, which is also a responsibility primarily upon them (Article 6 II *GG*). However, parents who are entitled and obliged to exercise parental custody should give consideration not only to dignity (Article 1 I *GG*) but also to freedom of personal development of the child (Article 2 I *GG*). Besides, the *GG* recognises equality between children born out of wedlock and children born in wedlock (Article 6 V *GG*), which was historically ignored by legislative authority and has only caught attention of lawmakers in the last twenty years.[83] It can be noted that the *GG* not only illustrates the relationship between parents and children, but also emphasises individuality and personal rights of the child.[84]

2.3.1.2 BGB

Rules concerning parental custody are in Title 5 of Section 2 of Book 4 (family law) of the *BGB*. To begin with the general principle, it is addressed that parents have the duty and right to care for their minor children in § 1626 I *BGB* which is followed by specific rules on parental custody for children born out of wedlock (§§ 1626a-e *BGB*). Then the content of parental custody (§§ 1631–1664 *BGB*) is elaborately regulated so that parents are shown how to exercise parental custody generally. Not only the normal case but also the exceptional cases have been considered by the lawmakers, in which court measures have to be taken to avert endangerment of the best interests of the child (§§ 1666–1667 *BGB*) or parental custody has to be reallocated following separation of parents (§ 1671 *BGB*). In addition, contact right of the child (§§ 1684–1685 *BGB*) which

---

82 *Grundgesetz* of 23 May 1949 (BGBl. I S. 1).

83 *Dethloff*, Familienrecht, § 1 Rn. 26.

84 *Dethloff*, Familienrecht, § 1 Rn. 32.

is closely linked to parental custody after separation of parents is also stipulated. In the last part of this Title, the principle of the best interests of the child (§ 1697a *BGB*) is enshrined as a guideline for the court to decide on issues related to parental custody.

2.3.1.3 FamFG

Proceedings related to family law in the *German Code of Civil Procedure* (also referred to as *ZPO*) have been modified and integrated into the *Act on Proceedings Concerning Family Matters and Matters of Non-Contentious Jurisdiction (FamFG)*[85] which replaced the *Act on Matters of Non-Contentious Jurisdiction*[86] and became effective on 1 September 2009. The new Act with a particular focus aims at simplifying and expediting procedures related to family law.[87]

According to the *FamFG*, the family court, replacing the guardianship court (Vormundschaftsgericht), shall have jurisdiction to legal disputes related to parental custody and right of contact. In 2013, summary procedure was introduced in § 155a *FamFG* to facilitate the transfer of the joint parental custody in § 1626a II 2 *BGB*, according to which the court may decide by means of written procedure without the *Youth Welfare Office* and the parents being heard.

2.3.1.4 Book VIII of Code of Social Law

The Book VIII of Code of Social Law (hereinafter referred to as *SGB VIII*) whose root can be found in the Reform of Child and Youth Welfare Service Act (Gesetz zur Neuordnung des Kinder- und Jugendhilferechts) in 1990 consists of 105 articles after having been revised in October 2015. It grants young people[88] the right to demand support to develop an independent and socially competent personality (§ 1 I *SGB VIII*). In addition, duties of the Youth Welfare Office are specified, which shall prevent the child from being discriminated and the child's interests from being injured, help the parents by offering them consultation and

---

85 The *FamFG* is short for *Act on Proceedings Concerning Family Matters and in Matters of Non-contentious Jurisdiction* (*Gesetz über das Verfahren in Familiensachen und Angelegenheiten der freiwilligen Gerichtsbarkeit*).

86 RGBl. I 1898, 189: *Das Gesetz über die Angelegenheiten der freiwilligen Gerichtsbarkeit* (hereinafter referred to as *FGG*).

87 *BT-Drucks.* 16/6308, 164; *Staudinger/Peschel-Gutzeit* (2015), Vorbemerkungen zu §§ 1626 ff., Rn. 80.

88 'Young people' refers to the child under the age of 14, the adolescent between the age of 14–18 and the young adults under the age of 27 according to Article 7 of the Code.

support, and pay contribution to maintain or create a positive living condition, a child- and family-orientated environment for the child (§ 1 III *SGB VIII*).

Furthermore, duty of parents to care for and educate their children and supervision of competent authorities on the performance of the parents are emphasised in § 1 *SGB VIII*, as in Article 6 II *GG*.

2.3.2 International Laws and Conventions, Regulations of EU

2.3.2.1 Convention on the Rights of the Child

To extend particular care to the child recognised in the Geneva Declaration of the Rights of the Child of 1924[89], the Declaration of the Rights of the Child of 1959[90], the Universal Declaration of Human Rights (in particular in Article 25)[91], the International Covenant on Civil and Political Rights[92] (in particular in Article 23 I and 24)[93], and in the International Covenant on Economic, Social and Cultural Rights[94] (in particular in Article 10), the Convention on the Rights of the Child (hereinafter referred to as CRC) ratified by the General Assembly of the United Nations on 20 November 1989 aims at calling upon all the member states to lay more emphasis on the primary care education of the child and to

---

89 Retrieved from http://www.un-documents.net/gdrc1924.htm on 12 September 2019.

90 It was adopted by the General Assembly on 20 November 1959.

91 Article 25 II: motherhood and childhood are entitled to special care and assistance. All children, whether born in or out of wedlock, shall enjoy the same social protection, retrieved from http://www.un.org/en/universal-declaration-human-rights/ on 12 September 2019.

92 Retrieved from http://www.ohchr.org/en/professionalinterest/pages/ccpr.aspx on 12 September 2019.

93 Article 23 I: the family is the natural and fundamental group unit of society and is entitled to protection by society and the State; Article 24 I: Every child shall have, without any discrimination as to race, colour, sex, language, religion, national or social origin, property or birth, the right to such measures of protection as are required by its status as a minor, on the part of its family, society and the State; Article 24 II: every child shall be registered immediately after birth and shall have a name, retrieved from http://www.ohchr.org/en/professionalinterest/pages/ccpr.aspx on 12 September 2019.

94 Article 10: the States Parties to the present Covenant recognise that: 1. The widest possible protection and assistance should be accorded to the family, which is the natural and fundamental group unit of society, particularly for its establishment and while it is responsible for the care and education of dependent children. Marriage must be entered into with the free consent of the intending spouses, retrieved from http://www.ohchr.org/EN/ProfessionalInterest/Pages/CESCR.aspx on 12 September 2019.

strengthen legal and other protection for the child before and after birth and international cooperation in securing the rights of the child.[95] Currently, 196 countries are parties to the treaty (some with stated reservations or interpretations) including every member of the United Nations except the United States of America.

The *CRC* defines a child as any human being under the age of 18, unless the age of majority is attained earlier by a state's own domestic legislation (Article 1). It is recognised that parents shall have the primary responsibility for the 'upbringing and development' of their children while state parties shall render appropriate assistance to parents in the performance of their child-rearing responsibilities (Article 18 I and II). In fulfilment of parental responsibilities or exercise of parental rights, parents shall take the 'evolving capacities of the child' into consideration (Article 5). In case the child must be separated from parents, its right to maintain a personal relationship with its parents should be respected if it is not contrary to its best interests (Article 9 III). Furthermore, the principle of the best interests of the child has been adopted which shall be 'a primary consideration' for all actions concerning children taken by public and private child welfare institutions, administrative authorities and legislative bodies (Article 3). In terms of equality between the child born in wedlock and out of wedlock, the *CRC* calls upon the member states to take all appropriate measures to protect the child from being discriminated (Article 2).

The *CRC* brings a new approach to rights of children which shall not be seen as in opposition to rights of adults or as an alternative to the rights of parents but as an integral part of human rights.[96] Not only with principles but also with concrete measures, the *CRC* has provided state parties guidance in legislation concerning the child.

Germany ratified the *CRC* in 1992[97], but declared reservation to Article 18 and insisted parents who had divorced or separated permanently or whose child was born out of wedlock should not exercise parental custody jointly. However, such a reservation was withdrawn in 2010.[98]

---

95 See Preamble of the Convention http://www.ohchr.org/en/professionalinterest/pages/crc.aspx, retrieved latest on 12 September 2019.

96 *Santos Pais*, 'General introduction to the Convention on the Rights of the Child: from its origin to its implementation', Defence for Children International, Selected essays on international children's rights (1993), Vol. 1, P. 1.

97 BGBl. II 1992, 990; See http://indicators.ohchr.org/, retrieved latest on 12 September 2019.

98 BGBl. II 2011, 600.

2.3.2.2 *Child Protection Convention of Hague Conference*

Considering the need to revise the Convention of 5 October 1961 concerning power of public authorities and the laws applicable in respect of the protection of minors and the need to improve the protection to children in international situations, the *Child Protection Convention of Hague Conference* of 19 October 1996[99] (hereinafter referred to as the *HCCH*), following guidance of the *CRC*, tries to avoid conflicts between different legal systems in respect of jurisdiction, applicable law, recognition and enforcement measures in protection of children by strengthening international cooperation. It is noted that the best interests of the child are a primary consideration in making decisions on jurisdiction, application of laws, enforcement, etc.

Although the Federal Republic of Germany had already ratified the Convention on 25 June 2009[100], it was not until 1 January 2011 that the convention came into force in Germany[101].

2.3.2.3 *European Convention on Human Rights*

Although the *European Convention on Human Rights*[102] (hereinafter referred to as *ECHR*) was drawn up with the focus on human rights of adults[103], children enjoy the same rights under this Convention as adults, as the *European Court for Human Rights* (hereinafter referred to as *ECtHR*) has accepted that 'everyone' in Article 1[104] includes children.[105] Therefore, not only parents but also children

---

99 Retrieved from http://www.hcch.net/index_en.php?act=conventions.text&cid=70 on 12 September 2019: *Convention of 19 October 1996 on Jurisdiction, Applicable Law, Recognition, Enforcement and Co-operation in Respect of Parental Responsibility and Measures for the Protection of Children.*

100 BGBl. II 2009, 602.

101 BGBl. II 2011, 1527.

102 Retrieved from http://www.echr.coe.int/Documents/Convention_ENG.pdf on 12 September 2019: the *European Convention on Human Rights* (*ECHR*) (formally the *Convention for the Protection of Human Rights and Fundamental Freedoms*) is an international treaty to protect human rights and fundamental freedoms in Europe freedoms. Drafted in 1950 by the then newly formed Council of Europe, the convention entered into force on 3 September 1953.

103 *Douglas*, The family and the state under European Convention on Human Rights, *International Journal of Law and the Family* 2: 76, 1998.

104 Article 1: the High Contracting Parties shall secure to everyone within their jurisdiction the rights and freedoms in this Convention.

105 *ECtHR*, Case of Nielsen v. Denmark, Judgement on 12 March 1987, Application no. 10929/84.

have the right to respect for their private and family life (Article 8 of *ECHR*). A public authority can only interfere with such a right when it is in accordance with the law and is necessary in a democratic society in the interests of national security, public safety or the economic well-being of the country, for the prevention of disorder or crime, for the protection of health or morals, or for the protection of the rights and freedoms of others. The *ECtHR* reiterates further that the notion of 'family life' under Article 8 of the Convention is not confined to marriage-based relationship and may encompass other *de facto* 'family' ties where parties are living together out of wedlock. A child born out of such a relationship is *ipso jure* part of that 'family' unit from the moment, and by the very fact of the birth. However, a mere biological kinship between a natural parent and a child, without any further legal or factual elements indicating the existence of a close personal relationship, is insufficient to claim the protection of Article 8.[106]

Not only Article 8 on respect of family life but also Article 14[107] against discrimination has been often invoked by parents who have been deprived of the right to exercise parental custody or the right to contact their children after separation or divorce. Decisions of the *ECtHR* based on Article 8 and 14 of *ECHR* have promoted legislative reform related to parental custody after separation and lawful interests of children born out of wedlock and the biological but not the legal fathers. Furthermore, the *ECHR* has also influenced domestic procedural laws by, for instance, requiring a national authority to provide an effective judicial remedy which the individual can seek in case of overlong procedure (Article 13 of *ECHR*).

2.3.2.4 Brussels IIa

Regulations of the *European Union* (hereinafter referred to as *EU*) are playing a more and more important role, since *EU*-regulations have been applied to the

---

106 *ECtHR*, Case of Anayo v. Germany, Judgement on 21 March 2011, Application no. 20578/07, Rn. 55–56 (In this case, the biological fatherhood is not contested by legal parents); *ECtHR*, Case of Schneider v. Germany, Judgement on 15 September 2011, Application no. 17080/07, Rn. 79–80 (In this case, the biological fatherhood is contested by legal parents).

107 Article 14 of the *ECHR*: all the rights and freedom set forth in this Convention shall be secured without discrimination on any ground such as sex, race, colour, language, religion, political or other opinion, national or social origin, association with a national minority, property, birth or other status.

core areas of civil law between the member states of *EU*[108]. Although *EU* has no direct competence to promulgate national family laws, many legal acts of the *EU* and decisions of the European Court of Justice establish 'minimum standards' for member states in legislation of family laws and regulations.[109]

In the field of parental custody, the most important European regulation should be *Council Regulation (EC) No. 2201/2003*[110] concerning jurisdiction and the recognition and enforcement of judgements in matrimonial matters and the matters of parental responsibility (hereinafter referred to as *Brussels IIa*). Having replaced the *Council Regulation (EC) No. 1347/2000*[111] and entered into force on 1 August 2004, the *Brussels IIa* is binding in its entirety and is directly applicable in member states in accordance with the Treaty establishing the European Community. The *Brussels IIa* has separated the jurisdiction in matters of parental responsibilities from the jurisdiction on the application for divorce, legal separation and marriage annulment, and takes the habitual residence of the children as the only criterion when deciding the jurisdiction in matters of parental responsibility.[112]

2.4 Summary

From the historical development of the legislation related to parental custody, it can be concluded that the social and legal status of the child whose rights and interests are taken more seriously has been improved, discrimination upon children born out of wedlock has been eliminated, rights of the parents towards the child have been overweighed by their obligation, mothers have won the fight for equality with fathers to take custody of their children and the public authorities have been undertaking necessary intervention to guarantee the best interests of

---

108 *Hau*, Europäische und autonome Zuständigkeitsgründe in Ehesachen mit Auslandsbezug, FPR 2002, 616.

109 *Scherpe*, European Family Law Volume I – The Impact of Institutions and Organisations on European Family Law, P. 264.

110 https://eur-lex.europa.eu/legal-content/DE/TXT/?uri=LEGISSUM:l33194 retrieved on 12 September 2019.

111 http://eur-lex.europa.eu/legal-content/EN/TXT/PDF/?uri=CELEX:32000R1347&from=D retrieved on 12 September 2019.

112 Article 8, Section 1: the courts of a Member State shall have jurisdiction in matters of parental responsibility over a child who is habitually resident in that Member State at the time the court is seised.

the child. However, reform on family laws will never be completed, as society never stops developing and no field of law is so closely linked as family law to it.

The domestic laws are influenced directly or indirectly by international laws or conventions. Both the *CRC* and *ECHR* have provided guideline and inspiration to legal reforms concerning parental custody in Germany. However, it is suggested that international or European conventions should provide for specific measures which the national authority should take to promote rights or welfare of the child, rather than just define a bottom line for them to follow.[113] Taking Article 2 of the first *Protocol to the Protection of the Human Rights and Fundamental Freedoms*, for example[114], the right to education is only granted to the child in a passive way; and the conventions could indicate member states further the ways to promote such rights of the child in a positive way. In addition to international or European conventions, the *HCCH* and the *Brussel IIa* also constitute an indispensable part of applicable laws on parental custody by providing applicable rules on jurisdiction, recognition and enforcement for cross-border cases involving parental custody. For member states of *EU*, in the case of discrepancies between *EU* and national law, the *EU* law prevails.[115]

113 *Dickens*, The modern function and limits of parental rights, Law Quarterly Review 97: 462, 1981.

114 It was signed in 1952 in Paris.

115 *Bernd von Hoffmann*, European Private International Law, Ars Aequi Libri 1998, P. 17: There are no supremacy clauses in any of European Union Treaties, but the European Court ruled that Community law is supreme (Flaminio v. ENEL, ECR 1964).

3 An Overview of the Legal Concept of 'Parental Custody'

3.1 Introduction

3.1.1 Concept of 'Parental Custody'

Since the entry into force of the *SorgRG*, 'parental custody' (Elterliche Sorge) has replaced the concept of 'parental authority' (Elterliche Gewalt) under which the focus was laid on parents' power and children were considered the property of their parental units. Such a change in legislation reflects the rise of the legal status of children and has redefined the relationship between parents and children which now emphasises parental responsibility, rather than parental rights[116].

3.1.2 Legal Nature

3.1.2.1 Right or Duty?

The concept of parental custody implies a legal relationship between parents and the child[117] which entails not only rights but also obligations between them. As provided for in the *GG*, *BGB* and *SGB VIII*, to care for and educate their children is not only the parents' natural rights, but also a duty primarily incumbent upon them.[118] The term 'parents' in Article 6 II 1 *GG* refers not only to the legal, but also the biological parents,[119] whereas § 1626 ff. *BGB* is solely based on legal parenthood.[120]

Parental custody is an absolute right of parents.[121] If any third party tries to violate such a right, parents can claim compensation for damages arising

---

116 *BT-Drucks.* 8/2788, 36; *Dethloff*, Familienrecht in Europa - Quo vadis? NJW 1–2/2018, 23 (28); *Zekoll/Reimann*, Introduction to German Law, P. 263; *Luthin*, Zur Neuregelung des elterlichen Sorgerechts, FamRZ 1979, 986.

117 *StichwortKo/Seebach* (2014), P. 488 Rn. 1.

118 *BVerfG*, Beschluss v. 17.2.1982 - 1 BvR 188/80 -, juris Rn. 34 = *BVerfGE* 60, 79, 88 = NJW 1982, 1379 = JZ 1982, 416 = FamRZ 1982, 567.

119 *Dethloff*, Familienrecht, § 1 Rn. 25; *BVerfG*, Beschluss v. 9.4.2003 - 1 BvR 1493/96 -, juris Rn. 54, 57 = *BVerfGE* 108, 82.

120 *Zorn*, Das Recht der elterlichen Sorge, P. 1 Rn. 2.

121 *Palandt/Götz* (2018), § 1626 Rn. 3.

therefrom according to § 823 I *BGB*.[122] In case a child is illegally withheld by any third party, either parent has the right to demand surrender of the child according to § 1632 I *BGB* and claim compensation for related expenses. Furthermore, the right to exercise parental custody is a very personal right of parents.[123] Therefore, it can generally neither be waived nor completely transferred to a third party. However, transfer of some parts of parental custody should not be excluded.[124] For instance, the child can be temporarily cared for by relatives or friends, or even be placed in a child's foster home if parents cannot exercise parental custody towards the child because of illness or employment.

Although rights and duties are inextricably connected, legislature has attempted to highlight duties of parents to their children,[125] which can be seen to some extent from the reversed position of the terms between 'right' and 'duty' in § 1626 I *BGB*. It is responsibility of parents that has dominated the concept of parenthood; right of parents to exercise parental custody is considered to be only of instrumental value which exists insofar as necessary for the fulfilment of parental duties.[126]

Parental custody not only indicates rights and obligations of parents, but also implies the children's rights towards their parents and state authorities. The *BVerfG* pointed out in its decision on 29 July 1968[127] that children should be entitled to fundamental rights in terms of parental custody, which enables them to approach the state authorities to seek protection, in case their rights in Article 1 I (Human dignity) and Article 2 I *GG* (Right to free development of the

---

122 *Heiß/Castellanos*, Gemeinsame Sorge und Kindeswohl nach neuem Recht, P. 43 Rn. 56; *BGH*, Urteil v. 24.4.1990 - VI ZR 110/89 -, juris Rn. 11 = NJW 1990, 2060 = FamRZ 1990, 966; *OLG Karlsruhe*, Urteil v. 21.12.2001 - 5 UF 78/01 -, juris Rn. 15, FamRZ 2002, 1056; *BGH*, Urteil v. 19.6.2002 - XII ZR 173/00 -, juris Rn. 11 = *BGHZ* 151, 155–164 = FamRZ 2002, 1099 = NJW 2002, 2566.

123 *Palandt/Götz* (2018), § 1626 Rn. 3; *Dethloff*, Familienrecht, § 13 Rn. 19.

124 *Palandt/Götz* (2018), § 1626 Rn. 3; *Staudinger/Peschel-Gutzeit* (2015), § 1626 Rn. 24–30; *StichwortKo/Seebach* (2014), P. 488 Rn. 1; *Gernhuber/Coester-Waltjen*, Familienrecht, § 57 Rn. 18.

125 *BVerfG*, Beschluss v. 9.4.2003 - 1 BvR 1493/96 -, juris Rn. 60, *BVerfGE* 108, 82 = NJW 2003, 2151 = FamRZ 2003, 816 (819) = FPR 2003, 471; *BVerfGE* 61, 358 (372); *Rauscher*, Familienrecht, S. 827 Rn. 952.

126 *Harris-Short, Miles, Rob*, Family Law, P. 578; *Staudinger/Peschel-Gutzeit* (2015), § 1626, Rn. 19.

127 *BVerfG*, Beschluss v. 29.7.1968 - 1 BvL 20/63, juris Rn. 58 = *BVerfGE* 24, 119 (144) = NJW 1968, 2233 = FamRZ 1968, 578.

personality) or Article 6 II (Caring and education from parents) are violated. Although children have always been under the protection of the *GG* (Article 6 II *GG*), their positive fundamental right is not explicitly stated in the *GG*. Therefore, there has been discussion on whether a child's fundamental right to demand parental custody or protection from state authorities should be enshrined in the *GG*.[128] Considering such a fundamental right which can be inferred from the current legal text (Article 6 II 1 *GG*), which has also been confirmed by the *BVerfG*, and the child is also legal subject (§ 1 *BGB*)[129], it is held that there is no further need to anchor it within the *GG*.[130]

3.1.2.2 Public or Private?

Family law governing family-related and domestic-related issues is a subcategory of private law[131] and is presented in Book 4 of the *BGB*. However, compared with the other branches of civil law, family law is more characterised by the intervention from state authorities. For instance, the state authorities shall supervise whether the parents have fulfilled their responsibilities under their duty of parental custody (Article 6 II 2 *GG*), and the family court can separate children from their parents in some particular circumstances or take measures to prevent the children's interests from being endangered (§ 1666 *BGB*). The reason why there is more intervention of state authorities in matters of family life than in other civil aspects might lie in the fact that social security depends to some extent on stability of families, because the society is made up of numerous families. In the United Kingdom, public child law has become a specialist area of practice, where social workers, legal associations and professional judges play different roles.[132]

However, as parental custody is primarily the right and responsibility of parents and state authorities can only interfere when necessary (§ 1666a *BGB*), the

---

128 *Seibert*, Verfassung und Kindschaftsrecht - Neue Entwicklungen und offene Fragen, FamRZ 1995, 1457 (1463); *Coester*, Verfassungsrechtliche Vorgaben für die gesetzliche Ausgestaltung des Sorgerechts nicht miteinander verheirateter Eltern, FPR 2005, 60; *Heilmann*, Schützt das Grundgesetz die Kinder nicht? Eine Betrachtung der bisherigen Kammerrechtsprechung des *BVerfG* im Jahr 2014, NJW 2014, 2909.

129 *Fröschle*, Sorge und Umgang in der Rechtspraxis, S. 8 Rn. 33; *Dethloff*, Familienrecht in Europa - Quo vadis? NJW 1–2/2018, 23 (27).

130 *Coester*, Sorgerecht nicht miteinander verheirateter Eltern, FamRZ 2012, 1337 (1342).

131 *Muscheler*, Familienrecht, P. 3 Rn. 7; *Dethloff*, Familienrecht, § 1 Rn. 8.

132 *Cretney*, Principles of Family Law, P. 691.

private legal nature of parental custody shall overweigh its public legal nature. Parents have the autonomy to reach an agreement on how to exercise parental custody after separation or divorce, provided it is not inconsistent with the best interests of the child (Article 6 II 1 *GG*). Therefore, it is necessary to examine the question where limits of the state interference in parental custody are and what the state's supportive role should entail, which will be elaborated in Chapter 6.

3.1.2.3 *Summary*

To summarise, 'parental custody' is a very complex legal term, where there are no clear boundaries between 'rights' and 'obligations', or between 'private' and 'public'. However, considering the change of concept and understanding towards relationship between parents and children and priority of parental autonomy over interference of state authorities concluded from Article 6 II 1 *GG*, parental custody is more characterised by obligations and its private nature.

3.1.3 Types of Parental Custody

3.1.3.1 *Care for the Person and Care for the Property*

Parental custody for minors includes care for the person of the child (Personensorge), care for the property (Vermögenssorge) of the child according to 1626 I *BGB* and representation the child (Vertretung des Kindes) according to § 1629 *BGB*.

Care for the person (§§ 1631–1632 *BGB*) entails all the matters which are beyond the care for the child's property. From naming, to nursing, to educating and financing the child, it covers many aspects of a child's life. Care for the person of a child reflects not only the factual but also the legal relationship between parents and children. The latter should not be prioritised but can be utilised to solve problems arising from the factual relationship.[133]

Care for the property is provided in § 1638 to § 1649 *BGB*, according to which parents have the right to manage all the property of the child, except that the ones which the child acquires from a testator or benefactor who opposes management of such property by the parents. However, parents shall not dispose of the property of the child at will, but follow the rules made either by the testator or benefactor (§ 1639 *BGB*) or by law[134]. If the child's interests are endangered

---

133 *Schwab*, Familienrecht, P. 347–348 Rn. 789.

134 For example, the parents shall invest the money which they do not need for the daily expense for the time being according to the principle of efficient management (§ 1642

by the parents' inappropriate management, the family court shall undertake measures to prevent it (§ 1667 *BGB*). Specific issues under care for the property and representation of the child will not be further discussed, as the focus of this thesis rests on the care for the person of the child.

3.1.3.2 Joint and Sole Parental Custody

a) Joint Parental Custody

Interpreted in a narrow sense, joint parental custody shall only refer to the parental custody shared jointly and equally by both parents. However, it was not until 1959 that the father was deprived of the right to make the final decision in case of disagreement with the mother so that parents finally had access to a substantially equal joint parental custody in the practice[135].

In an intact family where parents do not get separated or divorced, it is taken for granted that parents exercise joint parental custody towards their children. Parents are required to come to a mutual agreement when exercising parental custody jointly (§ 1627 II *BGB*). If they fail to reach an agreement in a single matter or a specific type of decisions which is of significant importance to the child, the family court may, upon application of one parent, transfer the right to decide upon one parent (§ 1628 I *BGB*).[136]

In the event of a separation or divorce, the parents according to current laws are still entitled to joint parental custody. However, there used to be much discussion concerning the question if parents after separation or divorce should exercise parental custody jointly.[137] Joint parental custody was once questioned with the argument that it was hardly plausible that joint parenting would be possible after separation or divorce if parents could not co-parent the child during the marriage or cohabitation. On 11 December 1970, the *LG Mannheim*, as the first court in Germany, delivered a decision which supported two parents' proposal for a joint parental custody after divorce by having argued that the wording of § 1671 IV 1 *BGB* is unclear and state intervention should be subsidiary to

---

BGB) and they shall not conduct new business in the name of the child without the approval of the family court (§ 1645 *BGB*).

135 *BVerfG*, Urteil v. 29.7.1959 -1 BvR 205/58 -, juris Rn. 26 = *BVerfGE* 10, 59 = NJW 1959, 1483.

136 *OLG Köln*, Beschluss v. 11.3.2008 - 4 UF 119/07 -, juris Rn. 4 = NJW-RR 2008, 1319, 1320 = FamRZ 2009, 62.

137 *Balloff*, Alleinerziehung und gemeinsame elterliche Sorge nach Trennung und Scheidung - Eine theoretische und empirische Vergleichsstudie, P. 267–287.

the parents' fundamental right in Article 6 II *GG* and the peace function of the laws.[138] Since the *KindRG* came into force, both parents are entitled to joint parental custody after separation or divorce. It is now also possible for the unmarried father to claim the joint parental custody without the mother's consent since the reform to parental custody of children born out of wedlock in 2013 (§ 1626a I 3 *BGB*).

For the divorced or separated parents who exercise joint parental custody towards the child, one parent will be usually designated as the 'resident' parent with whom the child resides habitually, while the other parent shall pay the child support to the resident parent. Residential status does not confer additional rights to the resident parent. It simply indicates with whom the child resides after separation or divorce. A common misperception among parents is the notion that joint parental custody means equal parenting time. Joint parental custody requires parents to cooperate and reach an agreement on all the most important matters concerning the children, and the parents shall keep a sustainable social relationship with each other.[139] If parents have serious and long-lasting problem to communicate with each other, they should not be granted or forced to exercise joint parental custody towards their children,[140] because it may have a negative impact on the children's development and interests, which depends on how long the conflicts between the parents last and their severity.[141]

---

138 *Lüderitz*, Übertragung der elterlichen Gewalt an beide Elternteile nach Scheidung, FamRZ 1971, 625; *LG Mannheim*, Beschluss v. 11.12.1970 - 4 b T 15/70, FamRZ 1971, 185.

139 *BGH, Beschluss* v. 15.6.2016 - XII ZB 419/15 -, juris Rn. 23 = FamRZ 2016, 1441; *BGH-Senatsbeschluss* v. 12.12.2007 - XII ZB 158/05, juris Rn. 6 = FamRZ 2008, 592 = NJW 2008, 994; *BT-Drucks.* 17/11048, 17.

140 *BT-Drucks.* 17/11048, 17; *BGH, Beschluss* v. 15.6.2016 - XII ZB 419/15 -, juris Rn. 24 = FamRZ 2016, 1441; *OLG Schleswig*, Beschluss v. 7.4.2014 - 15 UF 140/13 -, juris Rn. 19 = FamRZ 2014, 1374, 1375; *KG Berlin*, Beschluss v. 15.4.2014 - 19 UF 120/13 -, juris Rn. 6 = FamRZ 2014, 1375; *OLG Koblenz*, Beschluss v. 6.6.2013 - 13 UF 246/13 -, juris Rn. 10 = FamRZ 2014, 319; *OLG Stuttgart*, Beschluss v. 2.12.2014 - 11 UF 173/14 -, juris Rn. 17 = NJW 2015, 642 = FamRZ 2015, 674; *OLG Brandenburg*, Beschluss v. 17.6.2014 - 10 UF 5/14 -, juris Rn. 24 = FamRZ 2014, 1856; *Schilling*, Rechtliche Probleme bei der gemeinsamen Sorge nach Trennung bzw. Scheidung, NJW 2007, 3233, 3238.

141 *BGH*, Senatsbeschluss v. 29.9.1999 - XII ZB 3/99 -, juris Rn. 13 = FamRZ 1999, 1646, 1648.

b) Sole Parental Custody

The sole parental custody generally means that only one parent has the right of parental custody towards the child, for instance, the unmarried mother according to § 1626 III *BGB*. Either of the divorced or separated parents who are entitled to joint parental custody might in some circumstances apply to the court for withdrawal of the other parent's right of parental custody so that he or she may exercise the sole parental custody to the child, pursuant to § 1671 I, II *BGB*.

Although joint parental custody is considered a general rule for after separation or divorce (§ 1687 *BGB*), it cannot be concluded that joint parental custody is definitely more beneficial to the child than sole parental custody or the joint parental custody should be favoured over the sole parental custody by the courts under any circumstance.[142] Whether a child is put under joint or sole parental custody in any individual case should be decided according to the principle of the best interests of the child.[143]

3.1.4 Comparison with Other Legal Terms

3.1.4.1 Parental Responsibility

According to Article 6 II *GG*, to care for and bring up the child under parental custody is first and foremost the parents' responsibility. However, parental custody is only an important part, but not the entirety of the parental responsibility which also includes child support, the right of contact apart from parental custody.[144]

Parental responsibility encompasses all the rights, duties, powers, responsibilities and authority which a parent possesses in relation to the child and its property.[145] Legislators in certain countries prefer to replace the term 'parental rights' with 'parental responsibility', because the latter puts more emphasis on the responsibilities that parents have towards their children and attempts to end the prejudice that the child is dominated by its parents. The term 'parental responsibility' has also been adopted in some conventions and European regulations.

---

142 *OLG Frankfurt*, Beschluss v. 14.9.1998 - 3 UF 89/98 -, juris Rn. 8 = FamRZ 1999, 392.

143 *KG Berlin*, Beschluss v. 21.9.1999 - 17 UF 4806/99 -, juris Rn. 3 = FamRZ 2000, 502; *OLG Zweibrücken*, Beschluss v. 23.11.1999 - 5 UF 88/99 -, juris Rn. 36 = FamRZ 2000, 627 (629).

144 *Schwab*, Familienrecht, P. 282 Rn. 643.

145 *Boele-Woelki/Ferrand/González Beilfuss*, Principles of European family law regarding parental responsibilities, P. 14; Article 3 of the *Children Act* of 1989 in UK.

For example, it is agreed in the *HCCH*[146] that 'parental responsibility' includes parental authority or any analogous relationship of authority determining the rights, powers and responsibilities of parents, guardians or other legal representatives in relation to the person or the property of the child (Article 1, Section 1). It can be noted from above that parental responsibility is not a term contradictory to parental rights, and parental custody is considered the most important function of the parental responsibility to the child.

3.1.4.2 Guardianship, Legal Care and Curatorship

Guardianship in the *BGB* is designed for the children who are not subject to parental custody or whose parents are not entitled to care for the person or property of the child (Vormundschaft in § 1773 *BGB*), while legal care shall be arranged for the adults who cannot take care of their personal affairs in part or in its entirety because of psychological illness or physical, mental or psychological handicaps upon the application or *ex officio* (Rechtliche Betreuung in § 1900 *BGB*). A curator (Pfleger) shall be assigned to the child who is subject to parental custody or guardianship for the matters which parents or guardians are prevented from carrying out (§ 1909 *BGB*). The curatorship can also be ordered if the requirements for the ordering of a guardianship are satisfied but a guardian has not yet been appointed. Rules regarding parental custody in Title 5 (Parental custody from § 1626 to § 1698b *BGB*) of Section 2 (Relationship) in Book 4 (Family Law) of the *BGB* are not applied to matters of the child for whom a curator has been appointed (§ 1630 I *BGB*).

3.2 Care for the Person

3.2.1 Content

So far, there is no official definition which covers all that is included in the care for the person of a child, but the *BGB* has listed the most important aspects of caring for the person as follows:

- to care for, educate and supervise the children and decide on their residence (§ 1631 I);
- to help the children to make decision on the matters regarding training and occupation (§ 1631a);

146 For details of the *HCCH* see chapter 2.3.2.2.

- to deal with the accommodation matter for the children who are deprived of freedom (§1631b);
- to issue the claim of returning the children against any third party (§ 1632 I) and
- right to determine contact to the child (§ 1632 II).

In addition, the parent who exercises the parental custody towards the child shall register the birth of the child with the *Registry Office* (§ 19 of the *PStG*[147]) and shall share a residence with the child (§ 11 of the *BGB*).

Among these above-mentioned aspects, to care for and educate the child is the core of care for the person of the child and physical parental custody[148], which is also the research focus of this book.

3.2.2 Limitation to Parental Custody

3.2.2.1 Objectives of Parenting

So far, there has been no specific description in the *BGB* on the objectives of parenting.[149] However, it is generally accepted that a child is expected to be raised to become a useful member of society who can develop its abilities, its moral and social responsibility, as well as think and make decisions independently[150]. These are listed as principles[151] in the *Declaration of the Rights of the Child* of the United Nations and are the basis of the *CRC*. It is also provided for in Article 29 of *CRC* that the child's personality, talents and mental and physical abilities shall fully be developed by education which shall prepare the child for an active adult life in a free society. Additionally, the child's respect for its parents, for its own cultural identity, language and values, and for the cultural background and

---

147 BGBl. I 2007, 122: *Act on the Civil Status* (*Personenstandsgesetz*).

148 *Fröschle*, Sorge und Umgang in der Rechtspraxis, S. 82 Rn. 372.

149 *Palandt/Götz* (2018), § 1626 Rn. 22; *Fröschle*, Sorge und Umgang in der Rechtspraxis, S. 83 Rn. 374.

150 *Gernhuber/Coester-Waltjen*, Familienrecht, § 57 Rn. 74.

151 Principle 2 of *Declaration of the Rights of the Child*: the child shall enjoy special protection, and shall be given opportunities and facilities, by law and by other means, to enable him to develop physically, mentally, morally, spiritually and socially in a healthy and normal manner and in conditions of freedom and dignity. Principle 7: he shall be given an education which will promote his general culture and enable him, on a basis of equal opportunity, to develop his abilities, his individual judgement, and his sense of moral and social responsibility, and to become a useful member of society.

values of others should be fostered.[152] The child shall be brought up in a spirit of understanding, tolerance, friendship among peoples, peace and universal brotherhood, and in full consciousness that its energy and talents should be devoted to the service of its fellow men.[153] Therefore, parents should not only take care of the child's basic needs (food, clothes and education) and protect their legal interests, but also pay attention to the development of their abilities so that it may become an independent person who is willing to take responsibility and is socially competent.[154]

3.2.2.2 Limitation to Rights of Parents

A minor, as a human being, is entitled to fundamental rights provided for in the *GG*.[155] Therefore, parents in exercising parental custody shall not infringe upon these fundamental rights, particularly the personal rights of the child in Article 2 II *GG*,[156] because the fundamental rights in *GG* are an objective set of values which can be applied in every area of the law including family law, or rather parental custody.[157]

The right to exercise parental custody allows parents to choose the ways they wish to raise their children, which does not mean that parents can undertake anything they desire. In exercise of parental custody, the parents shall not endanger

---

152 http://www.ohchr.org/EN/Issues/Education/Training/Compilation/Pages/a)GeneralCommentNo1TheAimsofEducation(article29)(2001).aspx retrieved on 12 September 2019.

153 Principle 10, Declaration of the Rights of the Child.

154 See Article 1, 2 *GG*, relevant decisions are as follows: *BVerfG*, Beschluss v. 29.7.1968 - 1 BvL 20/63 -, juris Rn. 58 = *BVerfGE* 24, 119 (144) = NJW 1968, 2233 = FamRZ 1968, 578, 584; *BVerfG*, Urteil v. 01.4 2008 - 1 BvR 1620/04 -, juris Rn. 71 = FamRZ 2008, 845, 848; *OLG München*, Beschluss v. 17.10.2011 - 2 UF 990/11 -, juris Rn. 31 = FamRZ 2012, 1062; *BT-Drucks.* 8/2788, 34; *Staudinger/Coester* (2015), § 1671 Rn. 199.

155 *Hohm*, Grundrechtsträgerschaft und 'Grundrechtsmündigkeit' Minderjähriger am Beispiel öffentlicher Heimerziehung, NJW 1986, 3107; *BVerfG*, Beschluss v. 29.7.1968 - 1 BvL 20/63 -, juris Rn. 58 = *BVerfGE* 24, 119 (144) = NJW 1968, 2233; *BVerfG*, Beschluss v. 21.5.1974 - 1 BvL 22/71 -, juris Rn. 106 = *BVerfGE* 37, 217 (252) = NJW 1974, 1609; *BVerfG*, Beschluss v. 5.11.1980 - 1 BvR 349/80 -, juris Rn. 20 = *BVerfGE* 55, 171 (179) = NJW 1981, 217; *BVerfG*, Beschluss v. 17.2.1982 - 1 BvR 188/80 -, juris Rn. 34 = *BVerfGE* 60, 79 (88) = NJW 1982,1379 = JZ 1982, 416 = FamRZ 1982, 567.

156 *BVerfG*, Beschluss v. 13.5.1986 - 1 BvR 1542/84 -, juris Rn. 49 = *BVerfGE* 72, 155 = NJW 1986, 1859 = FamRZ 1986, 769 = JZ 1986, 632.

157 *Ossenbühl*, Die Interpretation der Grundrechte in der Rechtsprechung des Bundesverfassungsgerichts, NJW 1976, 2100, 2101.

the child's best interests,[158] and any decision made by parents for their children shall be pursuant to the best interests of the children (§ 1627 I *BGB*) which is the highest criterion in exercise of parental custody.[159] Furthermore, parents are required to avoid violence abuse and take consideration of the growing independence or autonomy of the child[160].

a) *Avoidance of Violence Abuse*

The *Law on Ban of Violence in Education and on Amendment of Children's Right for Support*[161] granted children the right to receive a nonviolent education in § 1631 II *BGB*. Ever since, it is forbidden to use violence to educate a child. According to § 1631 II *BGB*, corporal punishment, psychological injury and any degrading actions that will injure the child's dignity are prohibited. This is binding on parents, guardians, curators (§§ 1800, 1915 *BGB*) and all other legal guardians such as step-parents, life companion, life partner, relatives, friends, acquaintance, foster-parents as well as teachers in kindergarten. Thereby, obligation under Article 19 of the *CRC*, which requires all the member states of the convention to take the appropriate legislative measures to protect the child from being physically or psychologically mistreated, has been fulfilled in Germany. Besides, parents are obliged to protect children from any possible damage to their physical integrity, and either parent should try to prevent the other parent abusing the child.[162]

Despite the legal protection mentioned above, children never completely cease to suffer maltreatment at the hands of their parents. Although the severity of abuse, especially physical damage to children, can be determined by expert witness, many parents who abuse their children have avoided being charged or convicted. One important reason for this lies in the difficulty of proving their abusive behaviours, which leads to 'in dubio pro reo'.[163] Even if parents whose

---

158 *BVerfG*, Urteil v. 9.2.1982 - 1 BvR 845/79 -, juris Rn. 83 = *BVerfGE* 59, 360, 377 = NJW 1982, 1375; *BVerfG*, Beschluss v. 14.4.1987 - 1 BvR 332/86 -, juris Rn. 55 = *BVerfGE* 75, 201, 218 = NJW 1988, 125 = FamRZ 1987, 786.

159 *BVerfG*, Beschluss v. 17.2.1982 - 1 BvR 188/80 -, juris Rn. 51, = *BVerfGE* 60, 79, 88 = NJW 1982, 1379 = JZ 1982, 416 = FamRZ 1982, 567.

160 *Boele-Woelki/Ferrand/González Beilfuss*, Principles of European family law regarding parental responsibilities, 2007, P. 40 ff.

161 BGBl. I 2000, 1479: *Das Gesetz zur Ächtung der Gewalt in der Erziehung und zur Änderung des Kindesunterhaltsrechts* v. 2.11.2000.

162 *BGH*, Urteil von 3.7.2003 - 4 StR 190/03 -, juris Rn. 9.

163 *Doukkani-Bördner*, Kindesmisshandlungen im Haushalt der Eltern und elterliche Sorge, FamRZ 2016, 13–14.

children suffer from injuries are free from charge or conviction, their ability to care for the children should be questioned, and their rights under parental custody can be deprived.[164] However, before the decision concerning deprivation of parental custody is made, the court should assess the level of potential danger.

b) Consideration of the Growing Independence of the Child

Decisions made by parents in exercising parental custody are not always in accordance with the desire of the child to make its own decision, which generally lead to conflicts between parents' rights and the child's right for self-determination. Therefore, parents shall take into account the growing need and ability of the child to act independently and responsibly (§ 1626 II *BGB*).

aa) Abortion

Although a steady decrease of reported abortion was reported from 2008 to 2016 in Germany, the number of abortions in the first quarter of 2018 has been increased by 2.2 % compared with the same period a year before.[165] Among the 101,209 women who were reported to have had an abortion in 2017, there was around 3 % of them who were under the age of 18.[166]

In case of pregnancy of a minor, the legal abortion can only be carried out with consent of its parents, which, though not expressly stipulated by law, can be implied from parental custody in § 1626 and 1631 *BGB*. Contrary to the prevailing view that a minor can only have an abortion in the sense of § 218a *StGB* with her parents' consent,[167] it is held that a minor with the capability to discern and judge the consequences of an abortion can decide for herself whether to terminate her pregnancy.[168] To evaluate her capability, it is of significant importance to take

164 *Winkel*, Grenzüberschreitendes Sorge- und Umgangsrecht und dessen Vollstreckung, P. 7.

165 See Appendix 3.2, retrieved from https://www.destatis.de/DE/PresseService/Presse/Pressemitteilungen/2018/06/PD18_207_233.html on 12 September 2018.

166 https://www.destatis.de/DE/ZahlenFakten/GesellschaftStaat/Gesundheit/Schwangerschaftsabbrueche/Tabellen/Alter.html retrieved latest on 12 September 2019.

167 *OLG Hamburg*, Beschluss v. 5.3.2014 - 10 UF 25/14 -, juris Rn. 17 = NZFam 2014, 948, 949; *OLG Hamm*, Beschluss v. 16.7.1998 - 15 W 274/98 -, juris Rn. 5 = NJW 1998, 3424, 3425, and *AmtsG Celle*, Beschluss v. 9.2.1987 - 25 VII K3470 SH = FamRZ 1987, 738 (740) = NJW 1987, 2307, 2308; *Scherer*, Schwangerschaftsabbruch bei Minderjährigen und elterliche Zustimmung, FamRZ 1997, 589 (595).

168 It was held in the following decisions that minor children who had reached the age of 16 could by themselves decide termination of pregnancy in the court decisions: *AmtsG*

the age of a minor into consideration.[169] Although minors differ from each other in the degree of this ability and one minor at age of 14 might be more matured than another minor at the age of 16, a bottom line should be drawn to guarantee the best interests of children. Therefore, it is suggested that a pregnant minor under the age of 16 can generally only induce the abortion with the consent of both parents.[170] If the pregnant minor is not capable of making this decision, parents shall decide for them whether to terminate the pregnancy. However, parents shall not urge or force the pregnant minor to have an abortion.[171] If parents refuse to grant consent to an abortion desired by the minors, which is generally not deemed as abuse of parental right[172] or endangerment to the best interests of the child, the court can investigate the endangerment of the child's best interests from other aspects and then designate, for instance, an additional guardian to consent to the abortion in place of the parents according to § 1666 III 5 *BGB*.[173]

bb) Religion

Although religion is private, personal and intimately bound up with individual belief, desire and being,[174] parents generally choose a religion for their child very early. Some scholars consider decisions of parents on religion for their child a kind of violence towards the child.[175] In addition, it is suggested that the older a

---

Schlüchtern, Beschluss v. 29.4.1997 - X 17/97 -, juris Rn. 3 = FamRZ 1998, 968 = NJW 1998, 832 and *LG* München I, Beschluss v. 24.7.1978 - 13 T 8767/78 -, juris Rn. 12 = FamRZ 1979, 850 = NJW 1980, 646.

169 *Amend-Traut/Bongartz*, Der Schwangerschaftsabbruch bei Minderjährigen - rechtliche Perspektiven zwischen Selbstbestimmung und elterlicher Verantwortung, FamRZ 2016, 7.

170 *Amend-Traut/Bongartz*, FamRZ 2016, 12.

171 *Siedhoff*, Schwangerschaftsabbruch bei Minderjährigen und elterliche Zustimmung, FamRZ 1998, 8; *OLG Hamburg*, Beschluss v. 5.3.2014 - 10 UF 25/14 -, juris Rn. 22 = FamRZ 2014, 1213.

172 *OLG Naumburg*, Beschluss v. 19.11.2003 - 8 WF 152/03 -, juris Rn. 5 = FamRZ 2004, 1806.

173 *Staudinger/Coester* (2016), § 1666 Rn. 107; In the following court decisions, consent of parents who objected termination of the minor's pregnancy could be replaced: *OLG Hamburg*, Beschluss v. 5.3.2014 - 10 UF 25/14 -, juris Rn. 15 = FamRZ 2014, 1213; *LG Berlin*, Beschluss v. 20.11.1979 - 83 T 395/79 -, juris Rn. 17 = FamRZ 1980, 285, 286.

174 *Scherpe*, European Family Law Volume I - The Impact of Institutions and Organisations on European Family Law, P. 295; *Schwab*, Elterliche Sorge und Religion, FamRZ 2014, 1.

175 *Schwab*, Elterliche Sorge und Religion, FamRZ 2014, 2.

child is, the more it has a sense of identity.[176] Therefore, the child above a certain age can change the religion which it was committed to upon birth.

Although the *CRC* acknowledges the child's right of identity and religion in Article 8 and 14, there is little clarification on how these articles should be interpreted and applied in practice.[177] The *Law of Religious Education of Children* (short for *RKEG*) of 1921 which is still applicable nowadays[178] grants mothers the same rights as the fathers when deciding on the religious education of their children. Even if the parents are not very active in practising their religion or do not comply with religious rules, they can still decide their child's religion pursuant to § 3 II *RKEG*.[179] Furthermore, the *RKEG* imposes restrictions on the exercise of parental custody concerning religious issues. In accordance to Article 5 of this law, a minor who has reached the age of 14 has the right to make its own decision on its religious belief and a minor who has reached the age of 12 shall not be forced to change its religion that it chose previously.

c) *Supervision of State Authorities*

Parental custody can also be limited by the state authorities which shall watch over parents in exercise of parental custody (Article 6 II 2 *GG*).[180] Although the right of parents to care for and educate the child and their corresponding duty have been emphasised in Article 6 II 1 *GG*, duty of the state as a supervisor of parents' performance is also indicated.[181] The state shall, but can only interfere with decisions made by parents when it is necessary to prevent the child's best interests from being affected or damaged. For instance, if the physical, mental or psychological interests of the child or its property is endangered, and the parents do not want to or are not able to avert the danger, the family court can undertake measures necessary in accordance to § 1666 I, II *BGB*.

---

176 In the case S V S in 2012 Fam LR 148.

177 *Scherpe*, European Family Law Volume I - The Impact of Institutions and Organisations on European Family Law, P. 311.

178 *Law on the Religious Education for the Child* (*Gesetz über die religiöse Kindererziehung*) entered into force on 15 July 1921 (RGBI. 1921 I, S.939 ff.) and was revised in 2008.

179 *OLG Hamm*, Beschluss v. 29.3.2016 - II-2 UF 223/15 -, juris Rn. 31 = FamRZ 2016, 1382.

180 *Schumann*, Gutachten B 14.

181 *BVerfG*, Beschluss v. 29.7.1968 - 1 BvL 20/63 -, juris Rn. 40 = *BVerfGE* 24, 119 (143) = NJW 1968, 2233.

3.2.3 Duration, Suspension and Deprivation

3.2.3.1 Duration

A child should be under parental custody once it acquires legal capacity upon birth according to § 1 *BGB*.[182] Usually, parental custody ends when the child has reached the age of 18 (§ 1626 I 1 *BGB*)[183], or upon the death of its parents (§ 1677 *BGB*) or the child itself (§ 1698b *BGB*). Nevertheless, parental custody can be terminated if a third party adopts the child (§ 1755 *BGB*) or if the family court has withdrawn one parent's right to exercise parental custody completely (§ 1666 III 6 *BGB*) or transferred (§ 1671 I, II *BGB*) the right of parental custody from one parent to the other parent.

3.2.3.2 Suspension

a) Legal Hindrance

aa) Incapacity of Contracting in § 1673 BGB

According to § 1673 *BGB*, right to exercise parental custody of one parent should be suspended if he or she is contractually incapable or has limited capacity to contract, as it cannot be expected that a parent without or with only partial contractual capability has legal competence to care for the child. If a parent loses the capacity to contract only for a period of time, his or her right of parental custody can be transferred to the other parent or the court could take measures according to § 1666 II *BGB*.[184] Whether the parent who is partially contractually capable should be suspended from exercising parental custody should depend on how his or her partial capability is related to the exercise of parental custody. For underage parents, they still have the right to care for the person of the child together with the legal representative of that child, but they cannot represent the child (§ 1673 II 2 *BGB*). In case of different opinions between the legal representatives and the underage parents, opinions of the latter shall take precedence if the legal representative of the child is a guardian or curator (§ 1673 II 3 *BGB*).

---

182 *Gernhuber/Coester-Waltjen*, Familienrecht, § 57 Rn. 9; *Coester-Waltjen*, Der Schwangerschaftsabbruch und die Rolle des künftigen Vaters, NJW 1985, 2175, 2176; *Jagert*, Zur Frage der elterlichen Sorge über ein noch nicht geborenes Kind bei einem Elternstreit über einen zulässigen Schwangerschaftsabbruch, FamRZ 1985, 1173, 1174; *Roth-Stielow*, Nochmals: Der Schwangerschaftsabbruch und die Rolle des künftigen Vaters, NJW 1985, 2746.

183 *Gernhuber/Coester-Waltjen*, Familienrecht, § 57 Rn. 11–14.

184 *Staudinger/Coester* (2016), § 1673 Rn. 11.

bb) Confidential Birth in § 1674a BGB

Since 1 May 2014, mothers have been provided with the possibility of giving birth confidentially under a pseudonym pursuant to § 25 *SchKG*[185] to conform to the judgement of the *ECtHR* on 25 September 2012, according to which the anonymous birth of a child has violated Article 8 *ECHR* because of the infringement upon the right of the child to know its descent.[186] Mothers can make use of confidential delivery if they do not want others to learn of their pregnancy or delivery.[187] If the mother chooses to have a confidential birth, she will lose the right to exercise parental custody. However, such a right will revive if the family court establishes that the mother has provided the court with information required to enter the child's birth into the register (§ 1674a *BGB*).

b) Actual Hindrance (de facto) in § 1674 BGB

If the family court finds that one parent cannot exercise parental custody actually for a long period of time, it can suspend his or her parental custody which will revive as soon as the reasons for that suspension disappear (§ 1674 *BGB*). However, the discretion of the court to decide on the presence of an actual hindrance to parents in exercising parental custody might lead to uncertainty. There is no rule to determine how long the hindrance has to last so that the parental custody of a parent should be suspended. If the hindrance just occurs for a short period of time, there is no need to suspend the parental custody.

It could be a hindrance to exercise of parental custody if one parent could not care for the child because of his or her absence due to an overseas stay, detention or emigration. However, physical distance should not always be considered a hindrance to the exercise of parental custody if the relationship between parents and children is maintained and parents still can exercise parental custody with support from modern communication technologies.[188] Therefore, the necessity

---

185 *SchKG* is short for *Gesetz zur Vermeidung und Bewältigung von Schwangerschaftskonflikten* (Schwangerschaftskonfliktgesetz) v. 27.7.1992 (BGBl. I S. 1398). New rules concerning confidential birth were adopted in *SchKG* by *Gesetz zum Ausbau der Hilfen für Schwangere und zur Regelung der vertraulichen Geburt* v 28.8.2013 (BGBl. I S. 3458). For details see *Helms*, Die Einführung der sogenannten vertraulichen Geburt, FamRZ 2014, 609 ff. and *Schwedler*, Die Vertrauliche Geburt - Ein Meilensteil für Schwangere in Not? NZFam 2014, 193 ff.

186 *Henrich*, Anmerkung zum *EGMR* Urteil v. 25.9.2012 - 33783/09, FamRZ 2012, 1935.

187 *BT-Drucks.* 17/1284, 16.

188 *Staudinger/Coester* (2016), § 1674 Rn. 11; *Zorn*, Das Recht der elterlichen Sorge, P. 138–139 Rn. 238–239; *AG Ludwigslust*, Urteil v. 30.9.2009 - 5 F 144/09 -, juris Rn.

to deprive the parent of his or her parental custody who could not exercise parental custody because of long prison time is in practice criticised.[189] However, if a child who entered territory of the Federal Republic of Germany with the consent of its parents does not have any possibility of communicating with its parents, the court could suspend the parents' right to exercise parental custody and order a legal guardian for the child.[190] Apart from physical absence, mental or psychological illness could also prevent or hinder parents from exercising parental custody.[191]

c) Legal Consequences of Suspension

A parent who is hindered, due to factual (practical) or legal reasons, in exercising parental custody for a long time will generally not lose his or her legal status or right to parental custody, but only his or her power to exercise the parental custody.[192] If one of the parents exercising parental custody jointly is actually hindered to exercise parental custody or his or her parental custody has been suspended, the other parent can exercise the parental custody alone (§ 1678 I 1 *BGB*). However, if the parent who has the right of sole parental custody according to § 1626a III and § 1671 *BGB* experiences an actual hindrance to exercise parental custody, the other parent will not obtain right for parental custody ex lege automatically. Instead, only the court can transfer the sole parental custody to him or her *ex officio*, provided it cannot be foreseen that the reason for suspension would disappear and such a transfer is not inconsistent with the child's best interests (§ 1678 II *BGB*). It is noted that there are strict rules to be followed in respect to transfer of parental custody in § 1678 II *BGB* to avoid frequent change of parental custody and to maintain continuity in the child's living situation. Before such a transfer, opinions of parents, the child and the *Youth Welfare Office* have to be heard first. To guarantee the best interests of the child, a curator (Pfleger) and a guardian (Vormund) can be appointed by the court

---

40 = FamRZ 2010, 388; *OLG Nürnberg*, Beschluss v. 28.12.2005 - 10 UF 1260/05 -, juris Rn. 19 = FamRZ 2006, 878; *BGH*, Beschluss v. 6.10.2004 - XII ZB 80/04 -, juris Rn. 9 = FamRZ 2005, 29, 30.

189 *OLG Koblenz*, Beschluss v. 2.12.2011 - 13 UF 839/11 -, juris Rn. 9–10 = FamRZ 2012, 726.

190 *OLG Hamm*, Beschluss v. 10.8.2015 - 4 UF 117/15 -, juris Rn. 12.

191 *Staudinger/Coester* (2016), § 1674 Rn. 9; *Zorn*, Das Recht der elterlichen Sorge, P. 139 Rn. 239.

192 *Staudinger/Coester* (2016), § 1674 Rn. 1; *Zorn*, Das Recht der elterlichen Sorge, P. 138 Rn. 236.

(§§ 1909, 1915 and §§ 1773, 1774 *BGB*). However, the transfer of parental custody in § 1678 II *BGB* has priority over guardianship or curatorship, as they can only be substitutes of parental custody and cannot replace it.[193]

3.2.3.3 Deprivation

Parents can only be deprived of parental custody if the children's best interests are or will be endangered.[194] Before such a decision is made, the court shall undertake an intensive review of the fundamental rights with consideration of principle of proportionality.[195] The family court should not just focus on the parents' behaviours, but on the consequences arising from such behaviours. Therefore, the *BVerfG* requires the family court first to concretely describe and analyse the damage that is being or might be caused by the parents according to its nature, severity and the probability of occurrence before separating the child from its parents, keeping in mind the fundamental protection afforded.[196]

3.2.4 Limitation of Liability (§ 1664 *BGB*)

Damage caused by children to any third party should be reimbursed by parents based on their duty of supervision according to § 832 *BGB*.[197] However, parents in exercising parental custody are expected to take the same care in dealing with their own affairs (§ 1664 I *BGB*, *diligentia quam in suis*)[198] and therefore are only liable for damage caused by malicious intent and gross negligence (§ 277 *BGB*).[199] § 1664 *BGB* not only limits the parents' liability when exercising parental custody, but also provides (along with § 280 *BGB*) children with a legal basis to claim compensation if their parents fail to fulfil their duties of parental custody.[200] If both parents are responsible for the damage, they are liable as joint and several debtors (§ 1664 II *BGB*).

---

193 *Rotax*, Elterliche Sorge und Tod, FPR 2008, 151 ff.

194 *OLG Frankfurt*, Beschluss v. 13.7.2015 - 3 UF 251/14 -, juris Rn. 28 = FamRZ 2016, 247.

195 *BVerfG*, Beschluss v. 7.4.2014 - 1 BvR 3121/13 -, juris Rn. 29 = FamRZ 2014, 907; *Weber*, Die Entwicklung des Familienrechts seit Mitte 2013, NJW 2014, 3072.

196 *BVerfG*, Beschluss v. 19.11.2014 - 1 BvR 1178/14 -, juris Rn. 37 = FamRZ 2015, 112 = NJW 2015, 223.

197 *Staudinger/Peschel-Gutzeit* (2015), § 1626 Rn. 76.

198 *OLG Karlsruhe*, Urteil v. 3.5.2012 - 1 U 186/11 -, juris Rn. 29 = NJW 2012, 3043.

199 *Staudinger/Heilmann* (2016), § 1664 Rn. 30.

200 *Palandt/Götz* (2018), § 1664 Rn. 1; *MüKo/Huber* (2017), § 1664 Rn. 1; *Staudinger/Peschel-Gutzeit* (2015), § 1626 Rn. 74; *OLG Karlsruhe*, Beschluss v. 22.9.2014 - 18 WF 219/13 -, juris Rn. 18 = NJW 2015, 257; *OLG Hamm*, Urteil v 4.4.2014 - 9 U 145/

3.3 Principle of the Best Interests of the Child

3.3.1 Introduction

'The best interests' ('Wohl des Kindes' or 'Kindeswohl') in the context of parental custody in the *BGB*, which is synonymous with 'welfare' or 'well-being', extends to everything that relates to a child's development and its current and future life as a human being.[201] The principle of the best interests of the child also known as the welfare principle is not only adopted in conventions[202] but also in many domestic laws. However, legislatures throughout the world, due to varying legal cultures and national contexts, show different attitudes to the question whether the principle of the best interests of the child should be legally acknowledged as a guiding principle for the court when deciding upon issues related to parental custody.

In the past decades, the best interests of the child have increasingly become a guiding principle not only for legislative but also for judicative authorities.[203] In cases of separation or divorce where parental custody needs to be redistributed, the principle of 'the best interests of the child' can not only provide public authorities with legitimate grounds for intervention, but also help them, and especially the courts, to reach decisions.[204] However, any intervention by the public authorities to guarantee the best interests of children should be undertaken with due consideration to the principle of family autonomy which can be concluded from Article 6 II 1 *GG*. The principle of the best interests of the child, referred to as an open and undefined legal concept, needs to be interpreted by the judges as its content is not covered by the existing rules.[205]

---

13 -, juris Rn. 30; *OLG Karlsruhe*, Urteil v. 3.5.2012 - 1 U 186/11 -, juris Rn. 25 = NJW 2012, 3043; *OLG Saarbrücken*, Urteil v. 26.5.2011 - 8 U 519/09 - 136 -, juris Rn. 37 = FamRZ 2012, 235.

201 *Harris-Short, Miles, Rob*, Family Law, P. 540.

202 Principle 2 of the Declaration of Rights of the Child: in the enactment of laws for this purpose, the best interests of the child shall be the paramount consideration.

203 *Boele-Woelki/Ferrand/González Beilfuss*, Principles of European family law regarding parental responsibilities, 2007, 35 ff.; *Dethloff*, Familienrecht in Europa - Quo vadis? NJW 1–2/2018, 23 (27).

204 *Coester*, Das Kindeswohl als Rechtsbegriff, P. 134.

205 *Coester*, Das Kindeswohl als Rechtsbegriff, P. 162–163.

3.3.2 Evolution of Evaluation Criteria

3.3.2.1 Era of Gender Bias

Through the historical development of the laws pertaining to parental custody, as presented in Chapter 2, it can be seen that women were subordinate to their husbands for a long time. The father who had more opportunity to earn money and raise a whole family had authority not only over his wife but also over his children. The mother who took the principal responsibility to care for her child was not granted the right of parental custody, unless the father was deprived of his right or deceased. The 20th century has witnessed the continuing fight of women for equal treatment as men in every field, including custodian rights. Nowadays, some fathers complain that the courts are always biased in favour of the mother when determining the habitual residence of their children after separation or divorce, which the courts apparently deny.[206] However, it is not important to determine whether the gender bias revives, namely whether the courts now favour mothers when deciding on redistribution of parental custody after separation or divorce. Instead, what matters is to keep the relationship between the child and its parents insofar as it is in the child's best interests.

3.3.2.2 Priority of the Parent Without Fault

In Germany, before the *First Reform Law on the Marriage and Family Law* came into force, the parent whose fault had led to divorce would be deprived of his or her parental authority.[207] Since implementation of this Act, the court does not need to take the fault of the parents into consideration when deciding upon issues concerning parental custody, but only the child's best interests.

3.3.2.3 Doctrine of Primary Caretaker and Tender Years Preference

According to the doctrine of primary caretaker preference, the legal or physical custody shall be generally granted to the parent who primarily cared for the child before separation or divorce. The primary caretaker presumption is questioned, as it emphasises quantity of care instead of quality of care and cannot determine which parent is more suitable to be a custodian parent after separation or divorce.[208]

---

206 *Harris-Short, Miles, Rob*, Family Law, P. 744.

207 § 74 IV a.F of *Marriage Act* in 1946 and § 1626 III 2 a.F *BGB* of the *Law of the Equal Rights Between Men and Women in the Field of Civil Law* in 1957.

208 *Katz*, Family Law in America, P. 117.

This doctrine of primary caretaker preference is to some extent closely linked to the doctrine of 'tender years preference', according to which the mother generally exercises physical custody towards the child after separation or divorce, as the child at its early age is mainly cared for by its mother. This doctrine of tender years preference launched by feminists greatly influenced legislation with respect to parental custody in the 19th and 20th centuries.[209]

Both doctrine of primary caretaker and of tender years preference only focus custody disputes on custodian, rather than the child. Therefore, they cannot demonstrate what is in the best interests of the child. Although neither the doctrine of tender years preference nor the doctrine of primary caretaker principle was expressly stipulated in German law, the courts previously tended to decide in the mother's favour if the child was in the first years of its life.[210]

3.3.2.4 Principle of the Best Interests of the Child

The legal acknowledgement that the principle of the best interests of a child should be the decisive criterion in deciding upon issues concerning parental custody, however, does not help us determine what those best interests are in a particular case. It is more productive to discover how this principle can be best applied, and which specific criteria should be taken into consideration when determining the child's best interests.

Deciding what is in the child's best interests requires an analysis of many factors. Generally speaking, the parents' capability to care for their child; the continuity of the child's environment from both material and psychological perspective[211]; the psychosocial connection of the child to its parents, siblings, grandparents, and others with whom the child has a close relationship (§ 1682,

---

209 *Custody of Infants Act* 1839 and 1873.

210 *Lüderitz*, Die Rechtsstellung ehelicher Kinder nach Trennung ihrer Eltern im künftigen Recht der Bundesrepublik Deutschland, FamRZ 1975, 606.

211 *Coester*, Das Kindeswohl als Rechtsbegriff, P. 177: in the book of Goldstein, Freud, and Solnit *Beyond the Best Interests of the Child*, originally published in 1973, mental health concepts were integrated into the best interests test and the authors postulated that the child's most important emotional need after separation and divorce was psychological stability and preservation of key emotional relationships. They advocated that the court should identify the child's single 'psychological parent' and give that parent all custody rights. To the authors, the child's need for stability was so important that they advocated that the psychological parent should have the power to deny the other parent contact with the child.

§ 1685 I *BGB*) and the will of the child once it has reached a specific age[212] shall be taken into consideration by the court when deciding what is in the child's best interests.[213] However, whether the outcomes of the psychological experiments (on the mental health of the child or psychological connection between the parents and the child) are reliable, due to the current limitation of science and technology, is questionable.

When determining what the best interests are for a child, there is no fixed checklist which can be referred to in every situation, and applying this principle requires an individual assessment to be made in each case.[214]

3.3.3 In German Law

3.3.3.1 Introduction

Importance of the principle of the best interests of the child has also been recognised in German law. Already in the *Marriage Act of 1938*[215], it was proposed that the best interests of the child should act as the guideline for the distribution of the parental authority after divorce. Although the term 'the best interests of the child' has been used in the *Reform of Parental Custody Act* (§§ 1634, 1666, 1671, 1672, 1680, 1681 a.F *BGB*)[216], it was explicitly adopted into the *BGB* as a principle (§ 1697a[217]) by the *Act on the Reform of Parents and Children Law* in 1998. In the current *BGB*, 'the best interests of child' is mentioned thirty-five times, whereas it was only present once in the *BGB* of 1900 (§ 1666 *BGB* a.F of 1900), which reflects the significant change in the social status of the child and legislative guideline during the past century. Rules[218] demonstrating the principle of best interests of the child in the current *BGB* have been expressed in

212 According to § 1671 I 1, II 1 *BGB*, the transfer of the parental custody shall not be granted if the child beyond the age of 14 is against such a transfer, although the other parent or the mother has agreed with it.

213 *Schwab*, Handbuch des Scheidungsrechts (2013), P. 593 Rn. 105.

214 *Schwab*, Handbuch des Scheidungsrechts (2013), P. 594 Rn. 106.

215 RGBl I 807.

216 *Balloff*, Alleinerziehung und gemeinsame elterliche Sorge nach Trennung und Scheidung - Eine theoretische und empirische Vergleichsstudie, P. 192.

217 This Article was added into the *BGB* in 1998 by the *Reform Act on Parent and Child Law* (*KindRG*).

218 It is mentioned in § 1626 III, § 1627, § 1629, § 1631b, § 1666, § 1671, § 1678, § 1680, § 1681, § 1684, § 1685, § 1686, § 1686a, § 1687 II, § 1687b II, III, § 1688 III, § 1696 I, II, § 1697a, § 1741 I, § 1751 III, § 1757 IV, § 1761 II, § 1763 I, II, § 1764 IV *BGB*.

different ways. For example, it requires that transfer of the parental custody to an unmarried father in § 1671 II *BGB* shall be most conducive to the best interests of the child[219] (dem Kindeswohl am besten entspricht) on condition that a joint parental custody cannot be expected, while such a transfer will be granted by § 1626a *BGB* II if it is not inconsistent with the best interests of the child[220] (dem Kindeswohl nicht widerspricht). Other expressions concerning the best interests of the child can also be found in § 1687b *BGB* where all legal acts can be undertaken that are necessary to ensure the best interests of the child (die zum Wohl des Kindes notwendig/erforderlich ist). The *BGH* has pointed out that for the first time after § 1626a *BGB* and § 155 *FamFG* came into force on 19 May 2013, there is no substantial legal difference between the positive and negative criterion to evaluate the best interests of the child in § 1626a II 1 and § 1671 I 2 Nr. 2 *BGB*.[221]

3.3.3.2 Application Scope of This Principle

The principle of the best interests of the children shall be applied as the paramount guideline for the court when deciding upon any question concerning parental custody if it is not otherwise regulated in §§1626a II, 1671 I 1 and II 1, 1686 and 1686 I 2 *BGB*.[222] In addition, the principle of the best interests of the child provides justification for necessary intervention of public authorities with regard to the parent's performance in parental custody according to Article 2 II 2 *GG*.[223] Parents shall also follow the principle of the best interests of the child, who shall examine their performance and decisions related to parental custody with this principle, as provided for in § 1627 *BGB*.

3.3.3.3 Criteria to Evaluate the Best Interests of the Child

The principle of the best interests of the child requires comprehensively taking all aspects which could be important for the child and its future development

219 The same expression can be found in § 1697a where the principle of the best interests of the child was adopted as a legal principle.

220 Similar expression can be found in § 1671 III, § 1678 II, § 1680 II, § 1681 II, § 1686, § 1686 I 2 *BGB*.

221 *BGH*, Beschluss v. 15. Juni 2016 - XII ZB 419/15 -, juris Rn. 10, 15, 17 = NJW 2016, 2497 -2502 = FamRZ 2016, 1439–1444 = NZFam 2016, 795–800 = ZKJ 2016, 414–419 = FuR 2016, 576–578.

222 *Johannsen/Heinrich/Jaeger* (2015), § 1697a Rn. 1.

223 *Coester*, Das Kindeswohl als Rechtsbegriff, P. 173.

into account in each individual case.[224] In light of different family backgrounds and living conditions, evaluation of the best interests of the child should be conducted individually on a case-by-case basis.[225] Therefore, the court is obliged to examine every aspect that may be considered a criterion to evaluate the best interests of the child in each case.[226] Rather than simply determine which aspects will be of importance to the best interests of the child, the court should make a decision which is most beneficial to the child after having taken all the criteria into account.[227]

Generally, to decide what the best interests of the child in matters concerning parental custody are, the court shall take into consideration the capability of parents to care for the child, the continuity of the child's living circumstances, the connection between parents and child, and the will of the child.[228] However, there should not be a delineated or strict hierarchy of the criteria which are generally considered to impose influence upon the best interests of the child,[229] as a criterion which is less relevant to the best interests of the child in one case may be a crucial factor in another.[230]

a) Capability of Parents

To determine whether a parent is capable of caring for a child, the court shall uncover whether he or she can meet needs of the child for physical, mental and

---

224 *Rauscher*, Familienrecht, S. 832 Rn. 958.

225 *Schwab/Gottwald/Lettmaier*, 2017, P. 87, Rn. 196; *Staudinger/Coester* (2016), § 1671 Rn. 173; *Coester*, Kindeswohl, 143 ff.

226 *Staudinger/Coester* (2016), § 1671 Rn. 173; *Coester*, Kindeswohl, 465 ff.; *BVerfG*, Nichtannahmebeschluss v. 27.6.2008 - 1 BvR 1265/08 -, juris Rn. 19 = FamRZ 2009, 189, 190.

227 *Staudinger/Coester* (2016), § 1671 Rn. 174; *BGH*, Beschluss v. 11.7.1984 - IVb ZB 73/83 -, juris Rn. 7 = NJW 1985, 1702, 1703; *BGH*, Beschluss v. 6.12.1989 - IVb ZB 66/88 -, juris Rn. 8 = FamRZ 1990, 392, 393; *BGH*, Beschluss v. 28.4.2010 - XII ZB 81/09 -, juris Rn. 19 = FamRZ 2010, 1060.

228 *Fröschle*, Sorge und Umgang in der Rechtspraxis, P. 62 Rn. 281; *Staudinger/Coester* (2016), § 1671 Rn. 177.

229 *Staudinge/Coester* (2016), § 1671 Rn. 175.

230 *BGH*, Beschluss v. 15.6.2016 - XII ZB 419/15 -, juris Rn. 20 = FamRZ 2016, 1439, Rn. 20; *BGH*, Beschluss v. 16.3.2011 - XII ZB 407/10 -, juris Rn. 43 = FamRZ 2011, 796; *BGH*, Beschluss v. 28.4.2010 - XII ZB 81/09 -, juris Rn. 19 = FamRZ 2010, 1060; *KG Berlin*, Beschluss v. 14.3.2013 - 13 UF 234/12 -, juris Rn. 21 = FamRZ 2014, 50; *OLG Brandenburg*, Beschluss v. 11.4.2014 - 3 UF 50/13 -, juris Rn. 51; *OLG Brandenburg*, Beschluss v. 11.10.2012 - 13 UF 234/12 -, juris Rn. 64 = FamRZ 2013, 554.

health care, provide protection and whether he or she is a trustworthy person on whom the child can always rely.[231]

In the event of conflicts between parents on physical custody, a parent should not be transferred the right to exercise physical custody if he or she suffers from an illness that makes him incapable to care for the child and imposes negative influence on the child.[232] Generally, parents who suffer schizophrenia are unsuitable to care for children from the perspective of psychologists, while rights of parents who are alcoholic or afflicted by depression shall not always be excluded.[233] The financial situation of one parent could also be taken into consideration[234], but should be put behind the criteria related to personal aspects of children's best interests.[235] However, the financial situation of one parent would come to play a key role when the other parent could not guarantee the minimum economical standard[236] or the insecure financial situation of the other parent could lead to instability of the living environment of the child.[237]

There is no doubt that it is better for the best interests of the child if the parents, rather than a third party (for instance, the grandparents), care for the child.[238] That is the reason why physical parental custody is often granted to the

---

231 *OLG Brandenburg*, Beschluss v. 26.9.2016 - 10 UF 62/16 -, juris Rn. 38 = FamRZ 2016, 911.

232 *Pietzker*, Häufig vorkommende psychiatrische Erkrankungen im Sorge- und Umgangsverfahren - Beschreibung der Krankheitsbilder, FPR 2005, 222 ff.; *Kindler*, Folgewirkungen schwerer psychischer Erkrankungen mindestens eines Elternteils auf die Entwicklung von Kindern, FPR 2005, 227 ff.; *Lenz*, Kinder psychisch kranker Eltern - interinstitutionelle Kooperation als Voraussetzung für wirksame Hilfeleistungen, FPR 2005, 246; *Ehinger*, Die Regelung der elterlichen Sorge bei psychischer Erkrankung eines Elternteils oder beider Eltern im Überblick, FPR 2005, 253, 257.

233 *Arntzen*, Elterliche Sorge und Umgang mit Kindern: ein Grundriss der forensischen Familienpsychologie, P. 21.

234 *OLG Celle*, Beschluss v. 23.7.1984 - 12 UF 97/84 -, juris Rn. 5 = FamRZ 1984, 1035, 1036.

235 *OLG Brandenburg*, Beschluss v. 26.9.2016 - 10 UF 62/16 -, juris Rn. 92; *OLG Brandenburg*, Beschluss v. 9.5.2016 - 10 UF 117/15 -, juris Rn. 78 = NZFam 2016, 955; *OLG Hamburg*, Beschluss v. 17.12.2015 - 2 UF 107/14 -, juris Rn. 43 = FamRZ 2016, 912; *OLG Sachsen-Anhalt*, Beschluss v. 26.3.2010 - 8 UF 53/10 -, juris Rn. 16; *Johannsen/Henrich/Jaeger* (2015), § 1671 Rn. 53.

236 *OLG Bamberg*, Beschluss v. 23.7.1985 - 7 UF 42/85 = FamRZ 1985, 1175, 1178.

237 *OLG Celle*, Beschluss v. 23.7.1984 - 12 UF 97/84 -, juris Rn. 4–5 = FamRZ 1984, 1035, 1036; *OLG Hamm*, Beschluss v. 8.7.1988 - 5 UF 403/87 = FamRZ 1988, 1313 ff.

238 *OLG Brandenburg*, Beschluss v. 1.3.2001 - 9 WF 177/00 -, juris Rn. 10 = FamRZ 2001, 1021, 1022; *OLG Stuttgart*, Beschluss v. 25.2.1988 - 17 UF 17/88 -, juris Rn. 4 = NJW

parent who has more time to care for the child if other factors are almost equal between parents.[239] However, there is no general rule that a parent who does not need to work or who works less than the other parent should preferentially be granted the right of physical parental custody.[240]

Furthermore, it is believed that a parent who is willing and able to place personal tensions with the other parent second to the interests of the child, who tries not to get the child involved in parental conflicts, and always ensures the child feels cared for by both parents is more capable and qualified to care for the child.[241] If joint parental custody is not enforceable because of irreconcilable conflicts between parents, the connection tolerance of one parent could be decisive when deciding to whom the parental custody is transferred.[242] Contrarily, using a child as a weapon by one parent against the other is detrimental to the best interests of the child.

Foreign nationality and a possibility of emigration of parents generally plays an insignificant role in cross-border cases involving parental custody.[243] The court

---

1988, 2620, 2621; *OLG Bamberg*, Beschluss v. 3.11.1987 - 7 UF 47/87 -, juris Rn. 21 = FamRZ 1988, 750, 751; *BVerfG*, Beschluss v. 5.11.1980 - 1 BvR 349/80 -, juris Rn. 31 = *BVerfGE* 55, 171 = NJW 1981, 217, 219.

239 *OLG Köln*, Beschluss v. 14.11.2013 - II-10 UF 143/13 -, juris Rn. 21 = FamRZ 2014, 575; *OLG Stuttgart*, Beschluss v. 14.3.2007 - 16 UF 13/07 -, juris Rn. 5 = FamRZ 2007, 1266, 1267; *OLG Hamm*, Beschluss v. 14.2.2000 - 6 UF 141/99 -, juris Rn. 13 = FamRZ 2000, 1039, 1040.

240 *OLG Brandenburg*, Beschluss v. 26.9.2016 - 10 UF 62/16 -, juris Rn. 41; *OLG Brandenburg*, Beschluss v. 29.7.2013 - 3 UF 47/13 -, BeckRS 2013, 19107; *OLG Brandenburg*, Beschluss v. 6.8.2012 - 10 UF 139/11, BeckRS 2012, 18808; *OLG Brandenburg*, Beschluss v. 9.3.2009 - 10 UF 204/08, BeckRS 2009, 09543.

241 *Staudinger/Coester* (2016), § 1671 Rn 197; *BGH*, Beschluss v. 16.3.2011 - XII ZB 407/10 -, juris Rn. 54= FamRZ 2011, 796, Rn 54; *BVerfG*, Nichtannahmebeschluss v. 27.6.2008 - 1 BvR 1265/08 -, juris Rn. 22 = FamRZ 2009, 189, 190; *OLG Brandenburg*, Beschluss v. 1.3.2001 - 9 WF 177/00 -, juris Rn. 13–14 = FamRZ 2001, 1021, 1022; *OLG Hamm*, Beschluss v. 14.2.2000 - 6 UF 141/99 -, juris Rn. 14 = FamRZ 2000, 1039, 1040; *BGH*, Beschluss v. 11.7.1984 - IVb ZB 73/83 -, juris Rn. 19 = NJW 1985, 1702, 1704; *BVerfG*, Urteil v. 3.11.1982 - 1 BvL 25/80, 1 BvL 38/80, 1 BvL 40/80, 1 BvL 12/81 -, juris Rn. 48 = *BVerfGE* 61, 358 = FamRZ 1982, 1179 = NJW 1983, 101.

242 *OLG Brandenburg*, Beschluss v. 8.12.2014 - 10 UF 194/13 -, juris Rn. 47 = FamRZ 2015, 1304; *OLG Köln*, Beschluss v. 14.11.2013 - II-10 UF 143/13 -, juris Rn. 21= FamRZ 2014, 575; *KG Berlin*, Beschluss v. 24.4.2008 - 19 UF 12/08 -, juris Rn. 11 = FamRZ 2008, 2054.

243 *BGH*, Beschluss v. 16.3.2011 - XII ZB 407/10 -, juris Rn. 54 = FamRZ 2011, 796; *KG Berlin*, Beschluss v. 23.3.2009 - 16 UF 57/09 -, juris Rn. 2 = FamRZ 2009, 1762.

should not impose restrictions on the movement of a parent, which is counter to the personal rights and freedom of movement of that parent.[244] Moreover, a lack of proficiency in the German language of a parent, particularly when compared with the familial connection, the will of the child and the principle of continuity, should not be considered a key factor by the courts to deny his or her application for the transfer of parental custody if the parent assists the child to integrate better.

b) Connection of the Child

The *SorgRG* emphasised the connection between parents and children in decisions concerning transfer of parental custody after divorce of parents.[245] However, this criterion was removed from § 1671 a.F in the *KindRG* as there could be, besides connection of the child to parents, other criteria relevant in determining the best interests of the child.[246] However, the importance of connection of the child in determination of the best interests of the child is confirmed in the current *BGB*, namely in § 1626 III and § 1685 *BGB* indicating that it is in the best interests of the child to have contact with parents or other persons with whom it has important ties.

A child has connections not only to its parents, grandparents, siblings, but also guardians, friends, kindergarten and school. The closer the connections are, the more serious negative consequence might arise if the connections are broken. It should not be concluded which parent has a closer relationship to the child just by simply comparing the time each parent has spent caring for the child, because connection is not a simple measure of quantity of caring. On the contrary, the quality of the relationship should be greatly valued.[247]

If a child is mainly cared for by one parent or its grandparents before separation or divorce of its parents, the parent will generally be granted priority to decide habitual residence of the child after separation or divorce, on condition that both parents are capable of caring for the child.[248]

---

244 *Staudinger/Coester* (2016), § 1671 Rn. 211, 259; § 1666 Rn. 149.

245 § 1671 II a.F, BGBl. I 1976, 1064: the court should make a decision which is in the best interests of the child; thereunder, the connection of the child, in particular to its parents and siblings, should be taken into account.

246 *BT-Drucks.* 13/4899, P. 99.

247 *Staudinger/Coester* (2016), § 1671 Rn. 206; *Johannsen/Henrich/Jaeger* (2015), § 1671 Rn. 72; *Jopt*, Nacheheliche Elternschaft und Kindeswohl - Plädoyer für das gemeinsame Sorgerecht als anzustrebenden Regelfall, FamRZ 1987, 875, 876.

248 *Staudinger/Coester* (2016), § 1671 Rn. 222; *OLG Köln*, Beschluss v. 14.11.2013 - II-10 UF 143/13 -, juris Rn. 25 = FamRZ 2014, 575; *OLG Brandenburg*, Beschluss v. 1.3.2001 - 9 WF 177/00 -, juris Rn. 5 = FamRZ 2001, 1021, 1022.

c) *Will of the Child*

The will of a child which can be determined by hearing of the child according to § 159 *FamFG* is of great importance to determine the best interests of the child.[249] It has been acknowledged that a child has the fundamental right to express its own will.[250] The will of the child above the age of 14 was proposed in the draft of the *SorgRG* in 1979 to be a criterion when deciding on denial of contact right of one parent.[251] However, such a proposal was ultimately not adopted, given that it might impose excessive burden upon the child[252] and parents might try to unduly influence decisions of the child.[253]

The will of the child has achieved importance again in § 1671 I 1 *BGB* since the *KindRG* in 1998 and § 1671 II 2 *BGB* since the *NeheSorgRG* in 2013, according to which the child who has reached the age of 14 has the right to object to the transfer of parental custody. In addition, the age of 14 is considered a watershed to grant a child some rights in procedural law according to § 9 I 3[254], § 60[255] and § 159 I 1[256] *FamFG*. Although the lawmakers insist that only a child above the age of 14 has the necessary maturity and competence to judge and decide, it is believed in practice that the will of the child above the age of 12

---

249 *Dettenborn*, Kindeswohl und Kindeswille, Psychologische und rechtliche Aspekte, 83 ff.

250 *BVerfG*, Beschluss v. 27.6.2008 - 1 BvR 311/08 -, juris Rn. 30 = FamRZ 2008, 1737; *BVerfG*, Beschluss v. 5.11.1980 - 1 BvR 349/80 -, juris Rn. 20 = *BVerfGE* 55, 171 (179) = NJW 1981, 217; *BVerfG*, Beschluss v. 21.5.1974 - 1 BvL 22/71 -, juris Rn. 106 = *BVerfGE* 37, 217 (252) = NJW 1974, 1609.

251 *BT-Drucks.* 7/2060, 5.

252 *Arntzen*, Elterliche Sorge und Umgang mit Kindern: ein Grundriss der forensischen Familienpsychologie, P. 65.

253 *BT-Drucks.* 8/2788, 40, 61.

254 § 9 *FamFG* (capacity to participate in proceedings): (1) those persons with capacity to participate in proceedings are: 3) persons with limited capacity to contract pursuant to civil law, insofar as they have reached the age of 14 and they are asserting a right granted under civil law in the proceedings that affect them.

255 § 60 *FamFG* (Right of minors to a complaint on appeal): a child, who is subject to parental custody, or a ward subject to guardianship, may exercise its right to file a complaint on appeal without the cooperation of its legal representative in all matters that affect him. The same shall apply in other matters in which the child or ward is to be examined prior to a decision by the court. This shall not apply to persons who lack capacity to contract or who have not reached the age of 14 by the time of the issuance of the decision.

256 § 159 I 1 *FamFG* (In-hearing of the child): the court shall conduct an in-person hearing with the child when he has reached the age of 14.

can generally provide a somewhat reliable basis for a court decision,[257] and that the will of a child under the age of 14 who has in a particular case shown the necessary maturity to make decisions independently can be taken into consideration.[258] Therefore, it is held that there is no need to set a minimum age here,[259] and whether the will of a child under the age of 14 should be taken into consideration differs in each individual case.[260] It should be recognised that as a child matures, its will should be given more and more weight when reaching decisions that will affect its future.[261]

When evaluating the best interests of the child, taking the will of the child into consideration can uncover the inner connection between parents and children[262], but also allow the child to exercise the right to decide for himself

---

257 *OLG Brandenburg*, Beschluss v. 2.5.2017 - 10 UF 2/17 -, juris Rn. 50; *OLG Hamburg*, Beschluss v. 17.12.2015 - 2 UF 107/14 -, juris Rn. 41 = FamRZ 2016, 911; *OLG Zweibrücken*, Beschluss v. 23.2.2016 - 5 UF 145/15 = BeckRS 2016, 105893 Rn. 19; *BVerfG*, Nichtannahmebeschluss v. 25.4.2015 - 1 BvR 3326/14 -, juris Rn. 17; *OLG Brandenburg*, Beschluss v. 9.3.2009 - 10 UF 204/08 -, juris Rn. 63 = FamRZ 2009, 1759, 1760; *OLG Brandenburg*, Beschluss v. 16.4.2008 - 9 UF 191/07 -, juris Rn. 28 = FamRZ 2008, 1474, 1476; *OLG Brandenburg*, Beschluss v. 30.4.2003 - 10 UF 5/03 -, juris Rn. 19 = FamRZ 2003, 1953, 1954; *OLG Schleswig*, Beschluss v. 25.8.1989 - 13 UF 119/89 -, juris Rn. 14 = FamRZ 1990, 433, 434; *OLG Düsseldorf*, Beschluss v. 27.12.1982 - 3 UF 34/82 -, juris Rn. 32 = FamRZ 1983, 293, 295; *Johannsen/Henrich/Jaeger* (2015), § 1671 Rn 81.

258 *BGH*, Beschluss v. 28.4.2010 - XII ZB 81/09 -, juris Rn. 31 and 49 = FamRZ 2010, 1060.

259 *Staudinger/Coester* (2016), § 1671 Rn. 243; *MüKo/Hennemann* (2017), § 1671 Rn. 63.

260 *Boele-Woelki/Ferrand/González Beilfuss*, Principles of European family law regarding parental responsibilities, 2007, 55 ff., 244 ff.; The will of the child above 12 years can generally provide relatively reliable basis to a court decision: *OLG Hamburg*, Beschluss v. 17.12.2015 - 2 UF 107/14 -, juris Rn. 41 = FamRZ 2016, 909; *OLG Brandenburg*, Beschluss v. 2.12.2014 - 10 UF 74/14 -, juris Rn. 54 = FamRZ 2015, 1214; *OLG Brandenburg*, Beschluss v. 10.12.2009 - 10 WF 208/09 -, juris Rn. 54 = FamRZ 2010, 662 (664); The will of a child at the age of 11 should be taken into consideration: *BVerfG*, Beschluss v. 27.6.2008 - 1 BvR 311/08 -, juris Rn. 37–40 = FamRZ 2008, 1737 (1738); *AG Bremen*, Beschluss v. 20.7.2016 - 65 F 7360/15 SO -, juris Rn. 21; The will of the child above 10 years should be considered: *OLG Schleswig*, Beschluss v. 26.2.2003 - 10 UF 195/02 -, juris Rn. 6 = FamRZ 2003, 1494 (1495); *KG Berlin*, Beschluss v. 6.8.2009 - 13 UF 106/08 -, juris Rn. 44–46 = FamRZ 2010, 135 (137).

261 *OLG Nürnberg*, Beschluss v. 30.11.2016 - 7 UF 1309/16 -, juris Rn. 71 = NZFam 2017, 185; *OLG Köln*, Beschluss v. 8.6.2016 - II 10 UF 200/15 -, juris Rn. 8; *BVerfG*, Beschluss v. 27.6.2008 - 1 BvR 311/08 -, juris Rn. 12 = FamRZ 2008, 1738.

262 *BVerfG*, Beschluss v. 26.9.2006 - 1 BvR 1827/06 -, juris Rn. 14 = FamRZ 2007, 105; *BGH*, Beschluss v. 6.12.1989 - IVb ZB 66/88 -, juris Rn. 8 = FamRZ 1990, 392, 393.

granted by the constitution[263]. However, it might be in some cases very difficult to find out whether the child, especially the one trapped in conflict of loyalty towards parents,[264] has expressed its feeling truly without any influence from any parent.[265] Therefore, apart from judicial hearing and analysis of guardian ad litem, there is need to ask experts to provide professional opinions.[266] According to § 26 *FamFG*, the family court may designate an expert to evaluate whether the child has shown its true will and whether it can justify its will. This expert opinion can be used as an evidence according to § 30 I *FamFG* and § 411a *ZPO*.

The will of a child should not be a decisive factor for the court to reach a decision without taking other objective criteria into consideration.[267] The will of the child has less weight, for example, if the parent whom the child is in favour of is less capable of caring for the child than the other parent. In other situations, the court could consider the will of the child as a crucial element when deciding whether to transfer sole parental custody to the one parent if both parents are equally qualified to care for the child.[268] In the situation where the best interests of the child are endangered by either of the parents, the will of the child in favour of one parent or the other plays no significant role, and the court will decide according to § 1666 *BGB*.

The court shall take account of the will of the child according to the nature of the child's will and its age. Generally, a firm and consistent desire will be more influential[269] than a vague or inconsistent desire.[270] In addition, the older the

---

263 *BGH*, Beschluss v. 16.3.2011 - XII ZB 407/10 -, juris Rn. 46 = FamRZ 2011, 796; *BVerfG*, Beschluss v. 27.6.2008 - 1 BvR 311/08 -, juris Rn. 32 = FamRZ 2008, 1737; *Palandt/Götz* (2018), § 1671 Rn. 41; *Staudinger/Coester* (2016), § 1671 Rn. 235.

264 *BVerfG*, Nichtannahmebeschluss v. 22.9.2014 - 1 BvR 2102/14 -, juris Rn. 19 = FamRZ 2015, 210, 211 (The will of a 6- year-old child is less important than stability of its living environment).

265 *Arntzen*, Elterliche Sorge und Umgang mit Kindern: ein Grundriss der forensischen Familienpsychologie, P. 13.

266 *Staudinger/Coester* (2016), § 1671 Rn. 239, 245; *OLG Saarbrücken*, Beschluss v. 5.3.2013 - 6 UF 48/13 -, juris Rn. 10 = FamRZ 2013, 1231; Die Rüge durch den *EGMR* im Fall *BB und FB/Deutschland*, FamRZ 2013, 845 Rn. 50; *OLG Brandenburg*, Beschluss v. 24.2.2012 - 10 UF 360/11 -, juris Rn. 41 = ZKJ 2012, 308, 311.

267 *OLG Schleswig*, Beschluss v. 3.2.2012 - 10 WF 263/11 -, juris Rn. 8 = FamRZ 2012, 1066.

268 *KG Berlin*, Beschluss v. 6.8.2009 - 13 UF 106/08 -, juris Rn. 44–46 = FamRZ 2010, 135, 137; *BVerfG*, Beschluss v. 27.6.2008 - 1 BvR 311/08 -, juris Rn. 40 = FamRZ 2008, 1737, 1739.

269 *BVerfG*, Beschluss v. 27.6.2008 - 1 BvR 311/08 -, juris Rn. 39 = FamRZ 2008, 1737, 1738.

270 *OLG München*, Beschluss v. 17.10.2011 - 2 UF 990/11 -, juris Rn. 25 = FamRZ 2012, 1062, 1063; *OLG Thüringen*, Beschluss v. 21.2.2011 - 1 UF 273/10 -, juris Rn. 63 =

child is, the more important its will is.[271] Although the will of the child is an important criterion for decision-making processes of the court, the child who is not willing to express its opinions should have its will respected and the court should not try to peer into the mind of the child through psychological tests or by trick questions.[272]

d) *Principle of Continuity*

It cannot be denied or ignored that the continuity of living environment is of significance for healthy mental development of a child, which has been confirmed from courts of all levels.[273] To follow the principle of continuity, regard should be given not only to the external living conditions but also to personal connections of the child.[274] It is generally positive for a child's development if the primary caregiver can continue caring for the child after separation or divorce and its familiar environments such as school, play parks and friends remain.[275] Therefore, when implementing the principle of continuity, the court should learn which parent can best guarantee consistent and stable care and education in the future

---

FamRZ 2011, 1070, 1071; *OLG Köln*, Beschluss v. 28.8.2008 - 4 UF 102/08 -, juris Rn. 16 = FamRZ 2009, 434; *OLG Brandenburg*, Beschluss v. 16.4.2008 - 9 UF 191/07 -, juris Rn. 28 = FamRZ 2008, 1474, 1476; *OLG Koblenz*, Beschluss v. 20.8.2007 - 13 UF 166/07 -, juris Rn. 6 = FamRZ 2008, 2301, 2302.

271 *OLG Saarbrücken*, Beschluss v. 27.4.2016 - 6 UF 22/16 -, juris Rn. 13; *BGH*, Beschluss v. 16.3.2011 - XII ZB 407/10 -, juris Rn. 46 = FamRZ 2011, 796; *BGH*, Beschluss v. 28.4.2010 - XII ZB 81/09 -, juris Rn. 31 = FamRZ 2010, 1060; *KG Berlin*, Beschluss v. 6.8.2009 - 13 UF 106/08 -, juris Rn. 45 = FamRZ 2010, 135; *BVerfG*, Beschluss v. 27.6.2008 - 1 BvR 311/08 -, juris Rn. 32 = FamRZ 2008, 1737 (1738); *BVerfG*, Beschluss v. 26.9.2006 - 1 BvR 1827/06 -, juris Rn. 24 = FamRZ 2007, 105; *OLG Schleswig*, Beschluss v. 26.2.2003 - 10 UF 195/02 -, juris Rn. 6 = FamRZ 2003, 1494 (1495).

272 *Staudinger/Coester* (2016), § 1666 Rn 279; *KG Berlin*, Beschluss v. 10.11.1989 - 17 UF 2346/89 -, juris Rn. 32 = FamRZ 1990, 1383, 1384

273 *BVerfG*, Nichtannahmebeschluss v. 22.9.2014 - 1 BvR 2102/14 -, juris Rn.12, 15 = FamRZ 2015, 210, 211; *OLG Celle*, Beschluss v. 23.7.1984 - 12 UF 97/84 -, juris Rn. 3 = FamRZ 1984, 1035, 1036; *BVerfG*, Urteil v. 3.11.1982 - 1 BvL 25/80, 1 BvL 38/80, 1 BvL 40/80, 1 BvL 12/81 -, juris Rn. 47 = *BVerfGE* 61, 358 = FamRZ 1982, 1179 = NJW 1983, 101; *OLG Frankfurt*, Beschluss v. 10.2.1982 - 5 UF 190/81 = FamRZ 1982, 531.

274 *OLG Karlsruhe*, Beschluss v. 10.10.2007 - 2 WF 121/07 -, juris Rn. 23 = FamRZ 2008, 633, 634; *OLG Köln*, Beschluss v. 10.8.1982 - 21 UF 169/81 -, juris Rn. 33–35 = FamRZ 1982, 1232, 1233.

275 *BVerfG*, Beschluss v. 5.9.2007 - 1 BvR 1426/07 -, juris Rn. 19 = FamRZ 2007, 1797 with comment from *Völker*, FamRB 2008, 9.

after separation or divorce.[276] However, forced continuity is generally not in the best interests of the child and therefore will not be worth protection.[277]

The principle of continuity is of much greater importance to relatively young children than to the older children who have gained some independence from parents.[278] If, for example, a ten-year-old child is equally close to both parents and does not express its will, the principle of continuity can become a deciding factor in courts' decision in determining the future residence of the child.[279] However, continuity is not a key factor in decisions on transfer of the right to determine residence of a child who is no more than three years old and parents have lived separately in the marital home for nine months.[280]

e) An Example of Case-Law

aa) Legal Facts

The parents in this case married in 2008, and their two children M and N were born after marriage. They separated in November 2016 but still lived in the same apartment in A until the mother took the two children away from home to a women's shelter in December 2017. Since May 2018, M lives with his father in B, while the younger son N stays with his mother in the apartment in A where the parents lived together before separation. As M also lived and went to the school in A before May 2018, the father had to drive M from B to go to school in A because M could not register in the school of B without the consent of the mother. The mother applied to the local court for transfer of the sole parental custody so that she could decide on habitual residence, health care and school issues of M alone, while the father applied for transfer of the right to determine residence of M to him alone. In August 2018, the local court transferred the right to determine residence of M and to arrange school issues of M to the father. After the decision made by the court of first instance on 22 August 2018, the father registered

---

276 *BGH,* Beschluss v. 6.12.1989 - IVb ZB 66/88 -, juris Rn. 8 = FamRZ 1990, 392.

277 *BVerfG,* Beschluss v. 27.6.2008 - 1 BvR 1265/08 -, juris Rn. 23 = FamRZ 2009, 189.

278 *OLG München,* Beschluss v. 17.10.2011 - 2 UF 990/11 -, juris Rn. 21 = FamRZ 2012, 1062; *KG Berlin,* Beschluss v. 6.8.2009 - 13 UF 106/08 -, juris Rn. 43 = FamRZ 2010, 135 (137); *OLG Brandenburg,* Beschluss v. 1.3.2001 - 9 WF 177/00 -, juris Rn. 6 = FamRZ 2001, 1022; *OLG Köln,* Beschluss v. 10.8.1982 - 21 UF 169/81 -, juris Rn. 35 = FamRZ 1982, 1232, 1233.

279 *OLG Brandenburg,* Beschluss v. 6. 2.2013 - 9 UF 226/12 -, juris Rn. 28, 33.

280 *OLG Zweibrücken,* Beschluss v. 17.8.2000 - 5 UF 66/99 -, juris Rn. 29 = FamRZ 2001, 184, 185.

M for school in B. The mother filed a complaint against the decision of the court of first instance. However, the appeal of the mother was rejected.[281]

bb) Application of Criteria to Evaluate the Best Interests of the Child

The court of second instance examined in a first step whether the joint parental custody and in a second step whether transfer of the sole parental custody (or a part of it) to the father corresponded to the best interests of M. In the second step, the court took consideration of all the important aspects related to the child's interests into consideration, namely principle of continuity, connection and will of the child, and capability of parents (Rn. 30–33).

From perspective of principle of continuity, the court considered first whether parental responsibilities towards M have changed after separation of parents. During the marriage, M was equally cared for by both parents, and after separation of parents, M stayed almost the same time with each parent. Furthermore, the court checked whether social surroundings including friends' circles and school of the child have changed and whether such a change is detrimental to the best interests of the child. Although M only moved to B to live with his father in May 2018 and switched to the school in B after decision of the court of first instance had been made, M has got used to the new environment, which has been also confirmed by his teachers of the school in B and the guardian ad litem.

Although it cannot be concluded from the principle of continuity that the father should be transferred of the sole right to determine residence and school issues of the child, the following aspects of the connection and will of the child speak for such a transfer. The expert found that M has a more positive relationship with his father than with his mother, although M also maintains a very good relationship with the mother. Having considered that M would blame himself and the mother if the father could not be transferred the right to determine residence of M, the expert assessed that the only chance to maintain and stabilise a good relationship between M and both parents is that M would reside with his father habitually, while right of the mother to contact with M should be guaranteed (Rn. 48). Furthermore, the expert considered relationship between M and his younger brother who resides with the mother habitually should play a subordinate role to decide whether the mother should be transferred the right to determine residence of M (Rn. 49). In addition, will of M could reflect his relationship to his parents. According to the expert opinions, M's will to live with his

281 *OLG Karlsruhe*, Beschluss v. 22. 1.2019 - 20 UF 130/18 -, juris Rn. 24.

father was stable and genuine, although he might be manipulated or influenced by his father (Rn. 52).

Apart from the last aspects, the court also considered which parent could provide M a better care, education and chance to develop himself. In addition, the court attached importance to the question whether one parent would motivate the child to establish or maintain personal contact with the other parent. In this case, both parents were equally capable of promoting self-development of M and meeting his needs. However, compared with the mother who always recognised the importance of M's maintaining contact with his father and facilitated contact between them, the father who doubted the ability of the mother to educate and care for the child should be more cooperative to promote meaningful contact between M and his mother which is in the best interests of the child (Rn. 59).

After having weighed all the above-mentioned aspects, the court rejected the appeal of the mother. The father therefore kept the right to determine the residence of M and to decide on his school issues on the condition that he would guarantee contact between M and the mother and bring M to play therapy recommended by the expert (Rn. 62).

3.3.3.4 Conclusion

It can be concluded that capability of parents, the relationship of the child to its parents, the will of the child and the principle of continuity are the most important criteria when determining the best interests of the child. All these criteria mentioned above interweave and influence each other. As each child is different and lives in a different network of relationships, criteria applied to determine what is best for a particular child will be different from case to case.[282] One criterion which should be considered with priority in one case might be less important in the other case.[283] For instance, the personal connection of a child to one of its parent might not be considered if that parent imposes consistently negative influence on the child; and despite close connection to his or her child, the parent who is suitable and capable of caring for the child might not be transferred parental custody.[284]

---

282 *Herring*, Relational autonomy and family law, P. 46; *Rauscher*, Familienrecht, S. 832 Rn. 958.

283 *BGH*, Beschluss v. 15. 6. 2016 - XII ZB 419/15 -, juris Rn. 31 = FamRZ 2016, 1439; *OLG Brandenburg*, Beschluss v. 27.12.2016 - 10 UF 23/16 -, juris Rn. 70.

284 *BGH*, Beschluss v. 11.7.1984 - IVb ZB 73/83 -, juris Rn. 9 = NJW 1985, 1702; *OLG München*, Beschluss v. 12.4.1991 - 26 UF 1464/89 = FamRZ 1991, 1343, 1345; *OLG*

Although the principle of the best interests of children has been criticised for its uncertain evaluation criteria, potential abuse of the court's discretion, increased procedural cost and neglect of parents' interests, it is still widely applied because it represents an important social and moral value that children who are inevitably vulnerable and dependent must be protected from harm and given every opportunity to become healthy and well-adjusted adults.[285]

Frankfurt, Beschluss v. 14.9.1998 - 3 UF 89/98 -, juris Rn. 11 = FamRZ 1999, 392, 393; *Johannsen/Henrich/Jaeger* (2015), § 1671 Rn. 71.

285 *Cretney*, Principles of Family Law, P. 649.

4 Parental Custody for the Child Born in Wedlock

A child is born in wedlock if it is born during the marriage of its parents. The mother of a child born in wedlock is the woman who has given birth to that child, as is legally defined in § 1591 *BGB*. Although a child originates from the ovum (egg), the woman who donated the ovum cannot be called the legal mother of this child, because she has not delivered the child. The legal father of a child born in wedlock, who might not be the biological father, only refers to the one who is married to the mother at the time of birth of the child (§ 1592 *BGB*).

In an 'intact' family where the child is born in wedlock and its parents do not get separated (§ 1567 *BGB*)[286] or divorced (§ 1564 *BGB*), there are usually no conflicts between parents on the habitual residence of the child, child support or exercise of the contact right. Although not explicitly expressed in laws, parents who are already married at the time of birth of the children shall exercise joint parental custody, which requires parents to make decisions for their children jointly per § 1627 *BGB*. After separation or divorce, parents shall still exercise joint parental custody to their child born in wedlock since entry into force of the *KindRG* in 1998. However, either of the parents may apply to the family court for transfer of the whole or part of parental custody to them alone pursuant to § 1671 I *BGB* if they have lived apart for a period that is not merely temporary, and they have joint parental custody. If parents live apart because of separation or divorce, parental custody should be reallocated. Parents shall make agreement on issues concerning habitual residence of the child, exercise of contact rights, payment of child support, etc.

4.1 Joinder of Divorce Proceedings and Ancillary Proceedings

A marriage can be dissolved if the court grants the application of one or both spouses for divorce (§ 1564 I *BGB*). Application for divorce must contain the

286 § 1567 *BGB*: the spouses are living apart if there is no domestic community between them and a spouse recognisably does not intend to create this because he rejects conjugal community. Domestic community also no longer exists if the spouses live apart in the matrimonial home.

declaration whether a couple has reached an agreement on parental custody, right of contact, support to the minor children, alimony and legal distribution of marital home and household objects (§ 133 I 2 *FamFG*). Parental custody, right of contact and child support, though legally independent,[287] constitute the parental custody in a wide sense and are the most important issues related to the child after separation or divorce of parents. According to § 137 III *FamFG*, disputes on the transfer or deprivation of parental custody, right of contact or right to require surrender of the child shall be tried in combination (with divorce matters) in divorce proceedings. By combining divorce proceeding and the related issues in § 137 *FamFG*, the lawmakers aimed at, on the one hand, making parents aware of contingent consequences of divorce so that there would not be so many hasty divorces (warning function) and, on the other hand, preventing parents from getting out of marriage without reaching agreement on the other important issues (protection function).[288]

4.2 Determination of the Residence of the Child

Although parents are still entitled to joint parental custody after separation or divorce, the court, by determining habitual residence of the child, needs to decide whether the child should be mainly cared for by one parent or by both parents in turns if the parents cannot reach an agreement on the residence of the child. Following the guiding principle of the best interests of the child, the court shall take into account of factors elaborated in section 3.3.3.3 in determination of the residence of a child. Generally, there are three residence types for children whose parents get separated or divorced, namely the residence model, the nest model and switching model (hereinafter referred to as the Wechselmodell).

4.2.1 Residence Model (Residenzmodell)

The residence model practised by the great majority of the parents who get separated is the only model regulated by law in § 1687 *BGB*.[289] Under this model, the child resides with one parent (hereinafter referred to as the resident parent) and only has one habitual residence after the separation or divorce of its parents. The parent with whom the child does not live habitually (hereinafter referred to as the non-resident parent) is not freed of the obligation of parental custody and

287 *Mayer*, Der Kindesverbund - Ein Plädoyer, FamRZ 2016, 430.
288 *MüKo/Heiter* (2013), § 137 Rn. 2.
289 *Schumann*, B 9.

is entitled and obliged to maintain contact with the child. In addition, the non-resident parent must pay child support to the resident parent.

Under this model, the resident parent generally knows the child better and can make a better decision in the child's interests than the non-resident parent.[290] It is argued that this model might lead to alienation between the non-resident parent and the child because of the infrequent contact with each other. Moreover, it is criticised that the resident parent seems to exercise the sole parental custody in fact, which makes joint parental custody only exist in name. This is an important reason why the Wechselmodell has been under heated discussion.

4.2.2 Nest Model (Nestmodell)

The nest model[291] allows the child to stay in a fixed residence to which its parents should come to care for him by turns. This residence could be the one where the parents lived together before they got separated or divorced or could be the other residence bought or rented by parents only for the child. This model could avoid that the child must adapt to new living and schooling environment. It might be possible that there are only two residences in total, with one for the child as a nest residence and one for the parents to live in by turns. However, it is not practical for parents to share one residence after separation or divorce. Therefore, the nest model would not be practical if neither parent can afford a new residence or find a new residence (e.g., sharing the residence of his or her new partner).

4.2.3 Switching Model (Wechselmodell)

4.2.3.1 Introduction

a) Definition

The child to whom parents exercise joint parental custody usually resides with one parent habitually after separation or divorce of parents (§ 1687 I 2 *BGB*). Therefore, the non-resident parent generally cannot spend the same amount of time with the child as the resident parent. However, the non-resident parent can apply for the Wechselmodell which enables him or her to play the same role as the resident parent in caring for the child and to keep close contact with the child

290 *Luthin*, Gemeinsames Sorgerecht nach Scheidung, S. 59.

291 *Salzgeber*, Das Wechselmodell, NZFam 2014, 921 (923); *Kinderrechtekommission des Deutschen Familiengerichtstags e.V.*, Das Wechselmodell im deutschen Familienrecht, FamRZ 2014, 1157.

after separation or divorce.[292] The Wechselmodell can be assumed if parents care for the child in turns so that each parent undertakes about half of caring or educational tasks.[293] The Wechselmodell does not emphasise the equal distribution of caring time between parents, but the same responsibility both parents take towards the child.[294]

By reaching agreement on the Wechselmodell, parents tend to minimise the adverse consequences on the parent-child relationship brought by separation or divorce.[295] However, the Wechselmodell has meanwhile been challenged with the argument that a fixed life centre is more beneficial for the healthy development of a child.[296]

b) Precondition

Heilmann has listed preconditions for the granting of the Wechselmodell which is centred on the best interests of the child, according to which[297]:

- Sufficient capability of communication and cooperation of the parents, namely that they should have a sustainable social relationship and can reach an agreement on significant matters in exercise of parental custody;
- Both parents should be prepared and capable of meeting the increased requirement of communication in exercising the Wechselmodell;
- The child should have an almost equivalent connection to both parents;
- Both parents should be suitable to care for and educate the child;
- The Wechselmodell shall do justice to the will of the child;
- Some external conditions should also be fulfilled, for instance, short distance between parents' apartments.

---

292 *Dethloff/Kaesling*, Kindesunterhalt und Wechselmodell - Eine vergleichende Perspektive, FamRZ 2018, 73.

293 *OLG Dresden*, Beschluss v. 29.10.2015 - 20 UF 851/15 -, juris Rn. 18 = FamRZ 2016, 470; *BGH*, Beschluss v. 21.12.2005 - XII ZR 126/03 -, juris Rn. 9 = FamRZ 2006, 1015, with comment from *Luthin*.

294 *BGH*, Beschluss v. 5.11.2014 - XII ZB 599/13 -, juris Rn. 8 = FamRZ 2015, 236, 237.

295 *Maaß*, Keine Barunterhaltspflicht im echten Wechselmodell, FamRZ 2016, 603 (605).

296 *OLG Hamburg*, Beschluss v. 17.12.2015 - 2 UF 106/14 -, juris Rn. 27 = FamRZ 2016, 913; *OLG Karlsruhe*, Beschluss v. 5.11.2013 - 5 UF 27/13 -, juris Rn. 34 = FamRZ 2014, 1124; *OLG Dresden*, Beschluss v. 3.6.2004 - 21 UF 144/04 -, juris Rn. 13 = FamRZ 2005, 125; *Sünderhauf*, Vorurteile gegen das Wechselmodell: Was stimmt, was nicht? Argumente in der Rechtsprechung und Erkenntnisse aus der psychologischen Forschung, FamRB 2013, 333.

297 *Heilmann*, Kindeswohl und Wechselmodell, NJW 2015, 3346.

Hammer proposed to examine the best interests of the child in a court order of the Wechselmodell with two steps. In the first step, the court is to decide whether the Wechselmodell should be considered after analysing certain criteria (connection to parents, capability of parents, stability of living condition of the child, will of the child, and minimum level of cooperation and communication between parents) applied in proceedings related to § 1671 *BGB*, while in the second step the advantages and disadvantages of the Wechselmodell should be weighed against the other possible caring models.[298]

The Wechselmodell, which does not certainly reduce conflicts between parents[299], still requires parents to communicate and cooperate with each other. Therefore, the Wechselmodell shall not be ordered if parents are trapped in deep conflicts.[300] However, different approaches can be taken to avoid unnecessary burdens resulting from conflicts between parents exercising the Wechselmodell. For instance, the parents can try to communicate in writing (email, SMS and letters) or they can divide parental responsibilities beforehand.[301] In addition, researchers advise against ordering of the Wechselmodell for a child under the age of 3, to whose development a clear life centre is of great importance.[302]

4.2.3.2 Legal Issues in Dispute

Issues heatedly discussed are, for instance, whether the Wechselmodell should be regulated as a general rule and whether it can be ordered against the will of one parent.[303]

---

298 *Hammer*, Die gerichtliche Anordnung des Wechselmodells, FamRZ 2015, 1433 (1442).

299 *Salzgeber*, Das Wechselmodell, NZFam 2014, 921, 927.

300 *Heilmann*, Kindeswohl und Wechselmodell, NJW 2015, 3346 (3347); *OLG Schleswig*, Beschluss v. 16.6.2016 - 10 UF 197/15 -, juris Rn. 92 = FamRZ 2016, 1945.

301 *OLG Schleswig*, Beschluss v. 19.12.2013 - 15 UF 55/13 -, juris Rn. 50–52; *Sünderhauf*, Vorurteile gegen das Wechselmodell: was stimmt, was nicht? - Argumente in der Rechtsprechung und Erkenntnisse aus der psychologischen Forschung, FamRB 2013, 290.

302 *Rohmann*, Billigung nach § 156 *FamFG* Kindeswohlprüfung und Grenzen der Billigung, FPR 2013, 307 (311); *Salzgeber*, Das Wechselmodell, NZFam 2014, 921 (924).

303 *Hammer*, Die gerichtliche Anordnung des Wechselmodells, FamRZ 2015, 1433 (1434); *Hammer*, Anmerkung zum *OLG Hamburg*, Beschluss v. 17.12.2015 - 2 UF 106/14 = FamRZ 2016, 916.

a) As a General Rule?

It has been argued in some court decisions that the Wechselmodell is opposed to the residence model which, inferred from the provision of § 1687 *BGB*, should be the statutory guiding principle in the determination of the ways to care for the child after separation of parent.[304] On the question of whether the Wechselmodell should be introduced as a general rule of redistribution of parental care after separation if it is consistent with the best interests of the child, the *BVerfG* deems that it is not an obligation of legislature to stipulate the equal distribution of parental custody between parents as a general rule.[305] According to the *BVerfG*, § 1687 I *BGB* does not imply any discrimination in the sense of Article 3 III *GG* because of unequal distribution of parental custody; and such an inequality can be justified by the priority of guaranteeing the best interests of the child.[306]

b) Against Will of Parents?

It is unquestionable that parents whose autonomy in exercising parental custody is guaranteed by Article 6 II *GG* can apply for the Wechselmodell by mutual agreement. However, whether the Wechselmodell without agreement of the parents can be ordered by the court is at the centre of discussions.[307]

It is predominantly accepted that the Wechselmodell should generally not be ordered against will of the parents,[308] as the compulsory order of the

---

304 *OLG Koblenz*, Beschluss v. 6.2.2014 - 7 UF 797/13; *OLG Brandenburg*, Beschluss v. 7.6.2012 - 15 UF 314/11, juris Rn. 10 = FamRZ 2012, 1886.

305 *BVerfGE*, Nichtannahmebeschluss v. 24.6.2015 - 1 BvR 486/14 -, juris Rn. 12 = NJW 2015, 3366 (With comment from *Heilmann*, NJW 2015, 3346) = FamRZ 2015, 1585; *Fröschle*, Sorge und Umgang in der Rechtspraxis, S. 248 Rn. 1119a.

306 *BVerfGE*, Nichtannahmebeschluss v. 24.6.2015 - 1 BvR 486/14 -, juris Rn. 16.

307 *Schumann*, B 61, 65.

308 *Staudinger/Coester* (2016), § 1671 Rn. 23 and 60; *Salzgeber*, Das Wechselmodell, NZFam 2014, 921, 929; *OLG Thüringen*, Beschluss v. 12.9.2016 - 4 UF 678/15 -, juris Rn. 21 = FamRZ 2016, 2126; *OLG München*, Beschluss v. 31.8.2016 - 16 UF 1019/16 -, juris Rn. 12 = FamRZ 2016, 2120; *OLG Thüringen*, Beschluss v. 7.4.2016 - 2 UF 651/15 -, juris Rn. 15 = FamRZ 2016, 2122; *OLG Brandenburg*, Beschluss v. 15.2.2016 - 10 UF 213/14 -, juris Rn. 28 = FamRZ 2016, 1473; *AmtsG Konstanz*, Beschluss v 10.12.2015 - 6 F 126/14 -, juris Rn. 10 = FamRZ 2016, 476; *KG Berlin*, Beschluss v. 29.5.2015 - 18 UF 133/14 -, juris Rn. 11 = FamRZ 2015, 1910; *OLG Karlsruhe*, Beschluss v. 21.5.2015 - 18 UF 231/14 -, juris Rn. 20 = FamRZ 2015, 1736; *OLG Saarbrücken*, Beschluss v. 8.9.2014 - 6 UF 62/14 -, juris Rn. 14 = NJW-RR 2015, 135 = FamRZ 2015, 62; *OLG Naumburg*, Beschluss v. 8.8.2014 - 8 UF 152/14 -, juris Rn. 47 = FamRZ 2015, 764–765;

Wechselmodell might bring parents endless conflicts and therefore is not consistent with children's best interests.[309] Contrary to the prevailing view, it is held that the Wechselmodell can be ordered without consensus between parents.[310] Although it cannot be denied that the Wechselmodell will not be successfully carried out without cooperation, communication and compromise of parents,[311] will of parents nevertheless should not be considered a crucial criterion for the court to order the Wechselmodell. Instead, consensus between parents could be of subordinate importance.[312] The Wechselmodell is questionable if unwillingness of the other parent leads to substantial difficulties in communication between the parents and the potential escalation of conflicts between them, which is not correspondent to the best interests of the child. It is suggested that the court should take all relevant elements into account and evaluate disadvantages brought by the refusal of one parent and advantages of the Wechselmodell.[313]

c) *In Custody or Contact Proceedings?*

It has been deemed that the Wechselmodell which concerns determination of residence of the child and therefore should be part of parental custody cannot be ordered in the framework of the right of contact,[314] as right of contact with the child and right to determine residence for the child (§ 1631 I *BGB*) are

OLG Brandenburg, Beschluss v. 9.3.2009 - 10 UF 204/08 -, juris Rn. 78 = FamRZ 2009, 1759.

309 *Staudinger/Coester* (2016), § 1671 Rn. 261.

310 *OLG Hamburg*, Beschluss v. 17.12.2015 - 2 UF 106/14 -, juris Rn. 27 = FamRZ 2016, 912.

311 *OLG Thüringen*, Beschluss v. 12.9.2016 - 4 UF 678/15 -, juris Rn. 48 = FamRZ 2016, 2126; *OLG Saarbrücken*, Beschluss v. 8.9.2014 - 6 UF 62/14 -, juris Rn. 14 = NJW-RR 2015, 135 = FamRZ 2015, 62.

312 *OLG Schleswig*, Beschluss v. 19.12.2013 - 15 UF 55/13 -, juris Rn. 45, 58 (In this case, needs and wish of the child to participate equally in life of each parent overweigh the will of the parents).

313 *OLG Naumburg*, Beschluss v. 14.7.2014 - 4 UF 151/13 -, juris Rn. 6 = NJW 2015, 494 = FamRZ 2014, 1860.

314 *OLG Naumburg*, Beschluss v. 8.8.2014 - 8 UF 152/14 -, juris Rn. 47 = FamRZ 2015, 764–765; *OLG Karlsruhe*, Beschluss v. 21.5.2015 - 18 UF 231/14 -, juris Rn. 18, = FamRZ 2015, 1736; *BVerfG*, Nichtannahmebeschluss v. 24.6.2015 - 1 BvR 486/14 -, juris Rn. 12 = NJW 2015, 3366 = FamRZ 2015, 1585; *OLG Nürnberg*, Beschluss v. 8.12.2015 - 11 UF 1257/15 -, juris Rn. 41 = FamRZ 2016, 2119; *Hammer*, Die gerichtliche Anordnung des Wechselmodells, FamRZ 2015, 1433, 1439; Kinderrechtekommission des deutschen Familiengerichtstags, FamRZ 2014, 1157, 1163.

independent but place limits on each other.[315] Provisions on right of contact can therefore no longer be applied if the caring task is almost equally divided between parents so that the child has two life centres.[316] Contrarily, the *OLG Hamburg* considers it possible to grant the Wechsmodell which distributes the caring time equally between parents in proceedings regarding right of contact if it corresponds to the best interests of the child,[317] by arguing that the courts can make any decision which corresponds to the best interests of the child, as there are no concrete provisions on scope of the right of contact and ways to exercise it.[318] *Schumann*, maintaining that the caring model following separation of parents which does not concern status but exercise of parental care should not be dealt within the framework of § 1671 *BGB*, suggests that § 1628 *BGB* could be modified as follows to be applied for issues related to caring models[319]: 1. If the parents who exercise parental custody jointly but live apart permanently cannot make an agreement on caring model, the court can upon application of one parent order the caring model proposed by this parent if this caring model best corresponds to the best interests of the child after being taken into consideration of the actual situations and opportunity and as well as the interests of parents; 2. The court can limit the duration of the order under sentence 1 (probation period).

It is held that legal grounds for the order of the Wechselmodell can be found in both § 1671 I 1 *BGB* and § 1684 III *BGB*. According to § 1671 I 1 *BGB*, one parent can apply to the court for the periodical transfer of the right to determine residence of the child,[320] while according to § 1684 III *BGB*, the court can decide on how parents should exercise their right of contact concretely, as it is not provided for by law to what extent maximally the court can decide on the right of contact of the parents. However, no matter in which proceedings the Wechselmodell is

---

315 *OLG Karlsruhe*, Beschluss v. 21.5.2015 - 18 UF 231/14 -, juris Rn. 14 = FamRZ 2015, 1736).

316 *OLG Nürnberg*, Beschluss v. 8.12.2015 - 11 UF 1257/15 -, juris Rn. 41 = FamRZ 2016, 2119.

317 *OLG Hamburg*, Beschluss v. 17.12.2015 - 2 UF 106/14 -, juris Rn. 27 = FamRZ 2016, 912; Similar decision see *OLG Stuttgart*, Beschluss v. 23.08.2017 - 18 UF 104/17 -, juris Rn. 30 = FamRZ 2018, 35 (36 f.).

318 *OLG Hamburg*, Beschluss v. 17.12.2015 - 2 UF 106/14 -, juris Rn. 25 = FamRZ 2016, 913.

319 *Schumann*, B 69.

320 *Fröschle*, Sorge und Umgang in der Rechtspraxis, S. 96 Rn. 272.

ordered, the court shall examine in each individual case whether it is consistent with the best interests of the child.[321]

d) Positive Application of the Best Interests of the Child

Emphasis should be laid on the following aspects when deciding whether the Wechselmodell is in the best interests of the child. Generally, the Wechselmodell is not appropriate for the young children.[322] Not only the age but also the will of the child could be crucial for a court decision on the Wechselmodell which is seldom ordered against the will of a child.[323] Besides, the court should examine whether the parents maintain a sustainable social relationship and whether they have the minimal capability to communicate and cooperate with each other.[324] According to the prevailing view, the Wechselmodell will not serve the best interests of the child in case of deep conflicts between parents and therefore should not be considered from the very start.[325] In case that the Wechselmodell has been successfully practised by the parents or there are only disputes between them on whether to keep or extend this model, it will be deemed by the court to be consistent with the best interests of the child.[326]

Although there was only less than a third of parents practising Wechselmodell following separation in Germany, equally shared parental responsibility/care has become a trend in Germany.[327] However, the Wechselmodell though promoting the concept of equality between parents and rights of the father[328] should not be at cost of the best interests of the child.[329]

---

321 *BVerfG*, Nichtannahmebeschluss v. 24.6.2015 - 1 BvR 486/14 -, juris Rn. 21 = NJW 2015, 3366 = FamRZ 2015, 1585; *Heilmann*, Kindeswohl und Wechselmodell, NJW 2015, 3346 (3348).

322 *Löhnig*, Pendelkinder - Kindeswohl und gleichberechtigte, geteilte elterliche Verantwortung, NZFam 2016, 817; *Schumann*, B 64.

323 *Schumann*, B 64.

324 *Schumann*, B 65; *OLG Bamberg*, Beschluss v. 18.09.2017 - 2 UF 133/17 -, juris Rn. 32 = FamRZ 2018, 438 (440).

325 *Schumann*, B 67.

326 *Schumann*, B 62, 64.

327 *Schumann*, B 9.

328 See Resolution 2079 (2015) of Council of Europe on: http://assembly.coe.int/nw/xml/XRef/Xref-XML2HTML-EN.asp?fileid=22220 retrieved latest on 6 March 2019.

329 *Löhnig*, Pendelkinder - Kindeswohl und gleichberechtigte, geteilte elterliche Verantwortung, NZFam 2016, 817, 818.

e) *Current View of the* BGH

The *BGH* has finally taken a stand on the lasting controversy about whether the Wechselmodell can be ordered against the will of parents, (if so) upon which legal basis and according to which criterion the Wechselmodell can be ordered.[330] The *BGH* indicated that it cannot be inferred from § 1687 *BGB* that the residence model is a legal guideline for parental custody which excludes other ways to exercise parental custody, and that the child should be cared for mainly only by one parent after separation or divorce of parents. Furthermore, the *BGH* confirmed that the equal Wechselmodell enabling equal care between parents can also be ordered in proceedings concerning the right of contact.[331]

In determining whether to order the Wechselmodell, the best interests of the child, rather than mutual agreement between parents, shall be the essential criterion, which requires the court in each individual case to take all the elements into account that are of importance for the best interests of the child.[332] In addition, the equal Wechselmodell requires parents to have the minimal capability to communicate and cooperate with each other, because it is generally inconsistent with the best interests of the child if parents are trapped in serious conflicts.[333] From the perspective of the child, the Wechselmodell can only be ordered if the child maintains a sustainable relationship with both parents and should not be ordered as a way to promote willingness of parents to cooperate.[334] To investigate this, opinions of the child should be heard.[335]

330 *BGH*, Beschluss v. 1.2.2017 - XII ZB 601/15 = FamRZ 2017, 533.

331 *BGH*, Beschluss v. 1.2.2017 - XII ZB 601/15 = FamRZ 2017, 533, Rn. 18–19.

332 *BGH*, Beschluss v. 1.2.2017 - XII ZB 601/15 = FamRZ 2017, 533, Rn. 25–28.

333 *BGH*, Beschluss v. 1.2.2017 - XII ZB 601/15 = FamRZ 2017, 533, Rn.25, 31; More about consequences of conflicts between parents on the best interests of the child see: *Kindler/Walper*, Das Wechselmodell im Kontext elterlicher Konflikte, NZFam 2016, 820, 823; *Kostka*, Neue Erkenntnisse zum Wechselmodell, ZKJ 2014, 54; *Salzgeber*, Das Wechselmodell, NZFam 2014, 921, 929; *Hammer*, Die gerichtliche Anordnung des Wechselmodells, FamRZ 2015, 1433, 1441; *Finke*, Rechtliche Grundlagen und Ausgestaltung der Kindesbetreuung durch Eltern und Dritte, NZFam 2014, 865, 869.

334 *BGH*, Beschluss v. 1.2.2017 - XII ZB 601/15, FamRZ 2017, 533, Rn. 29.

335 *BGH*, Beschluss v. 1.2.2017 - XII ZB 601/15, FamRZ 2017, 533, Rn. 34.

4.2.3.3 *Problems in Practice*

So far, no research has proved whether the Wechselmodell has more positive impact on the child than the residence model[336], which seems to be preferred.[337] The following problems might occur in exercise of the Wechselmodell.

a) Physical Feasibility

The child not only profits but also might suffer from the Wechselmodell, as travel between two habitual residences, two different circles of friends and communication with the people from two different living environments might bring the child, especially the child at an early age, distraction, bewilderment and inconvenience. Therefore, this model is only practical when both parents do not live far away from one another so that the child does not need to switch schools all the time. Besides, it might not be feasible that the child after the separation or divorce of parents split its time between each parent.

b) Registration of Primary Residence

The child under the Wechselmodell has two habitual residences. However, parents can only choose one residence to register as the primary residence of the child.[338] Since registration of primary residence is a matter of everyday life in § 1687 I 3 *BGB*, either parent under Wechselmodell has the right to decide on it.[339] Therefore, the *BVerwG* requires parents first to determine the primary residence of the child, and if no agreement has been reached between the parents, the previous family residence where one parent still lives after separation shall be assumed as the primary residence of the child.[340]

c) Payment of Child Support

One of the biggest problems arising from the Wechselmodell is how child support should be paid if the child is equally cared for by its parents. The *BGH*

---

336 *Heilmann*, Kindeswohl und Wechselmodell, NJW 2015, 3346.

337 Deutscher Bundestag - Wissenschaftliche Dienste, Ausarbeitung v. 24.6.2015: WD 9-300-035/15, 6.

338 *BVerWG*, Urteil v. 30.9.2015 - 6 C 38.14 -, juris Rn. 24 = FamRZ 2016, 44 with comment from *Hammer*, NJW 2016, 99 (100).

339 *MüKo/Hennemann* (2017), § 1687 Rn. 4.

340 *BVerwG*, Urteil v. 30.9.2015 - 6 C 38.14, juris Rn. 24 = FamRZ 2016, 44 = NJW 2016, 99–101 (§ 1627 *BGB*: Determination of the main residence of the child in Wechselmodell) with comment from *Hammer*, NJW 2016, 99 (100).

pointed out in its decision in 2014 that payment of child support can be reduced by one or more levels of the Düsseldorf Table in the Wechselmodell where the child is cared for almost equally by both parents.[341] However, it is held by some scholars that in the Wechselmodell where caring work and parental responsibilities are equally distributed between parents, neither parent has the right to claim child support from the other parent; and the compensation for expenditure not relevant to daily life for the child can be claimed according to §§ 667, 670 *BGB*.[342] Such an opinion was criticised for not having taken different financial situation of both parents into account.[343]

To bring controversies on child support in the Wechselmodell to an end, the *BGH* explained its standpoints. It is explicitly indicated that parents in the Wechselmodell are not exempted from payment of child maintenance and that each parent is entitled to claim child maintenance from the other parent.[344] The maintenance is assessed according to incomes of both parents and covers the additional expenditure arising out of the Wechselmodell, in particular for accommodation and transport.[345] The child allowance which the resident parent receives under the residence model should be divided equally between parents under the Wechselmodell. One parent who carries out half of the caring work can claim the compensation of the child allowance from the other parent according to § 1612b *BGB*.[346]

---

341 *BGH*, Beschluss v. 5.11.2014 - XII ZB 599/13 -, juris Rn. 17 = FamRZ 2015, 236; *BGH*, Beschluss v. 12.3.2014 - XII ZB 234/13 -, juris Rn. 37–38 = FamRZ 2014, 917.

342 *Maaß*, keine Barunterhaltspflicht im echten Wechselmodell FamRZ 2016, 603 (609); *Maaß*, Wechselmodell ohne Barunterhaltspflicht! - Erwiderung auf die Stellungnahmen von Spangenberg, FamRZ 2016, 1426 und Wohlgemuth, FamRZ 2016, 1427, FamRZ 2016, 1428.

343 *Spangenberg*, Wechselmodell ohne Barunterhaltspflicht? - Stellungnahme zu Maaß FamRZ 2016, 603, FamRZ 2016, 1426; Further comments see: *Wohlgemuth*, zum Vorschlag von Maaß FamRZ 2016, 603, FamRZ 2016, 1427.

344 *BGH*, Beschluss v. 11.1.2017 - XII ZB 565/15 -, juris Rn. 20–21 = FamRZ 2017, 438; *BGH*, Beschluss v. 5.11.2014 - XII ZB 599/13 - juris Rn. 17 = FamRZ 2015, 236, 237; One of the local courts which made similar decision is: *OLG Dresden*, Beschluss 29.10.2015 - 20 UF 851/15 -, juris Rn.18 = FamRZ 2016, 470.

345 *BGH*, Beschluss v. 5.11.2014 - XII ZB 599/13 - juris Rn. 17 = FamRZ 2015, 236; *OLG Düsseldorf*, Beschluss v. 18.5.2015 - II-7 UF 10/15 -, juris Rn. 65 = FamRZ 2016, 142; *OLG Dresden*, Beschluss 29.10.2015 - 20 UF 851/15 -, juris Rn. 18 = FamRZ 2016, 470.

346 *BGH*, Beschluss v. 11.1.2017 - XII ZB 565/15 -, juris Rn. 47–48 = FamRZ 2017, 438; *BGH*, Beschluss v. 20.4.2016 - XII ZB 45/15 -, juris Rn. 21 = FamRZ 2016, 1051.

4.3 Exercise of Joint Parental Custody After Separation

4.3.1 Introduction

4.3.1.1 Scope of Application

§ 1687 *BGB* governs how joint parental custody is exercised after separation or divorce of parents, according to which a mutual agreement should be reached by parents to decide on matters of substantial importance for the child (§ 1687 I 1 *BGB*), while matters of everyday life of the child can be decided alone by the parent with whom the child habitually resides (§ 1687 I 2 *BGB*). Such a competence distribution is aimed at fostering a more effective exercise of joint parental custody. The best interests of the child can be better promoted if unnecessary constant meddling of the non-resident parent in everyday life matters of the child is avoided and the non-resident can participate in making decisions which are of substantial importance to the child.[347]

The application of § 1687 *BGB* requires first of all that parents have joint parental custody towards their child. In addition, the parents should have lived separately for a period that is not merely temporary. Therefore, § 1687 *BGB* will not apply if joint parental custody which has been changed to sole parental custody ends according to § 1671 *BGB* or the mother acquires the sole parental custody according to § 1626a III *BGB.* How joint parental custody is established (for the child born in wedlock upon birth, for the child born out of wedlock by declaration in § 1626a I 1 *BGB* or by court decision in § 1626a II *BGB*) is irrelevant to the application of § 1687 *BGB*.[348] In addition, § 1687 *BGB* cannot be applied if the life centre/habitual residence or caring model has not been determined.[349]

4.3.1.2 Distinction Between Matters of Everyday Life and of Significant Importance

Matters of everyday life of the child refers to the issues that come up frequently and do not have a significant influence on the development of the child, while matters of substantial significance for the child affect life of the child deeply and profoundly. *Schwab* criticised that it is a basic error for legislature to deem 'matters of everyday life' and 'matters of significant importance' as two definitions

347 *Staudinger/Salgo* (2014), § 1687 Rn. 34.
348 *MüKo/Hennemann* (2017), § 1687 Rn. 3.
349 *Johannsen/Henrich/Jaeger* (2015), § 1687 Rn. 4.

which are opposite to each other and noted that even matters of everyday life could exert significant influence on development of the child.[350]

Even though all matters could be categorised into either matters of everyday life or of significant importance, there should not be a fixed list or a forever valid formula to differentiate these two types of matters, because each individual case differs from every other.[351] Furthermore, to differentiate matters of great importance and of everyday life one needs to follow the principle of the best interests of the child in each individual case.[352]

In case there is difficulty in differentiating between 'matters of everyday life' and 'matters of significant importance', it is suggested by the *German Family Court Committee* (Deutscher Familiengerichtstag, hereinafter referred to as *DFGT*) that a decision in favour of 'matters of everyday life' should be made. The *DFGT* further suggested that a matter will only be considered a matter of significant importance when it can be proved that a matter will exert an influence to alter on the development of the child.[353]

4.3.2 Decision in Matters of Everyday Life of the Child

Matters of everyday life refer to the matters which frequently occur and exert no effects that are difficult to alter on the development of the child (§ 1687 I 3 *BGB*). The sole decision-making power in matters of everyday life is directly linked to the habitual residence of the child, and it shall change as habitual residence of the child changes. However, in the Wechselmodell, each parent has the right to decide on matters of everyday life of the child during the period where the child resides with him or her, although there should be only one primary residence registered.

There is a list of matters of everyday life of the child, including school issues (for instance, excuse for absence in the school in the event of illness, selection of private tutors); permission for leisure activities which do not pose extraordinary danger to the child (for instance, visiting friends, going to a party or disco); participation in a school trip; membership in a club; medical treatment of common children illnesses; routine visits or prevention-related medical care; nutrition;

---

350 *Schwab*, Elterliche Sorge bei Trennung und Scheidung der Eltern, FamRZ 1998, 457, 469.

351 *Staudinger/Salgo* (2014), § 1687 Rn. 35.

352 *Staudinger/Salgo* (2014), § 1687 Rn. 30; *BT-Drucks*. 13/4899, 111.

353 *Staudinger/Salgo* (2014), § 1687 Rn. 32.

bed time; TV consumption; opening of a bank account; management of the pocket money or small gifts, etc.[354]

Although the resident parent can decide alone in matters of everyday life of the child, the family court may restrict or exclude his or her powers under § 1687 I 2 and 4 *BGB* if this is necessary for the best interests of the child (§ 1687 II *BGB*). However, different opinions are held to the question of whether the courts can undertake such measure *ex officio* or only upon application (§ 1687 II *BGB*).[355]

4.3.3 Decision Concerning Matters of Great Importance for the Child

If parents who have joint parental custody towards their child live apart not merely temporarily, they should reach an agreement to decide on matters which are of substantial importance to the child (§ 1687 I 1 *BGB*). There is no legal definition to matters of substantial importance. However, matters which do not occur frequently, but exert great influence on development of the child can be presumed to be matters of substantial importance.[356] Ways to distribute care between parents after separation and determination of habitual residence for the child are without doubt matters of great importance for the child.[357] However, there are still certain matters of great importance which often come to be discussed in practice as follows.

4.3.3.1 Matters of Great Importance

a) School Issues

School issues such as course selection, private tutoring[358], participation in school trips[359] and picking children up from kindergarten[360] which are frequently to occur are considered matters of everyday life.[361] However, matters regarding choice or change of school which are considered as matters of significant

354 *Heiß/Castellanos*, Gemeinsame Sorge und Kindeswohl nach neuem Recht, Rn. 91.
355 *Staudinger/Salgo* (2014), § 1687 Rn. 55 (The court should decide upon application); *MüKo/Hennemann* (2017), § 1687 Rn. 23 (The court should decide ex officio).
356 *Fröschle*, Sorge und Umgang in der Rechtspraxis, S.144 Rn. 651–653; *MüKo/Hennemann* (2017), § 1687 Rn. 5.
357 *Palandt/Götz* (2018), § 1687 Rn. 4.
358 *OLG Naumburg*, Beschluss v. 14.6.2005 - 3 UF 55/05 -, juris Rn. 1 = FamRZ 2006, 1058.
359 *VG Berlin*, Beschluss v. 10.1.2013 - VG 3 L 1035.12 -, juris Rn. 6.
360 *OLG Bremen*, Beschluss v. 1.7.2008 - 4 UF 39/08 -, juris Rn. 4 = FamRZ 2009, 355.
361 *Staudinger/Salgo* (2014), § 1687 Rn. 43; *MüKo/Hennemann* (2017), § 1687 Rn. 16.

importance for the child should be decided jointly by parents who share joint parental custody to the child.[362]

b) Healthcare

Not all the measures concerning the child's healthcare are considered matters of significant importance for the child. The medical routine measures (such as preventive examination, recommended vaccination including influenza vaccination and treatment against infectious diseases) should be considered matters of everyday life in § 1687 I 3 *BGB*,[363] while deferrable operations (particularly those with risks and side effects), non-urgent blood transfusions, decision on abortion and termination of life-sustaining measures belong to matters of significant importance for the child[364]. However, in case of an emergency, the parent with whom the child is habitually residing at the time of emergency can decide alone whether a medical measure (for instance, tetanus vaccination, urgent and necessary blood transfusion) which has significant influence on the child should be undertaken, on the condition that these measures cannot be delayed (§§ 1687 I 5, 1629 I 4 *BGB*).[365]

aa) Vaccination

To the question whether a decision on vaccination of the child could be made just by one parent or shall be made under the agreement of both parents, there are controversial opinions in practice. It is considered by some courts to be a decision on matters of everyday life of the child for the parent with whom the

---

362 *BT-Drucks.* 13/4899, 107; *Johannsen/Henrich/Jaeger* (2015), § 1687 Rn. 4; *Schwab*, FamRZ 1998, 457, 469; *OLG Brandenburg*, Beschluss v. 13.7.2015 - 3 UF 155/14 -, juris Rn. 58; *OLG Schleswig*, Beschluss v. 7.12.2010 - 10 UF 186/10 -, juris Rn. 22 = FamRZ 2011, 1304; *AG Lemgo*, Beschluss v. 22.1.2003 - 8 F 26/03 -, juris Rn. 12 = FamRZ 2004, 49; *BVerfG*, Nichtannahmebeschluss v. 4.12.2002 - 1 BvR 1870/02, NJW 2003, 1031 = FamRZ 2003, 511; *OLG Hamm*, Urteil v. 19.4.1999 - 6 UF 205/98 -, juris Rn. 32 = FamRZ 2000, 26, 27; *OLG München*, Beschluss v. 13.7.1998 - 12 WF 966/98 -, juris Rn. 4 = FamRZ 1999, 111.

363 *BT-Drucks.* 13/4899, 107; *Schwab*, FamRZ 1998, 457, 469.

364 *OLG Brandenburg*, Beschluss v. 17.2.2000 - 10 UF 45/99 -, juris Rn. 23 = NJW 2000, 2361.

365 *Staudinger/Salgo* (2014), § 1687 Rn. 45; *Palandt/Götz* (2018), § 1626 Rn. 10; *BVerfG*, Einstweilige Anordnung (Temporary injunction) v. 6.6.2007 - 1 BvQ 18/07 -, juris Rn. 10 = FamRZ 2007, 2046; *Coester*, Kinderschutz - Übersicht zu den typischen Gefährdungslagen und aktuellen Probleme, FPR 2009, 549 (550).

child resides to decide on common vaccination recommended for medical care, for instance, the one against tetanus, diphtheria, whooping cough, measles and pneumococcus,[366] while vaccination is regarded by some courts as an issue that has significant impact on the child in the sense of § 1687 I 1 *BGB* with the argument that vaccination might bring about risks and complications for the child.[367] If parents exercising joint parental custody cannot reach an agreement on the vaccination of the child, the court may upon the application of one parent decide which parent shall make the final decision on this issue according to § 1628 *BGB*.[368] The courts, which pursuant to § 1628 *BGB* generally do not have the right to adjudicate on the merits, cannot decide on the necessity of vaccination of a child.[369] However, whether a vaccination is necessary for the child or the side effects or complications because of vaccination outweigh protective effects needs investigation and opinions of experts. Hence, it is suggested that the court should recommend certain authoritative organisations or institutes (for instance, *STIKO* short for *German Standing Vaccination* Committee) to the parents to acquire expertise on the decision of vaccination for the child.[370] It is generally considered to be consistent with the best interests of the child if the family court transfers decision on vaccination to the parent who advocates the vaccinations recommended by the *STIKO*.[371] However, only the disagreement on vaccination between parents shall not lead to transfer of parental custody in all matters concerning healthcare of the child.[372]

bb) Circumcision of Male Children

Though not categorised as a necessary medical measure, circumcision of male children should be considered a matter which exerts a significant influence on

---

366 *OLG Frankfurt*, Beschluss v. 7.6.2010 - 2 WF 117/10 -, juris Rn. 13 = FamRZ 2011, 47, 48; *AmtsG Darmstadt*, 11.6.2015 - 50 F 39/15 SO -, juris Rn. 14 = FamRZ 2016, 248.

367 *OLG Frankfurt*, Beschluss v. 4.9.2015 - 6 UF 150/15 -, juris Rn. 8 = FamRZ 2016, 834; *OLG Thüringen*, Beschluss v. 7.3.2016 - 4 UF 686/15-, juris Rn. 16 = FamRZ 2016, 1175; *KG Berlin*, Beschluss v. 18.5.2005 - 13 UF 12/05 = FamRZ 2006, 142.

368 *OLG Frankfurt*, Beschluss v. 4.9.2015 - 6 UF 150/15 -, juris Rn. 9 = FamRZ 2016, 834.

369 *BVerfG*, Nichtannahmebeschluss v. 4.12.2002 - 1 BvR 1870/02, juris Rn. 8 = NJW 2003, 1031 = FamRZ 2003, 511.

370 *Luthin*, Übertragung des Entscheidungsrechts betreffend Schutzimpfungen auf einen Elternteil, NZFam 2016, 431.

371 *BGH*, Beschluss v. 3.5.2017 - XII ZB 157/16, juris Rn. 27 = FamRZ 2017, 1057; *OLG Thüringen*, Beschluss v. 7.3.2016 - 4 UF 686/15 -, juris Rn. 25 = FamRZ 2016, 1175.

372 *OLG Thüringen*, Beschluss v. 7.3.2016 - 4 UF 686/15 -, juris Rn. 40 = FamRZ 2016, 1175.

them. Minor children who lack the ability to reason and judge can only be circumcised with the consent of parents on the condition that the operation is to be carried out in accordance with the rules of medical practice and it is not inconsistent with the best interests of the child (§ 1631 d *BGB*).

By having adopted § 1631 d *BGB*[373], the lawmakers intended to bring disputes arising from the circumcision to a Muslim child in Cologne[374] to an end. However, having been passed in a hurry, the new provision has caused a fierce reaction and has been criticised.[375] The first relevant court decision after entry of this law has shown that problems arising out of this matter cannot be solved in the short term.[376]

c) Religion

According to the prevailing view, religion is considered a matter of significant importance for a child under the age of 14.[377] However, it should be noted that not every decision related to religion is a matter of significant importance for the child, for instance, whether to attend divine service or comply with religious precepts provided by certain institutions. Only baptism (not the concrete date, but the decision to have the child baptised)[378]; registration for and deregistration

---

373 BGBl. I 2012, 2749: *Law on Scope of Parental Custody of Person in the Matter of Circumcision of Male Children* (*Gesetz über den Umfang der Personensorge bei einer Beschneidung des männlichen Kindes*).

374 *LG Köln*, Urteil v. 7.5.2012 - 151 Ns 169/11 -, juris Rn. 13 = NJW 2012, 2128: a Muslim doctor who had circumcised a 4-year-old child and therefore had been accused by the prosecutors in Cologne for intentional injury was acquitted by both the District Court and the Regional Court; *Klinkhammer*, Beschneidung männlicher Kleinkinder und gesetzliche Vertretung durch die Eltern, FamRZ 2012, 913 (915).

375 *Hauck*, Der Schutz von Minderjährigen bei Eingriffen in höchstpersönliche Rechte und Rechtsgüter, NJW 2012, 2398; *Mandla*, Gesetz über den Umfang der Personensorge bei einer Beschneidung des männlichen Kindes, FPR 2013, 244; *Peschel-Gutzeit*, Die neue Regelung zur Beschneidung des männlichen Kindes, NJW 2013, 3617; *Rixen*, Das Gesetz über den Umfang der Personensorge bei einer Beschneidung des männlichen Kindes, NJW 2013, 257; *Spickhoff*, Grund, Voraussetzungen und Grenzen des Sorgerechts bei Beschneidung männlicher Kinder, FamRZ 2013, 337; *Walter*, Der Gesetzesentwurf zur Beschneidung – Kritik und strafrechtliche Alternative, JZ 2012, 1110.

376 *OLG Hamm*, Beschluss v. 30.8.2013 - II-3 UF 133/13 -, juris Rn. 25 = FamRZ 2013, 1818.

377 *Staudinger/Salgo* (2014), § 1687 Rn. 37.

378 *AG Lübeck*, Beschluss v. 23.5.2002 - 129 F 116/02 -, juris Rn. 17 = FamRZ 2003, 549.

from religious education; and the withdrawal from the religious community belong to matters of significant importance for the child. If parents cannot reach an agreement on the matters of significant importance mentioned above, the family court shall have jurisdiction over this dispute upon application of one parent (§ 7 *RKEG*), and each parent can apply to the court for transfer of right to decide the religion of the child according to § 1628 *BGB*.

d) Trip Abroad

A trip abroad will be deemed as an issue which is of significant importance for the child in § 1687 I 1, 1628 *BGB* if there is a risk of kidnapping of the child or the child might be detained in non-European countries[379], or the destination of the trip is located in a political crisis region[380] or somewhere that has just undergone several terrorist attacks[381]. Apart from concrete risks, purpose of the trip is also an important criterion to determine whether the trip should be decided jointly by both parents. A short trip to the UK generally shall not be a significant issue for a child who has been brought up in an English culture and language.[382]

4.3.3.2 Court Decision in Case of Dissent Between Parents

If parents cannot reach an agreement on issues which are of significant importance for the child, the courts may, upon application of a parent, transfer decision-making power to one parent (§ 1628 *BGB*), rather than decide over such issues for the parents. A decision made by the *OLG Brandenburg* over a change of school of a child for its parents was considered to have violated not only the statutory law (§ 1628 *BGB*), but also the fundamental right of parents to care for and bring up the child according to Article 6 II 1 *GG*.[383]

---

379 *Menne*, Aktuelle Praxisfragen grenzüberschreitender Kindschaftssachen, FamRB 2015, 359.

380 *OLG Karlsruhe*, Beschluss v. 5.8.2014 - 5 WF 115/14, juris Rn. 23 = FamRZ 2015, 150 (Trip planned to east of Ukraine).

381 *OLG Frankfurt*, Beschluss v. 21.7.2016 - 5 UF 206/16 -, juris Rn. 11 = FamRZ 2016, 1595 (Trip to Turkey).

382 *KG Berlin*, Beschluss v. 1.8.2016 - 13 UF 106/16, juris Rn. 20 = FamRZ 2016, 2111.

383 *BVerfG*, Nichtannahmebeschluss v. 4.12. 2002 - 1 BvR 1870/02 -, juris Rn. 8 = NJW 2003, 1031–1032 = FamRZ 2003, 511–512 = ZfJ 2003, 233–234.

4.4 Right of Contact

Contact between the child and parents after separation or divorce of the parents is generally necessary and beneficial to the child (§ 1626 III 1 *BGB*). By maintaining contact with the child, the non-resident parent can continuously observe and witness the physical and mental condition of the child and its development. Furthermore, alienation of the relationship between parents and children can be prevented.[384]

Right of parental custody should not be a prerequisite for the exercise of the right of contact. Therefore, parents who are not entitled to parental custody still have the right to have contact with their child.[385] There is another misunderstanding regarding right of contact: it is generally taken for granted that the non-resident parent has the right to maintain contact with the child, while ignoring the right of the resident parent to contact the child during the contact between non-resident parent and the child. Even in the Wechselmodell, each parent is entitled to establish contact with the child.

4.4.1 Introduction

4.4.1.1 Legal Basis (§ 1626 III and § 1684 BGB*)*

Before the *KindRG* came into force, only the right of parents to contact with their children was highlighted (§ 1634 I 1 a.F *BGB*[386]), and the right of contact to the child born in wedlock and out of wedlock was separately and differently regulated in §§ 1634 and 1711 *BGB* a.F. The *KindRG* has brought about significant changes which constitute the legal basis of the current rules concerning the right

384 *BVerfG*, Beschluss v. 26.9.2006 - 1 BvR 1827/06 -, juris Rn. 12 = FamRZ 2007, 105; *OLG Braunschweig*, Beschluss v. 14.10.1998 - 1 UF 164/98 -, juris Rn. 3 = FamRZ 1999 185; *OLG Celle*, Beschluss v. 14.4.1998 - 19 UF 316/97 -, juris Rn. 10 = FamRZ 1998, 1458; *OLG Frankfurt*, Beschluss v. 29.1.1993 - 6 UF 125/92 -, juris Rn.4 = FamRZ 1993, 729; *OLG Hamm*, Beschluss v. 19.10.1989 - 5 UF 273/89, FamRZ 1990, 654; *BVerfG*, Beschluss v. 10.8.1989 - 2 BvR 67/85, FamRZ 1989, 1159; *BGH*, Beschluss v. 21.10.1964 - IV ZB 338/64 -, juris Rn. 25 = *BGHZ* 42, 364 = NJW 1965, 394 = FamRZ 1965, 130.

385 *Elden*, Der Umgang eines Elternteils mit den Kindern - eine in der Praxis oft schwierige Angelegenheit, NZFam 2017, 8; *Obermann*, Normative Strukturen des Umgangs, FamRZ 2016, 1033; *BVerfG*, Urteil v. 01.4 2008 - 1 BvR 1620/04, juris Rn. 74 = *BVerfGE* 121, 69 = FamRZ 2008, 845.

386 § 1634 I 1 a.F *BGB* (abolished since 1998, BGBl. I S. 2942): The parent who is not entitled to care for the person of the child has the right to have personal contact with the child.

of contact. It is first recognised in § 1626 III 1 *BGB* that contact to both parents generally conforms to the principle of best interests of the child, and other persons to whom the child has ties can maintain contact to the child as well if it is beneficial for the development of the child (§ 1626 III 2 *BGB*). Besides, different regulations concerning right of contact to the child born in wedlock and out of wedlock have been integrated into § 1684 *BGB*. While § 1626 III *BGB* contains the general rule concerning right of contact, § 1684 *BGB* describes how the right of contact should be concretely exercised. In addition, the non-resident parent has been granted the right to demand information about personal circumstances of the child insofar as it is compatible with the best interests of the child (§ 1686 *BGB*).

4.4.1.2 Legal Nature

a) Right and Duty of Parents

The right of contact of a parent stems from the natural parental right and responsibility, whose legal grounds can be found in Article 6 I GG and Article 8 I *ECHR* and § 1684 *BGB*.[387] Such a right of parents does not depend on whether they are entitled to exercise parental custody. Therefore, even the parent who is deprived of the right to exercise parental custody has the right to establish or maintain contact with his or her child.

The right of contact is a highly personal right of a parent. According to the prevailing view, it is also an absolute right as provided for in § 823 I *BGB*. Therefore, the parent whose right of contact has been infringed can claim compensation accordingly.[388]

Although it is uncontested that the right of parents to maintain contact with the child is a part of the parental right in Article 6 II 1 *GG* as the right to exercise parental custody,[389] no obligation has been imposed on the child to maintain contact with its parents[390], which could make claims of parents for contact against the wishes of the child unenforceable. Therefore, the right to contact with

---

387 *Johannsen-Henrich/Jaeger* (2010), § 1684 Rn. 6.

388 *BGH*, Urteil v. 19.6.2002 - XII ZR 173/00 -, juris Rn. 10–11 = *BGHZ* 151, 155–164 = FamRZ 2002, 1099 = NJW 2002, 2566.

389 *BVerfG*, Beschluss v. 5.2.2002 - 1 BvR 2029/00 -, juris Rn. 8 = FamRZ 2002, 809; *BVerfG*, Beschluss v. 15.6.1971 - 1 BvR 192/70 -, juris Rn. 22 = *BVerfGE* 31, 194 = FamRZ 1971, 421; *BGH*, Beschluss v. 21.10.1964 - IV ZB 338/64 -, juris Rn. 24 = *BGHZ* 42, 364 = NJW 1965, 394 = FamRZ 1965, 130.

390 *Obermann*, Normative Strukturen des Umgangs, FamRZ 2016, 1031.

the child of one parent cannot be invoked against the child who is unwilling to maintain contact with him or her, but only against the other parent who tries to hinder or prevent the contact.

It is not only a right, but also a duty for parents to have contact with their child (§ 1684 I 2 *BGB*). Such a duty shall be borne not only by the non-resident, but also the resident parent, who, according to § 1684 II *BGB*, shall not only refrain from preventing or impeding contact of the child with the other parent, but also try to influence the child positively who shows indifference towards or even refuses to maintain contact with the non-resident parent.[391]

b) Right of the Child

Right of contact used to be only addressed to parents, while the child was not entitled to it. Having realised that it is not only interests of parents, but also interests of the child that should be taken into account in legislation concerning the right of contact,[392] the right of the child to claim contact with its parents has been granted in the *KindRG* (§ 1684 I 1 *BGB*). Further emphasis on right of contact of the child is reflected by the change of the name of § 1684 *BGB* (from 'Right of contact of parents and children' in 1998 to 'Right of contact of children with parents' since 2002).

The right of contact in § 1684 I 1 *BGB* enables the child not only to claim contact with the non-resident parent but also to demand from the resident parent not to hinder its contact with the non-resident parent.

4.4.1.3 Ways and Place to Exercise Right of Contact

Parents can have personal contact with their children in many ways, among which writing letters and making calls used to be the common ways. With the new development of technology, letters between parents and child have nearly been replaced by emails, short messages and other modern means of communication. Ways to have contact with the children have been largely expanded, which, however, leads to various problems nowadays. For instance, it was questioned whether the parent with whom the child lived had the right to decide whether the child accepted the mobile phone from the other parent and how

391 *OLG Hamm*, Beschluss v. 12.12.2007 - 10 WF 196/07 -, juris Rn. 5; *Elden*, Der Umgang eines Elternteils mit den Kindern - eine in der Praxis oft schwierige Angelegenheit, NZFam 2017, 8.

392 *BT-Drucks.* 13/4899, 68, 93; *Schmid*, Juristische Grundsätze zu Umgangsmodellen, NZFam 2014, 881.

the mobile phone should be used to promote contact between child and parents, rather than bring trouble to the child and its resident family.[393] Considering that mobile phones are now used not only just as a communication tool, but also as a device with which children have access to online games and the internet, the resident parent has the right to decide whether the mobile phone from the non-resident parent as a gift can be accepted and can make any reasonable restriction on the use of the mobile phone.

The parent entitled to contact with the child can generally decide alone where the child should stay during the contact time.[394] If it does not endanger the best interests of the child, the non-resident parent can bring the child to his or her place of work.[395] However, the resident parent may interfere with decisions made by non-resident parent if it concerns a matter of significant importance under §§ 1687 I 1 and 1628 1 *BGB* for the child, because it is then no longer an issue related to right of contact but to exercise of parental custody.

4.4.2 Between Parents

Parents should first try to reach an agreement on exercise of the right of contact after separation or divorce, on which the court can only make a different decision if there is endangerment of the best interests of the child.[396] In case the parents are not able to come to a mutual agreement on how the right of contact shall be exercised after separation or divorce, or if the agreement they have made shall be changed, either of them can turn to the *Youth Welfare Office* for consultation and support (§ 18 III 3, 4 *SGB VIII*). The family court as well should facilitate that the parents reach an agreement on the exercise of the contact right by providing information on services offered by youth welfare associations (§ 156 I 2 *FamFG*) or ordering parents to individually or jointly participate in a free information interview concerning mediation or other conflict resolution methods outside of court (§ 156 I 3 *FamFG*). The court should decide the scope and exercise of the right to contact or exclude it by way of interlocutory order (§ 156 III 2 *FamFG*) if no agreement is reached at a court hearing pursuant to § 155 II *FamFG* after opinions of the child (§ 159 *FamFG*), parents (§ 160 *FamFG*) and

---

393 *Söpper*, Handy und Umgangsrecht, FamRZ 2002, 73.

394 *KG Berlin*, Beschluss v. 1.8.2016 - 13 UF 106/16 -, juris Rn. 20 = FamRZ 2016, 2113; *KG Berlin*, Beschluss v. 7.10.2015 - 13 WF 146/15 -, juris Rn. 8 = FamRZ 2016, 389.

395 *KG Berlin*, Beschluss v. 7.10.2015 - 13 WF 146/15 -, juris Rn. 8 = FamRZ 2016, 389.

396 *Staudinger/Rauscher* (2014), § 1684 Rn. 115, 118.

the *Youth Welfare Office* (§ 155 II 3 and § 162 I 1 *FamFG*) have been heard, but instead an order in § 156 I 3 *FamFG* is issued by the court.

4.4.2.1 Cooperative Behaviour Obligation in § 1684 II BGB

The contact right of one parent inevitably limits the right of the other parent to care for the person of the child, which might lead the resident parent to unwillingly make an agreement with the non-resident parent on the exercise of the contact right. However, a child can profit most from a reasonable agreement between parents on the exercise of the contact right which can avoid misunderstanding between parents and alienation of the relationship between the child and the non-resident parent.[397] Therefore, one parent should refrain from undertaking any actions that will injure the relationship between the child and the other parent or render difficult the upbringing of the child (§ 1684 II *BGB*).

a) Cooperative Behaviour Obligation of the Resident Parent

To fulfil the obligation arising from § 1684 II *BGB*, the resident parent should not only avoid alienation of relationship between the non-resident parent and the child (by, for instance, speaking ill of the non-resident parent), but also try to motivate the child to have contact with the non-resident parent as much as possible.[398] If the resident parent violates his or her obligation in § 1684 II *BGB* consistently and repeatedly, a contact supervisor (Umgangspflegschaft) shall be appointed.[399]

b) Cooperative Behaviour Obligation of the Non-resident Parent

The non-resident parent is also forbidden to undertake any action which is detrimental to the relationship between the child and the resident parent (§ 1684 II *BGB*). In addition, the non-resident should inform the resident parent of anything that is of substantial importance for the child during the contact. It is a violation of the cooperative behaviour obligation in § 1684 II *BGB* if the

397 *Schwab*, Familienrecht, P. 419 Rn. 956.

398 *OLG Saarbrücken*, Beschluss v. 30.10.2014 - 6 WF 186/14 -, juris Rn. 18 = FamRZ 2015, 863.

399 *OLG Brandenburg*, Beschluss v. 15.2.2016 - 10 UF 213/14 -, juris Rn. 37 = FamRZ 2016, 1473.

non-resident has contact with the child outside the determined contact period, which might lead to administrative penalties.[400]

c) *Claim for Compensation*

The non-resident parent can claim for compensation from the resident parent who prevents or thwarts his or her contact with the child according to § 1684 II *BGB* which has concretised § 280 *BGB* in the framework of the right of contact in family law.[401]

To decide whether a claim for compensation of one parent is justified, the court should determine whether he or her is accountable for the damage caused to himself or herself. Such a claim for compensation will not be granted if the non-resident parent's own negligence has largely contributed to the harm he or she suffered. Therefore, if the non-resident parent insists on going to meet the child despite having been notified of the child's absence, he or she does not have the right to claim damage from the resident parent.[402] However, the cancellation of an appointment between the non-resident parent and the child cannot be justified by refusal of the child, as the resident parent is obliged to influence the child positively and encourage the child to maintain contact with the non-resident parent.[403]

Compensation that the non-resident claims according to § 280 I 1 *BGB* includes wasted travel costs and loss of earnings.[404] The resident parent can also claim compensation from the non-resident parent for the child if he or she does not fulfil his or her obligation to exercise the right of contact.[405]

d) *Expenditure out of Right of Contact*

There is no statutory provision on who should bear the cost related to the right of contact, how it is paid and what amount it should be. Generally, the parent who

400 *KG Berlin*, Beschluss v. 13.2.2015 - 13 WF 203/14 -, juris Rn. 10–13 = FamRZ 2015, 940, with comment from *Spangenberg*, P. 1726 and with comment from *Söpper*, P. 2168.

401 *OLG Frankfurt*, Beschluss v. 21.7.2015 - 4 UF 379/14 -, juris Rn. 28 = FamRZ 2016, 387.

402 *OLG Frankfurt*, Beschluss v. 21.7.2015 - 4 UF 379/14 -, juris Rn. 34 = FamRZ 2016, 388.

403 *OLG Frankfurt*, Beschluss v. 21.7.2015 - 4 UF 379/14 -, juris Rn. 37 = FamRZ 2016, 388; *BGH*, Beschluss v. 1.2.2012 - XII ZB 188/11 -, juris Rn. 26 = FamRZ 2012, 533, 535; *BT-Drucks*. 16/6308, 218.

404 *OLG Frankfurt*, Beschluss v. 21.7.2015 - 4 UF 379/14 -, juris Rn. 39 = FamRZ 2016, 388.

405 *Dethloff*, Familienrecht, § 13 Rn. 194.

has the right of contact with the child bears expenses arising out of the exercise of this right[406] if it is not otherwise agreed between the parents.[407] The court, therefore, shall in every individual case take into consideration whether the way the right of contact is exercised is reasonable for the non-resident parent so that it will not be an extra financial burden for the non-resident parent.[408] However, the resident parent shall provide financial or organisational support if exercise of the contact right of the non-resident parent becomes more difficult because of him or her (for instance, movement).[409] Considering there is no legal basis in family law for the non-resident parent to claim compensation for expenditure out of his or her contact right, it is held that one parent can file a lawsuit against the resident parent according to § 242 *BGB* or § 266 I 5 *FamFG* if the unreasonable increased expenditure is solely due to decision of the other parent without reasonable justification.

4.4.2.2 Right to Demand Information on Personal Circumstances of the Child

According to § 1686 *BGB*, each parent who has a legitimate interest in obtaining information about the child's personal circumstances may request such information from the other parent in so far as it is not contrary to the child's best interests. It is noted that only legal parents (with exception to the biological but not the legal fathers in § 1686a) are entitled to such a right. The one obliged to provide information pursuant to § 1686 *BGB* is not limited to the resident parent but extended to the parent who has the right to contact with the child[410] and

406 *Schwab*, Handbuch des Scheidungsrechts (2013), P. 657 Rn. 234; *MüKo/Hennemann* (2017), § 1684 Rn. 41; *Johannsen/Henrich/Jaeger* (2015), § 1684 Rn. 30; *Staudinger/Rauscher* (2014), § 1684 Rn. 135.

407 *OLG Zweibrücken*, Beschluss v. 28.7.1998 - 5 UF 20/98 -, juris Rn. 39 = FamRZ 1998, 1465; *BGH*, Urteil v. 9.11.1994 - XII ZR 206/93 -, juris Rn. 12 = FamRZ 1995, 215.

408 *BVerfG*, Beschluss v. 5.2.2002 - 1 BvR 2029/00 -, juris Rn. 8 = FamRZ 2002, 809.

409 *OLG Nürnberg*, Beschluss v. 26.11.2013 - 10 UF 173/13 -, juris Rn. 21 = NJW - RR 2014, 644; *BVerfG*, Beschluss v. 5.2.2002 - 1 BvR 2029/00 -, juris Rn. 8 = FamRZ 2002, 809 (In this case, the resident parent is obliged to take the child to airport).

410 *MüKo/Henneman* (2017), § 1686 Rn. 5; *Palandt/Götz* (2018), § 1686 Rn. 4; *Staudinger/Rauscher* (2014), § 1686 Rn. 5; *BGH*, Beschluss v. 14.12.2016 - XII ZB 345/16 -, juris Rn. 13 = FamRZ 2017, 378; *OLG Brandenburg*, Beschluss v. 17.1.2007 - 10 WF 193/06 -, juris Rn. 9 = FamRZ 2007, 2003.

intermediaries who are comparable to non-resident parents (for instance, the *Youth Welfare Office*).[411]

A justified interest in the sense of § 1686 *BGB* only exists if the claimant cannot acquire information on the development and personal circumstances of the child in other reasonable ways without jeopardising the legislative purpose of the contact right and acting against the child's will.[412] Parents should first try to obtain information on personal circumstances of the child during the contact with child by means of, for instance, conversation with the child. It is also a duty for the non-resident parent who exercises parental custody jointly with the resident parent to collect information on the schooling performance of the child directly from school.[413]

The personal circumstances in § 1686 *BGB* include all the essential circumstances of the child, particularly performance at school, extracurricular activities, health status and social development.[414] However, the will of the child who shows sufficient maturity and ability in self-determination should be taken into account if the child refuses to expose the personal information related to its very personal matters (e.g., its health status) to its parents.[415] Although the opinion of the child needs to be heard in certain cases, the child generally should not get involved in the claim arising from § 1686 *BGB*.[416]

---

411 *BGH*, Beschluss v. 14.12.2016 - XII ZB 345/16 -, juris Rn. 18 = FamRZ 2017, 378; *OLG Hamm*, Beschluss v. 1.8.2016 - II-4 UF 99/16 -, juris Rn. 10 = FamRZ 2017, 384; *Gottschalk*, in: *Heilmann*, Praxiskommentar Kindschaftsrecht, § 1686 Rn. 5; *Staudinger/Rauscher* (2014), § 1686 Rn. 5; *MüKo/Henneman* (2017), § 1686 Rn. 6; *Palandt/Götz* (2018), § 1686 Rn. 3; *Johannsen/Henrich/Jaeger* (2015), § 1686 Rn. 1.

412 *BGH*, Beschluss v. 14.12.2016 - XII ZB 345/16 -, juris Rn. 25 = FamRZ 2017, 378; *OLG Jena*, Beschluss v. 13.5.2016 - 1 UF 109/16 -, juris Rn. 13; *OLG Brandenburg*, Beschluss v. 11.4.2014 - 3 UF 50/13 -, juris Rn. 61; *Staudinger/Rauscher* (2014), § 1686 Rn. 7; *MüKo/Henneman* (2017), § 1686 Rn. 7.

413 *OLG Brandenburg*, Beschluss v. 9.5.2016 - 10 UF 117/15 -, juris Rn. 49 = NZFam 2016, 955.

414 *BGH*, Beschluss v. 14.12.2016 - XII ZB 345/16 -, juris Rn. 30 = FamRZ 2017, 378; *OLG Hamm*, Beschluss v. 1.8.2016 - II-4 UF 99/16 -, juris Rn. 8 = FamRZ 2017, 384; *MüKo/Henneman* (2017), § 1686 Rn. 10; *Gottschalk*, in: *Heilmann*, Praxiskommentar Kindschaftsrecht, § 1686 Rn. 10; *Staudinger/Rauscher* (2014), § 1686 Rn. 13.

415 *OLG Köln*, Beschluss v. 28.6.2016 - 10 UF 21/15 -, juris Rn. 20 = FamRZ 2017, 385.

416 *MüKo/Henneman* (2017), § 1686 Rn. 5.

4.4.3 Court Orders by the Family Court

In 2017, there were 54 374 proceedings[417] on right of contact instituted by parents who could not reach an agreement on the exercise of right of contact or who did not follow previous court decisions on the right of contact. In proceedings concerning the right of contact, the court can not only decide upon the extent of the right of contact (§ 1684 III *BGB*) and specify the ways to exercise it but also restrict or even exclude the right of contact of parents (§ 1684 IV *BGB*).

4.4.3.1 Arrangement of the Contact by Court (§ 1684 III BGB*)*

a) Criteria

The court can arrange the contact without being limited to application of parents but only follow the principle of the best interests of the child which requires it to consider all the relevant circumstances in each individual case.[418] Crucial criteria to determine frequency and duration of contact are age and resilience of the child, inner connection between the child and the non-resident parent, distance between residence of resident and non-resident parent, and disposable time of the child and parents.[419] For young children, shorter visitation might be more appropriate.[420] A longer visitation with overnight stay could be considered if a young child has an intimate relationship with the non-resident parent.[421]

b) Appointment of a Contact Supervisor (§ 1684 III 3 BGB*)*

If one parent permanently or repeatedly violates his or her obligation under § 1684 II *BGB* to help the other parent maintain contact with the child, the court can appoint a contact supervisor (Umgangspflegschaft, § 1684 III 3 *BGB*).[422] Such

---

417 Statistisches Bundesamt, Familiengerichte 2017 - Fachserie 10 Reihe 2.2, Tabelle 2.1.

418 *Staudinger/Rauscher* (2014), § 1684 Rn. 163; *BVerfG*, Beschluss v. 7.3.2005 - 1 BvR 552/04 -, juris Rn. 9 = FamRZ 2005, 871; *BVerfG*, Beschluss v. 25.10.1994 - 1 BvR 1197/93 -, Rn. 28 = FamRZ 1995, 86, 87.

419 *Palandt/Götz* (2018), § 1684 Rn. 14.

420 *OLG Brandenburg*, Beschluss v. 8.8.2001 - 9 UF 28/01 -, juris Rn. 13. = FamRZ 2002, 414.

421 *Palandt/Götz* (2018), § 1684 Rn. 15.

422 *OLG Saarbrücken*, Beschluss v. 28.1.2015 - 6 UF 145/14 -, juris Rn. 10; *ECtHR*, Case of Kuppinger v. Germany, Judgement on 15 January 2015, Application no. 62198/11, Rn. 44; *OLG Brandenburg*, Beschluss v. 15.2.2016 - 10 UF 213/14 -, juris Rn. 37 = FamRZ 2016, 1473.

an appointment should generally be only for a limited duration,[423] but can be extended upon application of parents or if from the perspective of the court an extension is necessary to get the parents to solve problems in exercise of the contact right with the child.[424] In case the will of the child not to maintain contact with the non-resident parent becomes stronger after several years' appointment of the contact supervisor, the court can subsequently order an accompanied contact.[425] §§ 1909 ff. *BGB* are applied for selection of a contact supervisor who can be the *Youth Welfare Office*, professionals from a counselling centre or a person with whom the child has a connection.[426] A contact supervisor has the right to demand surrender of the child to carry out contact and determine where the child resides during the contact period (§ 1684 III 4 *BGB*). He or she should report to the court about exercise of the contact between the child and parents, although it cannot be guaranteed that report of contact supervisors is always objective. Parents have the right to apply to the court for dismissal of the contact supervisor, but such an application can only be granted if another contact supervisor is appointed.

4.4.3.2 Restriction and Exclusion of Right of Contact (§ 1684 IV BGB*)*

a) Principle of Proportionality

The family court may restrict or exclude the right of contact or enforcement of earlier decisions on the right of contact if it is necessary to protect the best interests of the children (§ 1684 IV 1, 2 *BGB*). However, not only the restriction but also exclusion of the contact right of one parent should follow the principle of proportionality, which requires the court to take both the best interests of the child and the fundamental rights of parents into consideration.[427] Before the non-resident parent is excluded from exercising the right of contact with his or her child, the court should consider if there is a less harsh measure, for instance, restriction of the right of contact or order of an accompanied contact, that can be

423 *Staudinger/Rauscher* (2014), § 1684 Rn. 115.

424 *BT-Drucks*. 16/6308, 346.

425 *OLG Celle*, Beschluss v. 3.12.2014 - 19 UF 129/14 -, juris Rn. 10 = FamRZ 2015, 769.

426 *BT-Drucks*. 16/6308, 346; About selection and appointment of a contact supervisor see: *Kohler*, Vom Umgang mit der Umgangspflegschaft, JAmt 2010, 226; *Zivier*, Die neuen gesetzlichen Regelungen zur Umgangspflegschaft, ZKJ 2010, 306, 307.

427 *BVerfG*, Nichtannahmebeschluss v. 17.9.2016 - BvR 1547/16 -, juris Rn. 19.

taken; it is also suggested that an expert opinion should be obtained to evaluate the necessity to exclude one parent's right of contact.[428]

Generally, a long-term exclusion of the right of contact requires serious and lasting endangerment of the best interests of the child (for instance, child maltreatment[429] and abuse[430], psychological illness,[431] addiction,[432] domestic violence,[433] risk of kidnapping,[434] alienation[435] and resistance of the child[436]),[437] whereas the right of contact can be excluded for a short term, even if it is not necessary to avert such an endangerment.[438] Once endangerment of the child's best interests disappears, the court should lift the exclusion of right of contact.[439] Right of contact can be excluded for a limited period if an accompanied contact cannot be ordered because of endangerment of the best interests of the child,[440] or if the non-resident parent refuses an accompanied contact.[441]

---

428 *OLG Schleswig*, Beschluss v. 22.9.2015 - 10 UF 105/15 -, juris Rn. 33 = FamRZ 2016, 483.

429 *MüKo/Hennemann* (2017), § 1684 Rn. 77; *OLG Karlsruhe*, Beschluss v. 5.5.2008 - 16 UF 3/08 -, juris Rn. 24–28 = FamRZ 2009, 130.

430 *MüKo/Hennemann* (2017), § 1684 Rn. 78; *Scharl/Schmid*, Sucht und Persönlichkeitsstörung in Kindschaftssachen, FamRB 2013, 224 (227).

431 *MüKo/Hennemann* (2017), § 1684 Rn. 82; *Scharl/Schmid*, Sucht und Persönlichkeitsstörung in Kindschaftssachen, FamRB 2013, 224 (226).

432 *MüKo/Hennemann* (2017), § 1684 Rn. 81; *OLG Koblenz*, Beschluss v. 24.5.2006 - 11 UF 60/06 -, juris Rn. 10 = FamRZ 2007, 926.

433 *MüKo/Hennemann* (2017), § 1684 Rn. 71; *OLG Köln*, Beschluss v. 23.3.2005 - 4 UF 119/04 -, juris Rn. 20 = FamRZ 2005, 2011.

434 *MüKo/Hennemann* (2017), § 1684 Rn. 76; *OLG Hamm*, Beschluss v. 10.5.2010 - II-6 UF 184/09 -, juris Rn. 17–19 = FamRZ 2010, 1574.

435 *MüKo/Hennemann* (2017), § 1684 Rn. 83; *OLG Zweibrücken*, Entscheidung v. 9.5.2005 - 6 UF 4/05 = FamRZ 2006, 144.

436 *OLG Schleswig*, Beschluss v. 22.9.2015 - 10 UF 105/15 -, juris Rn. 46 = NZFam 2016, 29–31; *OLG Koblenz*, Beschluss v. 21.5.2003 - 13 UF 230/03 = FamRZ 2004, 288.

437 *MüKo/Hennemann* (2017), § 1684 Rn. 67; *Palandt/Götz* (2018), § 1684 Rn. 36.

438 *OLG Nürnberg*, Beschluss v. 19.7.2016 - 7 UF 746/16 -, juris Rn. 43 = FamRZ 2017, 298; *OLG Brandenburg*, Beschluss v. 6.10.2015 - 10 UF 57/13 -, juris 36–37, 45, 49; *OLG Stuttgart*, Beschluss v. 23.2.2015 - 15 UF 192/13 -, juris Rn. 19 = FamRZ 2015, 1727.

439 *BVerfG*, Nichtannahmebeschluss v. 25.4.2015 - 1 BvR 3326/14 -, juris Rn. 27 = NJW 2015, 2561 = FamRZ 2015, 1093 (with comment from *Fischer*, FamRZ 2015, 1169).

440 *MüKo/Hennemann* (2017), § 1684 Rn. 67.

441 *MüKo/Hennemann* (2017), § 1684 Rn. 68.

b) *Accompanied Contact*

aa) *General Rules*

Accompanied contact as a restriction to the right of contact is a less severe measure than withdrawal of contact right, and order of accompanied contact still needs to follow the principle of proportionality. Although it is clear that accompanied contact can only be ordered by the family court (§ 1684 IV *BGB*) it does not indicate whether the accompanied contact is ordered *ex officio* or upon application of parents.

bb) *Presence of a Third Party*

Accompanied contact is practicable only when a third party is willing to be present during the contact (§ 1684 IV 3 *BGB*). Therefore, the family court cannot force a third party to accompany the contact between the child and its non-resident parent,[442] which has been confirmed by the *BVerfG*[443]. The *BVerfG* further indicates that the family court has no authority to order the *Youth Welfare Office* and the voluntary associations providing youth welfare service to be present during the contact between the child and the non-resident parent. Although parents have the right to sue state associations which provide youth welfare services before administrative courts for support to exercise the right of contact (§ 18 III 3, 4 *SGB VIII*), it would be unrealistic for the family court to suspend proceedings concerning contact right and wait for the decision of the administrative court.

A third party in § 1684 IV 3 *BGB* can be either a private individual or an association. The family court is obliged to investigate *ex officio* whether a third party is suitable to accompany the contact.[444] In cases where the child suffers from mental problems because of the contact or the non-resident parent is suspected of assaulting the child sexually, psychological experts or the *Youth Welfare Office* are more suitable to be a third party compared with friends or relatives without professional knowledge.[445]

---

442 *OLG Frankfurt*, Beschluss v. 24.3.2015 - 5 UF 270/14 -, juris Rn. 9; *OLG Schleswig*, Beschluss v. 23.3.2015 - 10 UF 6/15 -, juris Rn. 28, 34; *Palandt/Götz* (2018), § 1684 Rn. 35; *Staudinger/Rauscher* (2014), § 1684 Rn. 319; *Weber*, Die Entwicklung des Familienrechts seit Mitte 2014, NJW 2015, 3068, 3079; *BT-Drucks.* 13/4899, 106; *Staudinger/Rauscher* (2014), § 1684 Rn. 319.

443 *BVerfG*, Beschluss v. 29.07.2015 - 1 BvR 1468/15 -, juris Rn. 5 = NJW 2015, 3563 = FamRZ 2015, 1686.

444 *OLG Schleswig*, Beschluss v. 23.3.2015 -10 UF 6/15 -, juris Rn. 28 = FamRZ 2015, 1040.

445 *Staudinger/Rauscher* (2014), § 1684 Rn. 321.

cc) Comparison with Contact Supervisor

The accompanied contact and the contact supervisor play different roles to guarantee an effective exercise of the contact right. A contact supervisor who is not inevitably related to restriction to contact right[446] is generally ordered in case where the resident parent hinders the non-resident parent from establishing contact with the child, while the accompanied contact, as a way to restrict the contact right, guarantees that the best interests of the child will not be endangered during contact with the non-resident parent. If required, both accompanied contact and contact supervisor can be ordered in parallel in the same case.[447]

4.4.3.3 No Compulsion for the Child to Have Contact with Parents

Refusal of the child to have contact with one parent does not always reflect its own will but might result from the loyalty to the other parent.[448] Therefore, if a child refuses to have contact with its parent, the court shall conduct an investigation to find out the reasons for such a refusal and try to make a decision which takes into account the true will of the child.[449] A child who shows serious unwillingness to maintain contact with its parent should not be ordered to receive therapy unless it has been proved that this child suffers from a mental illness.[450] Besides, it should be found out whether the resident parent has the ability to convey a positive image of the non-resident parent and whether he or she can recognise the needs of the child in a family situation full of serious controversies.[451]

It has been generally acknowledged in practice that a child showing a serious unwillingness which conforms to its psychological conditions and state of maturity should not be forced to maintain contact with the non-resident parent,

---

446 *Fröschle*, Sorge und Umgang in der Rechtspraxis, S. 260 Rn. 1184.

447 *Staudinger/Rauscher* (2014), § 1684 Rn. 309a.

448 *ECtHR*, Case of Kuppinger v. Germany, Judgement on 15 January 2015, Application no. 62198/11, Rn. 42; *BVerfG*, Nichtannahmebeschluss v. 2.4.2001 - 1 BvR 212/98 -, juris Rn. 4 = FamRZ 2001, 1057.

449 *BVerfG*, Nichtannahmebeschluss v. 25.4.2015 - 1 BvR 3326/14 -, juris Rn. 18 = NJW 2015, 2561 = FamRZ 2015, 1093; *BVerfG*, Beschluss v. 31.5.1983 - 1 BvL 11/80 -, juris Rn. 39 = *BVerfGE* 64, 180 (191).

450 *BVerfG*, Beschluss v. 28.2.2012 - 1 BvR 3116/11 -, juris Rn. 31 = *BVerfGK* 19, 295 (304); *BVerfG*, Nichtannahmebeschluss v. 17.9.2016 - BvR 1547/16 -, juris Rn. 35.

451 *BVerfG*, Nichtannahmebeschluss v. 25.4.2015 - 1 BvR 3326/14 -, juris Rn. 20 = NJW 2015, 2561 = FamRZ 2015, 1093 (with comment from *Fischer*, FamRZ 2015, 1169).

even if the child might be consciously or unconsciously influenced, because the forced contact might bring the child more harm than benefits.[452] However, if the influenced will of the child does not correspond to the fact that the child and its non-resident parent have been maintaining a good relationship, the court shall not take the unwillingness of the child into account.[453]

4.4.4 Administrative Means of Coercion and Enforcement in §§ 89, 90 *FamFG*

4.4.4.1 Two Means of Coercion

Administrative means of coercion in § 89 *FamFG* not only aim at warning the non-compliance of parents with court decisions concerning the right of contact, but also aim at punishing parents for their non-compliance.[454]

The court might impose an administrative fine (each time not exceeding 25,000 euro) on the parent who does not comply with an enforcement instrument requiring surrender of the person of the child and rules concerning contact. Therefore, an administrative fine cannot be ordered against the parent who does not follow the court order to talk with the other parent, as there is no relevant legal basis.[455] If the situation still cannot be alleviated by administrative fine, the court might order administrative detention (§ 89 I *FamFG*). It is noted that administrative detention cannot generally be imposed without prior imposition of an administrative fine, unless contact can still not be enforced even if administrative fine has been imposed several times.[456] If the obligated person demonstrates that he or she is not liable for the non-compliance (§ 89 IV 1 *FamFG*), the coercive measures in § 89 I *FamFG* should not be imposed.

---

452 *BVerfG*, Nichtannahmebeschluss v. 25.4.2015 - 1 BvR 3326/14 -, juris Rn. 17 = NJW 2015, 2561 = FamRZ 2015, 1093 (with comment from *Fischer*, FamRZ 2015, 1169); *OLG Naumburg*, Beschluss v. 12.8.2014 - 8 UF 124/14 -, juris Rn. 44 = FamRZ 2015, 767; *ECtHR*, Case of Kuppinger v. Germany, Judgement on 15 January 2015, Application no. 62198/11, Rn. 80.

453 *BVerfG*, Beschluss v. 25.4.2015 - 1 BvR 3326/14 -, juris Rn. 17.

454 *OLG Saarbrücken*, Beschluss v. 30.10.2014 - 6 WF 186/14 -, juris Rn. 5 = FamRZ 2015, 863.

455 *KG Berlin*, Beschluss v. 17.6.2015 - 18 WF 109/14 -, juris Rn. 12.

456 *Elden*, Der Umgang eines Elternteils mit den Kindern - eine in der Praxis oft schwierige Angelegenheit, NZFam 2017, 9.

4.4.4.2 Principle of Proportionality

Based on the expert opinion that order of an administrative fine generally does not impose a beneficial influence on normalisation of the living situation or mental health of the child,[457] the *BGH* suggests that the administrative coercion should be ordered only if it is suitable for achieving the anticipated results.[458] The enforcement measures which are improper, unrealistic or endanger the best interests of the child are also not advocated by the *ECtHR*.[459]

4.4.4.3 Enforcement in § 90 FamFG

The court may order enforcement through direct coercion if the administrative means of coercion have been or are likely to be unsuccessful or immediate enforcement of the decision is necessary (§ 90 I *FamFG*). However, direct enforcement should not be permitted, when the child is to be surrendered for the purpose of exercising rights of contact (§ 90 II 1 *FamFG*).[460]

4.4.5 Need for Further Reform

4.4.5.1 Stricter Burden of Proof

Although the *KindRG* has already brought significant change to provisions regarding the right of contact, there is still room to improve the relevant legislation. For instance, parents who desire to visit the child shall not only prove that they are keeping a good contact with the child, but also prove the desired contact with the child is consistent with the best interests of the child,[461] as a frequent contact with the child does not certainly serve the best interests of the child.[462]

---

457 *BVerfG*, Nichtannahmebeschluss v. 17.9.2016 - BvR 1547/16 -, juris Rn. 31.

458 *BVerfG*, Nichtannahmebeschluss v. 17.9.2016 - BvR 1547/16 -, juris Rn. 33.

459 *ECtHR*, Case of Tsikakis v. Deutschland, Judgement on 10 February 2011, Application no. 1521/06, Rn. 80.

460 *Elden*, Der Umgang eines Elternteils mit den Kindern - eine in der Praxis oft schwierige Angelegenheit, NZFam 2017, 9.

461 *Schleicher*, Jugend- und Familienrecht, P. 339.

462 *Kostka*, Elterliche Sorge und Umgang bei Trennung und Scheidung - unter besonderer Berücksichtigung der Perspektive des Kindes, FPR 2005, 89 (94).

4.4.5.2 *More Punitive Measures*

The *ECtHR* has criticised that the administrative fine (300 euro) imposed by the trial court in the case of *Kuppinger v. Germany*[463] was not sufficient to make her change her attitude and behaviour towards the contact right of the father, especially when the maximal administrative fine by domestic law is 25,000 euro. Therefore, the administrative fine imposed on the parent who does not comply with enforcement instruments concerning contact with the child could be increased in practice. In addition, for the parents who have not fulfilled their obligations to keep contact with the child, certain punitive measures or penalties that have influence on their rights to claim reestablishment of a contact with the child should be provided for.

4.4.5.3 *More Effective Legal Protection*

The duration of proceedings concerning right of contact is of particular importance, because there is generally no effective contact between the non-resident parent and the child during proceedings, which might lead to increasing alienation between them.[464] The risk that the child will have prejudice towards the non-resident parent will be higher, as proceedings are delayed.[465] Therefore, effective remedy should be legally provided so that proceedings concerning the right of contact can be settled in a timely manner.

In the judgement on 15 January 2015, the *ECtHR* deemed that the legal remedy provided by the German state authorities to the applicant is not sufficient to meet the state's positive obligations under Article 8 *ECHR* in proceedings relating to a parent's contact right with his young child.[466] Although the applicant could lodge a compensation claim according to § 198 *GVG*, it would not definitely encourage the trial court to expedite contact proceedings so that the right to respect private life would not risk becoming illusory. Therefore, it is suggested that legislature could place a legal remedy which is not compensatory but also

---

463 *ECtHR*, Case of Kuppinger v. Germany, Judgement on 15 January 2015, Application no. 62198/11, Rn. 105–106.

464 *Vogel*, Die Untätigkeitsbeschwerde im Familienrecht, FPR 2009, 165.

465 *Motzer*, Neue Tendenzen beim Umgangsrecht, FPR 2007, 275 (278).

466 *ECtHR*, Case of Kuppinger v. Germany, Judgement on 15 January 2015, Application no. 62198/11, Rn. 141.

preventive for proceedings, for instance, in proceedings concerning right of contact, in which the length of the proceedings has a clear impact on family life.[467]

4.5 Transfer from Joint Parental Custody to Sole Parental Custody According to § 1671 I *BGB* After Separation

4.5.1 Introduction

According to § 1671 I 1 *BGB*, a parent under certain conditions can apply to the court for transfer of parental custody or of part[468] of it to him or her alone. Parents in § 1671 *BGB* are legal parents whose parenthood has been legally established according to §§ 1591, 1592 or 1754 I *BGB*. Moreover, they should be parents who exercise joint parental custody towards their joint minor children. Whether the parents are married or how they established the joint parental custody to the child (through marriage or declaration or court order) will not prevent one parent from exercising his or her right to apply for transfer of parental custody according to § 1671 I 1 *BGB*.[469] Furthermore, parents under § 1671 I 1 *BGB* must have got divorced or separated for a period that is not merely temporary[470].

4.5.2 § 1671 I 2 Nr. 1 *BGB*

The application for transfer of sole parental custody shall be granted if the other parent consents and the child who has reached fourteen years does not object to the transfer (§ 1671 I 2 Nr. 1 *BGB*). If the child objects to the transfer, the court shall consider whether the application can be granted according to § 1671 I 2 Nr. 2 *BGB*. Therefore, objection of the child will not inevitably lead to dismissal of the application.[471] Provided that consensus between parents which is not consistent with the best interests of the child has not been objected by the child, the courts shall take measures according to §§ 1666 and 1666a *BGB*, which is implied by § 1671 IV *BGB*.

---

467 *ECtHR*, Case of Kuppinger v. Germany, Judgement on 15 January 2015, Application no. 62198/11, Rn. 137.

468 A part of parental custody is, for instance, determination of habitual residence of the child, religious education or healthcare, etc.

469 *Staudinger/Coester* (2016), § 1671 Rn. 24.

470 *Staudinger/Coester* (2016), § 1671 Rn. 38.

471 *Schwab/Motzer*, Handbuch des Scheidungsrechts (2013), P. 588, Rn. 91; *OLG Schleswig*, Beschluss v. 3.2.2012 - 10 WF 263/11 -, juris Rn. 8 = FamRZ 2012, 1066.

4.5.3 § 1671 I 2 Nr. 2 *BGB*

If parents cannot reach an agreement on the transfer of sole parental custody or the child above fourteen years opposes the agreement between the parents, the court shall decide whether to grant the application for transfer of sole parental custody according to § 1671 I 2 Nr. 2 *BGB*, which requires that both withdrawal of the joint parental custody and transfer of the sole parental custody to the applicant should be most conducive to the best interests of the child. Therefore, the court should examine the best interests of the child in two steps, namely it should not only decide whether to withdraw joint parental custody, but also decide whether to transfer sole parental custody to the applicant.[472]

4.5.3.1 Examination of Withdrawal of Joint Parental Custody

Joint parental custody which is not definitely beneficial to the child after separation or divorce of parents should not take precedence over sole parental custody in any case,[473] and a forced joint parental custody is not always conducive to the best interests of the child.[474] To decide whether joint parental custody should survive or should be withdrawn after separation of parents, the court should follow the principles of the best interests of the child[475]: which requires the court to consider the capability of parents to care for the child, continuity of living environment of the child, connection between the child and parents, and the will of the child.[476] In addition, it should find out whether parents are deeply trapped

472 *OLG Celle*, Beschluss v. 17.8.2015 - 15 UF 44/15 -, juris Rn. 13 = FamRZ 2016, 385; *OLG Stuttgart*, Beschluss v. 24.8.2016 - 17 UF 40/16 -, juris Rn. 14 = NZFam 2016, 1204.

473 *BVerfG*, Beschluss v. 18.12.2003 - 1 BvR 1140/03 -, juris Rn. 10 = FamRZ 2004, 354, 355 = FPR 2004, 260; *BVerfG*, Beschluss v. 11.5.2005 - XII ZB 33/04 -, juris Rn. 6 = FamRZ 2005, 1167; *BVerfG*, Beschluss v. 29.5.2006 - 1 BvR 430/03 -, juris Rn. 13 = FamRZ 2007, 1876; *BGH*, Beschluss v. 12.12.2007 - XII ZB 158/05 -, juris Rn. 14 = FamRZ 2008, 592 = NJW 2008, 994; *OLG Celle*, Beschluss v. 17.8.2015 - 15 UF 44/15 -, juris Rn 9. = FamRZ 2016, 385.

474 *BT-Drucks*. 13/4899, 58; *BT-Drucks*. 13/8511, 66; *BVerfG*, Beschluss v. 21.7.2010 - 1 BvR 420/09 -, juris Rn. 51 = *BVerfGE* 127, 132 (155 ff.) = NJW 2010, 3008 (3012) = FamRZ 2010, 1403 = FPR 2010, 465; *OLG Saarbrücken*, Beschluss v. 26.8.2009 - 6 UF 68/09 -, juris Rn. 18 = FamRZ 2010, 385; *BGH*, Beschluss v. 12.12.2007 - XII ZB 158/05 -, juris Rn. 15 = FamRZ 2008, 592 = NJW 2008, 994.

475 *AG Gelnhausen*, Beschluss v. 15.7.2016 - 62 F 4/16 -, juris Rn. 23.

476 *OLG Brandenburg*, Beschluss v. 2.5.2017 - 10 UF 2/17 -, juris Rn. 41; *OLG Brandenburg*, Beschluss v. 19.7.2016 - 10 UF 8/16 -, juris Rn. 26; *OLG Brandenburg*, Beschluss v. 27.12.2016 - 10 UF 23/16 -, juris Rn. 67–68; *OLG Brandenburg*, Beschluss v. 9.5.2016

in conflicts and whether they have problems to cooperate and communicate with each other.

It is normal for parents to have disputes in exercise of parental custody, but not every tension or conflict between parents will lead to termination of joint parental custody. Only when they cannot agree on matters of significant importance for the child in the sense of § 1687 I 2 *BGB* can the joint parental custody be withdrawn.[477] Most importantly, the court should assess the impact on the development and interests of the child resulting from insufficient capability of the parents to reach an agreement.[478] Joint parental custody is generally not consistent with the best interests of the child if parents have a lasting and far-reaching conflict.[479] Such a conflict can be presumed from a number of reports of criminal acts against each other.[480]

The joint parental custody might be not conceivable if parents are not willing or able to cooperate or communicate with each other.[481] Especially when both parents allege that communication and cooperation between them is impossible, which can be seen from mutual distrust, reproaches, reciprocal claims[482] and also

- 10 UF 117/15 -, juris Rn. 28–29 = NZFam 2016, 955; *AG Gelnhausen*, Beschluss v. 15.7.2016 - 62 F 4/16 -, juris Rn. 24.

477 *OLG Brandenburg*, Beschluss v. 27.12.2016 - 10 UF 23/16 -, juris Rn. 23; *BGH*, Beschluss v. 15.6.2016 - XII ZB 419/15 -, juris Rn. 21–23 = FamRZ 2016, 1439; *OLG Brandenburg*, Beschluss v. 15.2.2016 - 10 UF 216/14 -, juris Rn. 39; *OLG Brandenburg*, Beschluss v. 17.3.2014 - 10 UF 244/13-, juris Rn. 22 = FamRZ 2014, 1714; *BGH*, Beschluss v. 12.12.2007 - XII ZB27 158/05 -, juris Rn. 13 = FamRZ 2008, 592 = NJW 2008, 994; *OLG Hamm*, Beschluss v. 16.11.2006 - 3 UF 112/06 -, juris Rn. 27 = FamRZ 2007, 757; *KG Berlin*, Beschluss v. 22.9.2006 - 25 UF 21/06 -, juris Rn. 17 = FamRZ 2007, 754; *OLG Celle*, Beschluss v. 15.12.2003 - 10 UF 267/03 -, juris Rn. 8 = FamRZ 2004, 1667; *OLG Celle*, Beschluss v. 14.11.2002 - 12 UF 81/02 -, juris Rn. 8–10 = FamRZ 2003, 1488.

478 *OLG Brandenburg*, Beschluss v. 17.3.2014 - 10 UF 244/13 -, juris Rn. 23 = FamRZ 2014, 1714.

479 *OLG Brandenburg*, Beschluss v. 27.12.2016 - 10 UF 23/16 -, juris Rn. 23; *OLG Schleswig*, Beschluss v. 16.6.2016 - 10 UF 197/15 -, juris Rn. 52 = FamRZ 2016, 1945; *BGH*, Beschluss v. 15.6.2016 - XII ZB 419/15 -, juris Rn. 21 = FamRZ 2016, 1439.

480 *OLG Nürnberg*, Beschluss v. 29.6.2016 - 7 UF 625/16 -, juris Rn. 39.

481 *OLG Köln*, Beschluss v. 11.10.2002 - 4 UF 24/02 -, juris Rn. 5 = FamRZ 2003, 1036.

482 *OLG Frankfurt*, Beschluss v. 2.2.2017 - 7 UF 2/17 -, juris Rn. 11; *OLG Stuttgart*, Beschluss v. 24.8.2016 - 17 UF 40/16 -, juris Rn. 23 = NZFam 2016, 1204; *OLG Brandenburg*, Beschluss v. 19.7.2016 - 10 UF 8/16 -, juris Rn. 22 (In this case, one parent lodged a lawsuit against the other parent); *OLG Frankfurt*, Beschluss v. 15.3.2006 - 4 UF 112/

confirmed by expert opinions, guardians ad litem or the *Youth Welfare Office*, the court can come to the conclusion that the parents lack the minimal ability to communicate and cooperate with each other.[483] The mere fact that parents only communicate with each other in written form will not lead to withdrawal of the joint parental custody if it does not impose a burden on the child. Joint parental custody can be terminated, even if only one parent is held accountable for the failure of cooperation necessary for exercise of joint parental custody.[484]

The court must dismiss the application of one parent for sole parental custody, having considered that parents despite problems in communication still maintain a sustainable social relationship and have the minimum ability to reach an agreement.[485] An application of a mother for sole parental custody should also not be granted if grounds against joint parental custody probably or certainly will disappear in the short term. For instance, the joint parental custody should remain if the father who has addiction problem (for instance, with alcohol) has shown regret of his previous behaviour and has authorised the mother to care for the child during his treatment.[486]

4.5.3.2 Examination of Transfer of Sole Parental Custody

In this phase, all the elements relevant to the best interests of the child should be examined as in the first phase so that the sole parental custody will not be transferred to an improper applicant.[487] The *BVerfG* has indicated that transfer of the sole parental custody to one parent according to § 1671 I 2 Nr. 2 *BGB* does not require endangerment of the best interests of the child and can be ordered if exercise of joint parental custody (which should not be assumed as a rule) is not consistent with the best interests of the child.[488] Furthermore, it is noted that the court should not transfer sole parental custody completely to one parent if the

---

05 -, juris Rn. 5 = FamRZ 2006, 1627 (Joint parental custody is withdrawn because the parents cannot undertake responsibility jointly because of breach of trust).

483 *OLG Stuttgart*, Beschluss v. 24.8.2016 - 17 UF 40/16 -, juris Rn. 18 = NZFam 2016, 1204.

484 *OLG Nürnberg*, Beschluss v. 29.6.2016 - 7 UF 625/16 -, juris Rn. 36; *OLG Brandenburg*, Beschluss v. 15.2.2016 - 10 UF 216/14 -, juris Rn. 39.

485 *OLG Hamburg*, Beschluss v. 17.12.2015 - 2 UF 107/14 -, juris Rn. 29 = FamRZ 2016, 910.

486 *OLG Köln*, Beschluss v. 26.3.2015 - 26 UF 21/15 -, juris Rn. 16 = FamRZ 2015, 2180.

487 *BGH*, Beschluss v. 12.12.2007 - XII ZB27 158/05 -, juris Rn. 19 = FamRZ 2008, 592 = NJW 2008, 994.

488 *BVerfG*, Nichtannahmebeschluss v. 4.8.2015 - 1 BvR 1388/15 -, juris Rn. 5.

deep and lasting conflicts between parents on important issues of the child can be solved by transfer of partial parental custody.[489]

489 *BVerfG*, Beschluss v. 11.5.2005 - XII ZB 33/04 -, juris Rn. 9 = FamRZ 2005, 1167.

5 Parental Custody for the Child Born Out of Wedlock

According to statistics published by the Federal Statistical Office, children born out of wedlock in 2017 accounted for 34.75 % of all children born in this year, while the proportion of children born out of wedlock in 1970 was only 7.23 %.[490]

There has been always different legislation for the relationship between parents and the child born out of wedlock and in wedlock, although it is required by Article 6 V *GG* that they should be provided the same opportunities to develop themselves physically and mentally and enjoy the same social status. How to realise substantial equality between children born out of wedlock and in wedlock shall first be the task of the legislature who has kept on pushing through legal reforms since entry into force of the *BGB*.[491]

5.1 Historical Development of the Legal Status of the 'Illegitimate' Child

5.1.1 Before the Entry into Force of the *BGB*

Looking through the history of Europe, it can be noted that children born out of wedlock were discriminated against. In the *Roman Kingdom* (*Regnum Romanum*), a child born out of wedlock had no *pater familias* and was free from parental authority (*sui iruis*) from its birth.[492] The father in the early Middle Ages still had the right to acknowledge his child born out of wedlock and its right as a successor, while the relationship between the father and the child born out of wedlock during the late Middle Ages was cut off and the legal status of the non-marital child was largely weakened.[493] The *General State Laws for the Prussian States* of 1794 not only denied an illegitimate child any relationship with its father, but also with its mother's relatives.[494]

490 Retrieved from https://de.statista.com/statistik/daten/studie/1324/umfrage/uneheliche-kinder-anteil-an-allen-geburten/ on 12 September 2019.

491 *Muscheler*, Familienrecht, P. 104 Rn. 207.

492 *Manthe*, Geschichte des römischen Rechts, P. 30.

493 *Schwab*, Familienrecht, P. 287 Rn. 652.

494 *Dethloff*, Familienrecht, § 9 Rn. 5.

5.1.2 From 1 January 1900 to 23 May 1949

According to the *BGB* of 1900, the child born out of wedlock was not related to its father (§ 1589 II a.F)[495] but legally related to its mother and relatives of its mother (§ 1705 a.F).[496] However, the father of a child born out of wedlock[497] should pay child support until his non-marital child reached the age of 16 (§ 1708 I a.F).[498] Although the mother had the right and duty to care for the person of her child born out of wedlock, she was not entitled to parental authority towards the child and could not legally represent her child (§ 1707 a.F).[499]

5.1.3 Since the Entry into Force of the Basic Law

5.1.3.1 Revision of Family Law of 11 August 1961

Although significant changes on the right of the mother to parental authority had been brought about by the *Law on Equal Status Between Men and Women*, rules concerning the legal relationship between parents and children born out of wedlock remained untouched. The amendment in the *Revision of Family Law* in 1961[500] granted the unmarried mother for the first time the right to exercise parental authority over her child born out of wedlock.[501] Furthermore, fathers were required to pay child support to their non-marital children who had not reached the age of 18. However, all the reform approaches failed, and a new law concerning the child born out of wedlock was called for by the *BVerfG*.[502]

---

495 § 1589 II *BGB* of 1900: the child born out of wedlock is not related to his father.

496 § 1705 *BGB* of 1900: the child born out of wedlock shall have the same legal status as the child born in wedlock with respect to relationship with the mother and her relatives.

497 According § 1717 I *BGB*, the father of a child born out of wedlock in §§ 1708–1716 referred to the man who had sexual intercourse with the mother of this child during the conception, unless it was apparent that another man had sexual intercourse with the mother during this period.

498 § 1708 I *BGB* of 1900.

499 § 1707 *BGB* of 1900.

500 BGBl. I 1961, 1221: *Familienrechtsänderungsgesetz* of 11 August1961.

501 *Balloff*, Alleinerziehung und gemeinsame elterliche Sorge nach Trennung und Scheidung - Eine theoretische und empirische Vergleichsstudie, P. 195.

502 *BVerfG*, Beschluss v. 29.1.1969 - 1 BvR 26/66 -, juris Rn. 64 = *BVerfGE* 25, 167 = NJW 1969, 597.

5.1.3.2 Act on Children Born Out of Wedlock of 19 August 1969

The *Act on Children Born out of Wedlock*[503] abolished the provision of § 1589 II a.F *BGB* which denied the legal relationship between children born out of wedlock and their father and the relatives from the side of the father. However, the mother generally was by law the one who had parental authority over the minor child born out of marriage (§ 1705 a.F).[504] According to this law, a child born out of wedlock legitimated or adopted by its biological father could acquire the same legal status as the child born in wedlock had, and the father thereby became entitled to parental authority, while the mother lost the right of parental authority at the same time (§ 1738 a.F).[505] In addition, this law provided for the first time the opportunity for the father to have contact with his children born out of wedlock. However, it was the one (usually the mother) who was entitled to care for the person of the child who had the right to determine whether and how the father should have personal contact with the child (§ 1711 a.F).[506] Although there was a significant change brought by this law in the relationship between children born out of wedlock and their fathers, inequality between the father and mother concerning the exercise of parental authority over their non-marital child was still not removed.

5.1.3.3 Reform of Parental Custody Act of 18 July 1979

The *Reform of Parental Custody Act*[507] enabled the parents who were not entitled to care for the person of the child, including the father of a child born out of wedlock, to maintain contact with their child (§ 1634 I a.F).[508] Besides, the father of a child born out of wedlock was granted the right to request information about the personal circumstances of the child (§ 1634 III a.F).[509]

Before the *KindRG* in 1998, only the parents who had got married could exercise joint parental custody to their children. However, it was in practice criticised that the father of a child born out of wedlock should not be excluded from the right to exercise joint parental custody. The *BVerfG* in its decision on

503 BGBl. I 1969, 1243: *Nichtehelichengesetz* of 19 August1969.
504 § 1705 a.F (abolished), BGBl. I 1969, 1248.
505 § 1738 a.F (abolished), BGBl. I 1969, 1249.
506 § 1711 a.F (abolished), BGBl. I 1969, 1248.
507 BGBl. I 1979, 1061: *Gesetz zur Neuregelung des Rechts der elterlichen Sorge.*
508 § 1634 I a.F (abolished), BGBl. I 1979, 1063.
509 § 1634 III a.F, BGBl. I 1979, 1063.

7 May 1991[510] declared this inconsistent with Article 6 II *GG* if the parents who lived together with their children born out of wedlock and were willing and could take joint responsibility to them were excluded the right for joint parental custody, which was in fact in the best interests of the children. Later, the *BVerfG*-[511]confirmed on the matters regarding legitimation and adoption that the father whose paternity had been established enjoyed the basic right in Article 6 II 1 *GG*. These decisions of the *BVerfG* sped up the legal reform on parental custody for children born out of wedlock.

5.1.3.4 Reform of Parents and Child Act of 1 July 1998

The reform[512] made an effort to eliminate the difference between children born out of and in wedlock, first by having removed the legal term 'illegitimate children' from the *BGB*. Since the entry into force of this Act, children born out of wedlock are no longer described as illegitimate children but as children whose parents are not married to each other.

As regard to the right of contact, the *Reform of Parents and Child Act* in 1998 incorporated § 1634 a.F *BGB* and § 1711 a.F *BGB* where a right of contact for children born in wedlock and out of wedlock was, respectively, regulated into § 1684 *BGB* which is equally applicable for these two types of children.

Furthermore, the right of the father to legitimate the children born out of wedlock, which brought about the consequence that the mother would lose the right and duty to exercise parental authority to her own children, was withdrawn by this reform law. Instead, doors have been opened for unwed parents to exercise joint parental custody towards their children born out of wedlock (§ 1626a I 1 and 2 *BGB*). However, if parents did not submit a declaration for joint parental custody or concluded a marriage according to § 1626 I 1 and 2 *BGB*, the sole parental custody was only left to the mother. An application of the father for transfer of joint parental custody towards the child born out of wedlock was only possible with consent of the mother (§ 1672 I *BGB* a.F). Therefore, it was criticised by not only the *ECtHR*[513] but also the *BVerfG*[514] that the biological father

---

510 *BVerfG*, Beschluss v. 7.5.1991 - 1 BvL 32/88 -, juris Rn. 34 = *BVerfGE* 84, 168 = NJW 1991, 1944 = FamRZ 1991, 913.

511 *BVerfG*, Beschluss v. 7.3.1995 - 1 BvR 790/91-, juris Rn. 61 = *BVerfGE* 92, 158, 178.

512 BGBl. I 1998, 2942: *Kindschaftsrechtsreformgesetz*.

513 *ECtHR*, Case of Zaunegger v. Germany, Judgement on 3 March 2010, Application no. 22028/24 = NJW 2010, 501 (504).

514 *BVerfG*, Beschluss v. 21.7.2010 - 1 BvR 420/09 -, juris Rn. 76 = *BVerfGE* 127, 132 (155 ff.) = NJW 2010, 3008 (3012 f.) = FamRZ 2010, 1403 = FPR 2010, 465.

should be granted the right to apply to the court for judicial review of whether the exclusion of his right to exercise parental custody could be justified from perspective of the best interests of the child.

5.1.3.5 Reform of Act of Parental Custody of the Unmarried Parents of 19 May 2013

This Act[515] opened another door for unmarried parents to have access to the joint parental custody for their children born out of wedlock. They can, besides by concluding a marriage or submitting a declaration for joint parental custody, apply to the family court for the transfer of partial or whole parental custody (§ 1626a I 3 *BGB*). If the child is under the sole parental custody of the mother, the father can apply to the family court for transfer of partial or whole parental custody according to § 1671 II *BGB*. Such a transfer will be granted by the court if the mother consents and the transfer is not inconsistent with the best interests of the child, and the child older than fourteen does not object to the transfer (§ 1671 II 1 *BGB*); or if the joint parental custody is out of question and it is expected that the transfer is most conducive to the best interests of the child (§ 1671 II 2 *BGB*).

5.1.3.6 Act to Strengthen Rights of the Biological but not the Legal Father

The *Act to Strengthen Rights of the Biological but not the Legal Father* in 2013[516], despite the existence of the legal father, grants the biological father the right to establish contact with the child and demand information about the child under certain circumstances (§ 1686a *BGB*). Correspondingly, a new provision (§ 167a *FamFG*) was adopted in the *FamFG* to implement the procedure with respect to exercise of the right under § 1686a *BGB*.

Such a reform has led to debates over constitutionality, legal justification and application of the new rules which have promoted the legal rights of the biological (but not the legal) father. Some scholars pointed out that more obligation should be imposed on the biological father as he enjoys more rights, or it

---

515 BGBl. I 2013, 795: *Gesetz zur Reform der elterlichen Sorge nicht miteinander verheirateter Eltern.*

516 BGBl. I 2013, 2176: *Gesetz zur Stärkung der Rechte des leiblichen, nicht rechtlichen Vaters.*

will result in imbalance between his rights and obligation towards the child.[517] Moreover, it has been criticised that the right of the biological father to contact with the child or to information might pose threat to the existing family where the mother and the legal father live and which is under protection of Article 6 I *GG*.[518] However, although always denied by the *BVerfG*[519], it could in some cases be in the best interests of the child to have two legal fathers.[520]

5.1.4 Conclusion

For a long time, legislatures thought it would be justifiable to grant the mother sole parental custody towards the child born out of wedlock as a general rule. One of the most important reasons lay in the closest connection between the child and the mother shown not only during the pregnancy but also after the birth of the child, which guaranteed that the child had a person at birth who could act for it in a legally binding way.[521] Contrarily, it could not be taken for granted that a father of a child born out of wedlock would want to bear joint parental custody with the mother as a legal father upon birth of the child.

However, legislative justification of sole parental custody of the mother was questioned to be inconsistent with Article 6 II and Article 3 II *GG* which lays emphasis on equality between parents in exercising the natural rights to care for and bring up the child. The historical development of legislation on parental custody of the child born out of wedlock has seen not only the promotion of the legal rights of the legal father, but also those of the biological but not the legal father. However, promotion of rights of both legal and biological father should be always subordinate to the best interests of the child which should be a guideline for further legal reforms on parental custody of the child born out of wedlock.

---

517 *Peschel-Gutezeit*, Der doppelte Vater - Kritische Überlegung zum Gesetz zur Stärkung der Rechte des leiblichen, nicht rechtlichen Vaters, NJW 2013, 2469.

518 *Hoffmann*, Das Gesetz zur Stärkung der Rechte des leiblichen, nicht rechtlichen Vaters, FamRZ 2013, 1077; *Lang*, Entwurf eines Gesetzes zur Stärkung der Rechte des leiblichen, nicht rechtlichen Vaters, FPR 2013, 233; *Peschel-Gutezeit*, Der doppelte Vater - Kritische Überlegung zum Gesetz zur Stärkung der Rechte des leiblichen, nicht rechtlichen Vaters, NJW 2013, 2465.

519 *Zorn*, Das Recht der elterlichen Sorge, P. 90, Rn. 155.

520 *Plettenberg*, Vater, Vater, Mutter, Kind - Ein Plädoyer für die rechtliche Mehrvaterschaft, P. 140.

521 *BT-Drucks.* 13/4899, 60, 100; *ECtHR*, Case of Zaunegger v. Germany, Judgement on 3 March 2010, Application no. 22028/04, Rn. 18.

5.2 Types of Parental Custody of Children Born Out of Wedlock

5.2.1 Sole Parental Custody of the Mother in § 1626a III *BGB*

According to § 1626a III *BGB*, a mother acquires the sole parental custody automatically to the child born out of wedlock if neither a declaration of joint parental custody (§ 1626a I 1 *BGB*) has been submitted nor a marriage has been concluded by the parents (§ 1626a I 2 *BGB*), and an application for transfer of joint parental custody of the fathers has not been granted by the family court (§ 1626a I 3 and II *BGB*).

5.2.2 Sole Parental Custody of the Father Through Court Decision According to § 1671 II *BGB*

The father of a child born out of wedlock towards whom the mother exercises sole parental custody can apply to the court for a complete transfer of parental custody. Preconditions for the granting of such an application are similar to the ones for the application of parents who exercise joint parental custody and are separated for a period that is not merely temporary in § 1671 I *BGB*.

The application of the father of a child born out of wedlock for transfer of sole parental custody to him shall be granted by the court under the condition that the mother consents to it unless the transfer is not contradictory to the best interests of the child or the child above the age of 14 does not object to such a transfer (§ 1671 II 1 *BGB*). In addition, the application of the father of a child born out of wedlock for transfer of sole parental custody can also be ordered if joint parental custody does not come into question, and it is expected that the transfer of the sole parental custody to the father is in the best interests of the child (§ 1671 II 2 *BGB*). The criteria to evaluate the best interests of the child in § 1671 II *BGB* are the same as the ones in § 1671 I *BGB* which has been elaborated in section 4.5.3.

5.2.3 Joint Parental Custody Through Declaration in § 1626a I 1 *BGB*

5.2.3.1 Formality

Legal parents who are not married to each other at the birth of their joint child can make a declaration that they wish to take on joint parental custody for the child. The number of declarations has sharply risen during the past years.[522] Such a declaration needs to be notarised to become effective (§ 1626d I *BGB*). If either of the parents is not sufficiently proficient in the German language, an interpreter is needed for the official notarisation according to § 16 III 1 *BeurkG*[523]. However, the declaration might be invalid if the interpreter should not participate in notarisation because of his or her relationship with one parent in accordance with § 16 III 2 in conjunction with § 7 Nr. 3 *BeurkG*.[524] The notary office shall notify the competent *Youth Welfare Office* of the declaration without any undue delay.

It is pointed out by the lawmakers in the explanatory memorandum that parents do not need to specify how they will exercise parental custody jointly, but just to submit their declaration of the joint parental custody.[525] An examination of the best interests of the child following declaration of joint parental custody is not required.[526]

Parents cannot make a declaration that they will only exercise part of parental custody jointly.[527] If one parent finds it necessary to exercise part of parental custody solely, he can apply to the court for it according to § 1671 I 2 Nr. 1 *BGB*. However, it is suggested that declaration of partial parental custody should be accepted de lege ferenda,[528] and that parents should be granted the right to make a declaration concerning joint exercise of partial parental custody.[529]

5.2.3.2 Time of the Declaration

The declaration can be delivered before the birth of the child (§ 1626b II *BGB*), but not before the conception, but there is no fixed date before which parents

522 In the year of 2004, there were only 87 366 declaration, while in the year of 2015 there were 180 006 declaration, Statistisches Bundesamts, Statistiken der Kinder- und Jugendhilfe - Pflegschaften, Vormundschaften, Beistandschaften, Pflegeerlaubnis, Sorgerechtsentzug, Sorgeerklärung 2015, Tabelle 3.

523 *Notification Law* (*Beurkundungsgesetz*), BGBl. I 1969, 1513, revised by BGBl. I 2015, 2090.

524 *OLG Frankfurt*, Beschluss v. 1.2.2016 - 5 UF 286/15 -, juris Rn. 7 = FamRZ 2016, 2017.

525 *BT-Drucks*. 13/4899, 93.

526 *BT-Drucks*. 13/4899, 59.

527 *BT-Drucks*. 17/11048, 30; *BGH*, Beschluss v. 15.11.2007 - XII ZB 136/04 -, juris Rn. 32, 34 = NJW 2008, 662; *Staudinger/Coester* (2015), § 1626a Rn. 59.

528 *Bamberger/Roth/Veit* (2015), § 1626a Rn. 10.2.

529 *Coester*, Sorgerecht nicht miteinander verheirateter Eltern, FamRZ 2012, 1337 (1344).

shall make a joint declaration. Such a joint declaration will come into force only when the child is born.[530]

5.2.3.3 *Legal Nature*

The declaration of joint parental custody is considered a contract between the mother and father, as it is only the legally binding expression of one's own will and it can become effective the moment it is made. Such a declaration, according to the prevailing view, is only a declaration of the intention to concretise the right to exercise parental custody derived from Article 6 II 1 *GG*.[531]

If joint parental custody has been established by such a declaration of the parents, it cannot be removed by another joint declaration, but only by a court decision. For example, one of the parents who have already separated can apply to the court for sole parental custody according to § 1671 I *BGB*.

5.2.4 Joint Parental Custody Through Marriage in § 1626a I 2 *BGB*

Parents who did not get married at birth of their child can acquire joint parental custody by marriage (§ 1626a I 2 *BGB*). Upon marriage, the sole parental custody according to § 1626a III *BGB* or § 1671 *BGB* changes to joint parental custody automatically, on the condition that one of the parents was entitled to sole parental custody before the marriage.[532] For instance, in case parents have married once before and the sole parental custody was transferred to one parent on occasion of divorce, joint parental custody can be reestablished upon the de novo marriage, without the need to invoke § 1696 *BGB* and to evaluate the best interests of the child again.[533] If the sole parental custody of one of the parents before marriage is limited, the other parent can only get a limited right to exercise parental care upon marriage.

530 *Schwab*, Familienrecht, P. 340 Rn. 771.

531 *Lipp*, Das elterliche Sorgerecht für das nichteheliche Kind nach dem Kindschaftsreformgesetz (*KindRG*), FamRZ 1998, 65, 70; *MüKo/Huber* (2017), § 1626a Rn. 25.

532 *Zorn*, Das Recht der elterlichen Sorge, P. 112 Rn. 194; *MüKo/Huber* (2017), § 1626a Rn. 37.

533 *MüKo/Huber* (2017), § 1626a Rn. 37.

5.2.5 Joint Parental Custody Acquired by Court Order in § 1626a I 3, II *BGB*

The court decision of the *BVerfG* on 21 July 2010[534] has opened another door for unmarried parents to have access to joint parental custody. Following this decision, the family court would grant the application of one unmarried parent for the transfer of joint parental custody provided that it was expected to be in the best interests of the child. However, since the entry into force of the *Reform of Act of Parental Custody of the Unmarried Parents* on 19 May 2013, such an application can be granted if it is not inconsistent to the best interests of the children (§ 1626a I 3, II *BGB*).

5.2.5.1 Legal Requirements

The parent who submits such an application must be the legal parent of the child. Not only the father, but also the mother has the right to apply for transfer of joint parental custody.[535]

5.2.5.2 Criteria to Decide on Transfer of Joint Parental Custody

a) Negative Assessment Criterion

It has been held that the new provision § 1626a II 2 *BGB* has introduced a statutory guiding principle and legal presumption in favour of joint parental custody towards the child born out of wedlock.[536] Therefore, the criterion on transfer of joint parental custody is less strict than the one on transfer of sole parental custody.[537] An application for transfer of joint parental custody should be granted if it is not inconsistent with children's best interests (§ 1626a II 1 *BGB*). A positive assessment of the question of whether joint parental custody is in the best interests of the child is not necessary.[538] Therefore, the applicant is not required

---

534 *BVerfG*, Beschluss v. 21.7.2010 - 1 BvR 420/09 -, juris Rn. 46 = *BVerfGE* 127, 132 (155) = NJW 2010, 3008 (3012) = FamRZ 2010, 1403 = FPR 2010, 465.

535 *BT-Drucks*. 17/11048, 6; *Palandt/Götz* (2018), § 1626a Rn. 9.

536 *BT-Drucks*. 17/11048, 12, S. 17; *OLG Brandenburg*, Beschluss v. 3.8.2015 - 13 UF 190/14 -, juris Rn. 49 = FamRZ 2016, 240; *OLG Brandenburg*, Beschluss v. 16.7.2015 - 10 UF 209/14 -, juris Rn. 23 = FamRZ 2015, 1207; *OLG Nürnberg*, Beschluss v. 9.12.2013 - 7 UF 1195/13 -, juris Rn. 54 = FamRZ 2014, 571, 572.

537 *Palandt/Götz* (2018), § 1626a Rn. 11.

538 *OLG Brandenburg*, Beschluss v. 3.8.2015 - 13 UF 190/14 -, juris Rn. 49 = FamRZ 2016, 240; *OLG Brandenburg*, Beschluss v. 16.7.2015 - 10 UF 209/14 -, juris Rn. 25 = FamRZ 2015, 1207; *KG Berlin*, Beschluss v. 3.7.2015 - 19 UF 9/15 -, juris Rn. 22 = FamRZ 2015,

to prove how joint parental custody will promote the best interests of the child, whereas the respondent is obliged to present grounds which speak against joint parental custody.[539] The family court only looks into grounds which speak against joint parental custody. An application for joint parental custody cannot be dismissed unless it was convinced with considerable certainty that joint parental custody would be detrimental to the best interests of the child.[540]

Although the court under guidance of the negative assessment criterion is not required to assess positively if the transfer of joint parental custody according to § 1626a II *BGB* is in the best interests of the child, it shall make sure parents have the minimum ability to reach agreement. Therefore, parents should be willing and capable to communicate and cooperate with each other in exercising the parental custody jointly, or it will be inconsistent with the best interests of the child.[541] Furthermore, there should not be endless insurmountable conflicts between parents which could be exacerbated by transfer of joint parental custody.[542] This negative assessment criterion, however, can hardly be applied in the case where the *Youth Welfare Office* and the parents' opinion has not been heard (§ 1626 II 2 *BGB* and § 155a III *FamFG*)[543]

2069; *OLG Karlsruhe*, Beschluss *v.* 26.3.2015 - 18 UF 304/14 -, juris Rn. 14 = FamRZ 2015, 2168; *OLG Brandenburg*, Beschluss v. 23.3.2015 - 13 UF 240/14 -, juris Rn. 22 = FamRZ 2015, 1203; *OLG Brandenburg*, Beschluss v. 12.3.2015 - 9 UF 214/14 -, juris Rn. 12; *OLG Brandenburg*, Beschluss v. 22.10.2014 - 13 UF 206/13 -, juris Rn. 11 = NJW 2015, 964 = FamRZ 2015, 760; *OLG Brandenburg*, Beschluss v. 19.9.2013 - 9 UF 96/11 -, juris Rn. 33 = NJW 2014, 233–235; *Huber/Antomo*, Die Neuregelung der elterlichen Sorge nicht miteinander verheirateter Eltern, FamRZ 2012, 1257 (1263); *Heilmann*, Die Reform des Sorgerechts nicht miteinander verheirateter Eltern - Das Ende eines Irrwegs? NJW 2013, 1473 (1474).

539 *OLG Brandenburg*, Beschluss v. 22.10.2014 - 13 UF 206/13 -, juris Rn. 12 = NJW 2015, 964 = FamRZ 2015, 760.

540 *OLG Brandenburg*, Beschluss v. 3.8.2015 - 13 UF 190/14 -, juris Rn. 59 = FamRZ 2016, 243; *OLG Nürnberg*, Beschluss v. 9.12.2013 - 7 UF 1195/13 -, juris Rn. 54 = FamRZ 2014, 571, 572.

541 *BT-Drucks*. 17/11048, 17; *Palandt/Götz* (2018), § 1626a Rn. 11a; *OLG Naumburg*, Beschluss v. 11.08.2014 - 3 UF 130/14 -, juris Rn. 10 = FamRZ 2015, 764; *OLG Brandenburg*, Beschluss v. 19.9.2013 - 9 UF 96/11 -, juris Rn. 32–34 = NJW 2014, 233–235.

542 *OLG Brandenburg*, Beschluss v. 19.9.2013 - 9 UF 96/11 -, juris Rn. 46 = NJW 2014, 233–235.

543 *Fahl*, § 1626a *BGB* und das Kindeswohl - Reformbedarf wegen Verstoßes gegen die UN-Kinderrechtskonvention (Rn. 156), NZFam 2014, 155.

b) Positive Assessment Criterion

While some courts stick to the statutory presumption in favour of joint parental custody in § 1626a II *BGB*, some hold that it cannot be presumed from § 1626a II *BGB* that joint parental custody should take precedence over sole parental custody for the child born out of wedlock.[544] It is further maintained by the courts refusing legal presumption in favour of joint parental custody that criteria applied to evaluate whether transfer of joint parental custody in § 1626a I 3, II *BGB* is inconsistent with the best interests of the child should be the same as the positive assessment criterion applied in § 1671 I 2 Nr. 2 *BGB* for withdrawal of joint parental custody,[545] which has already been confirmed by the *BGH*.[546]

In proceedings concerning the transfer of joint parental custody according to § 1626a I 3 *BGB*, the court in each individual case should weigh circumstances not only against but also for the joint parental custody as in proceedings concerning withdrawal of joint parental custody pursuant to § 1671 I 2 Nr. 2 *BGB*.[547] The wish of one parent not to exercise joint parental custody or the subjective reservation to the other parent alone cannot shake the presumption of the joint parental custody.[548] In addition, the court shall also regard whether parents are willing and able to cooperate with each other, and whether there is a sustainable social relationship between parents.[549] The ability of parents to

---

544 *OLG Frankfurt*, Beschluss v. 7.10.2013 - 5 UF 88/13 -, juris Rn. 2 = NJW 2014, 2201; *OLG Stuttgart*, Beschluss am 2.12.2014 - 11 UF 173/14 -, juris Rn. 14 = NJW 2015, 642 = FamRZ 2015, 674–675; *OLG Hamm*, Beschluss v. 24.5.2016 - II-3 UF 139/15 -, juris Rn. 43 = FuR 2017, 95; *OLG Karlsruhe*, Beschluss v. 2.4.2015 - 18 UF 253/14 -, juris Rn. 15; *OLG Karlsruhe*, Beschluss v. 20.6.2013 - 18 UF 38/13 -, juris Rn. 12 = FamRZ 2014, 490.

545 *KG Berlin*, Beschluss v. 22.12.2016 - 25 UF 23/16 -, juris Rn. 16; *OLG Stuttgart*, Beschluss am 2.12.2014 - 11 UF 173/14 -, juris Rn. 10 = NJW 2015, 642 = FamRZ 2015, 674–675.

546 *BGH*, Beschluss v. 15.6.2016 - XII ZB 419/15 -, juris Rn. 10 = NJW 2016, 2497–2502 = FamRZ 2016, 1439–1444 = NZFam 2016, 795–800 = ZKJ 2016, 414–419 = FuR 2016, 576–578.

547 *OLG Bremen*, Beschluss v. 16.12.2016 - 5 UF 110/16 -, juris Rn. 7; *BGH*, Beschluss v. 15.6.2016 - XII ZB 419/15 -, juris Rn. 19 = NJW 2016, 2497–2502 = FamRZ 2016, 1439–1444 = NZFam 2016, 795–800 = ZKJ 2016, 414–419 = FuR 2016, 576–578.

548 *OLG Hamm*, Beschluss v. 19.9.2016 – II-5 UF 174/16 -, juris Rn. 21–22 = FuR 2016, 722–723.

549 *OLG Koblenz*, Beschluss v. 6.2.2017 - 13 UF 696/16 -, juris Rn. 11; *KG Berlin*, Beschluss v. 22.12.2016 - 25 UF 23/16 -, juris Rn. 16; *OLG Bremen*, Beschluss v. 16.12.2016 - 5

communicate shall not come into question if they can only communicate well on WhatsApp.[550]

It is normal that parents hold different opinions towards how to exercise parental custody.[551] However, a lasting and profound conflict between parents is generally not consistent with the best interests of the child.[552] Therefore, it is very necessary for the court to examine *ex officio* whether parents can reach agreement on important matters of the child, for instance, its life centre, in the case related to transfer of joint parental custody.[553]

c) *Study on Decisions of Local Courts*

When deciding whether an application of a father for joint parental custody should be granted, it is necessary for the court to investigate the legal grounds against joint parental custody according to § 1626a II 2 *BGB*. In decisions where the joint parental custody did not come into question,[554] those grounds which are contradictory to the best interests of the child emerge if the parents lack the minimal capability to communicate and cooperate with each other or they are incapable of reaching an agreement on the child's issues of great significance. On the contrary, the application of a father of a child born out of wedlock according to § 1626a I 3, II *BGB* is generally granted if the joint parental custody is not

---

UF 110/16, juris Rn. 9; *OLG Hamm*, Beschluss v. 24.5.2016 - II-3 UF 139/15 -, juris Rn. 45 = FuR 2017, 95; *OLG Hamm*, Beschluss v. 9.3.2016 - II-2 WF 38/16 -, juris Rn. 17; *KG Berlin*, Beschluss v. 15.4.2014 - 19 UF 120/13 -, juris Rn. 6 = FamRZ 2014, 1375; *OLG Celle*, Beschluss v. 19.5.2014 - 10 UF 91/14 -, juris Rn. 11= NZFam 2014, 738; *OLG Schleswig*, Beschluss v. 7.4.2014 - 15 UF 140/13 -, juris Rn. 19 = FamRZ 2014, 1374.

550 *OLG Saarbrücken*, Beschluss v. 27.4.2016 - 6 UF 22/16 -, juris Rn. 17.

551 *OLG Karlsruhe*, Beschluss *v.* 26.3.2015 - 18 UF 304/14 -, juris Rn. 14 = FamRZ 2015, 2168.

552 *KG Berlin*, Beschluss v. 22.12.2016 - 25 UF 23/16 -, juris Rn. 16; *BGH*, Beschluss v. 15.6.2016 - XII ZB 419/15 -, juris Rn. 24 = NJW 2016, 2497–2502 = FamRZ 2016, 1439–1444 = NZFam 2016, 795–800 = ZKJ 2016, 414–419 = FuR 2016, 576–578; *OLG Schleswig*, Beschluss v. 7.4.2014 - 15 UF 140/13 -, juris Rn. 19 = FamRZ 2014, 1374.

553 *Staudinger/Salgo* (2014), § 1687 Rn. 38a; *OLG Hamm*, Beschluss v. 19.9.2016 - II-5 UF 174/16 -, juris Rn. 20 = FuR 2016, 722–723.

554 *OLG Koblenz*, Beschluss v. 6.2.2017 - 13 UF 696/16 -, juris Rn. 11–13; *OLG Bremen*, Beschluss v. 16.12.2016 - 5 UF 110/16 -, juris Rn. 9–10; *KG Berlin*, Beschluss v. 15.4.2014 - 19 UF 120/13 -, juris Rn. 12 = FamRZ 2014, 1375.

inconsistent with the best interests of the child and the legal grounds against the joint parental custody has neither been presented nor detected.[555]

d) Decision of BGH *on 15 June 2016*

It is indicated by the *BGH* that the best interests of the child should be taken as a primary criterion not only in the positive assessment of children's best interests in § 1671 I 2 Nr. 2 *BGB* but also in the so-called negative assessment in § 1626a II *BGB*.[556] Even in the negative evaluation, it is necessary for the courts to take all the facts which are for or against joint parental custody into account (Rn. 19). The *BGH* has also restricted the application of the rebuttable presumption in § 1626a II *BGB* – joint parental custody should not be ordered through speedy procedure if any concrete circumstance is presented or manifest which is not consistent with the best interests of the child (Rn. 32 and 38).

On the crucial evaluation criteria of the best interests of the child, it is noted by the *BGH* that one-sided denial of one parent might not be contradictory to the best interests of the child and therefore will not exclude the joint parental custody (Rn. 22). However, it is generally considered to be detrimental to the best interests of the child if parents, though communicating with each other, frequently cannot exchange opinions on issues concerning the child objectively and reach an agreement in an appropriate manner (Rn. 25).

5.2.5.3 Proceedings for Transfer of Joint Parental Custody (§ 155a FamFG*)*

§ 155a *FamFG* introduces a summary procedure to respond to § 1626a I 3, II *BGB*. Such a procedure can only be applied in proceedings concerning transfer

---

555 *OLG Hamm*, Beschluss v. 19.9.2016 - II-5 UF 174/16 -, juris Rn. 17, 20 = FuR 2016, 722–723; *OLG Saarbrücken*, Beschluss v. 27.4.2016 - 6 UF 22/16 -, juris Rn. 12; *OLG Brandenburg*, Beschluss v. 3.8.2015 - 13 UF 190/14 -, juris Rn. 60 = FamRZ 2016, 240; *OLG Brandenburg*, Beschluss v. 26.3.2015 - 13 UF 209/14 -, juris Rn. 21; *OLG Karlsruhe*, Beschluss *v.* 26.3.2015 - 18 UF 304/14 -, juris Rn. 12, 17; *OLG Brandenburg*, Beschluss v. 22.10.2014 - 13 UF 206/13 -, juris Rn. 10, 16 = NJW 2015, 964 = FamRZ 2015, 760; *OLG Naumburg*, Beschluss v. 11.08.2014 - 3 UF 130/14 -, juris Rn. 10–11 = FamRZ 2015, 763 (The legal grounds against joint parental custody are not present if the parents only have problems to reach agreement on exercise of contact right).

556 *BGH*, Beschluss v. 15.6.2016 - XII ZB 419/15 -, juris Rn. 14; *BT-Drucks*. 17/11048, 14: The primary criterion of a decision according to § 1626a II *BGB* is the best interests of the child.

of joint parental custody pursuant to § 1626a II *BGB* if no grounds against joint parental custody are presented or otherwise manifest (§ 1626a II 2 *BGB*).[557] Whether these grounds can shake the legal presumption in § 1626a II 2 *BGB*, which is irrelevant to application of summary procedure, shall be examined pursuant to substantive laws.[558]

According to § 155a III 1, IV 1 *FamFG*, the decision on transfer of joint parental custody pursuant to § 1626a II *BGB* should generally be made in a speedy and written procedure without hearing of the *Youth Welfare Office* and the parents if no grounds which speak against joint parental custody have been found or presented. Although it should be generally examined in summary procedure whether opinions of the child should be heard according to § 159 *FamFG*,[559] it, however, would be still difficult to find grounds which might be against the joint parental custody without hearing opinions of the parents or the *Youth Welfare Office*.[560] Therefore, application of the summary procedure has been restricted by some courts which exclude summary procedure if any indication related to evaluation of children's best interests becomes known.[561] Furthermore, § 155a II *FamFG* which allows the mother to comment on the application of the father but after six weeks upon the child's birth is criticised for not being unjust for the father.[562]

---

557 *OLG Hamm*, Beschluss v. 19.9.2016 - II-5 UF 174/16 -, juris Rn. 17 = FuR 2016, 722–723.

558 *OLG Karlsruhe*, Beschluss v. 13.6.2014 - 18 UF 103/14 -, juris Rn. 19 = NJW 2014, 3044 = FamRZ 2014, 1797.

559 *OLG Brandenburg*, Beschluss v. 22.10.2014 - 13 UF 206/13 -, juris Rn. 32 = NJW 2015, 964 = FamRZ 2015, 760; *OLG Brandenburg*, Beschluss v. 16.7.2015 - 10 UF 209/14 -, juris Rn. 42 = FamRZ 2015, 1207.

560 *Coester*, Sorgerecht nicht miteinander verheirateter Eltern, FamRZ 2012, 1337 (1341); *Keuter*, Vereinfachtes Verfahren zur Übertragung der gemeinsamen elterlichen Sorge - ein Fremdkörper in Kindschaftssachen, FamRZ 2015, 825 (827); *Huber/Antomo*, Die Neuregelung der elterlichen Sorge nicht miteinander verheirateter Eltern, FamRZ 2012, 1257 (1264).

561 *OLG Bremen*, Beschluss v. 1.4.2015 - 4 UF 33/15 -, juris Rn. 6 = FamRZ 2015, 2170, with comment from *Keuter*, FamRZ 2016, 473; *OLG Thüringen*, Beschluss v. 19.1.2015 - 1 UF 727/13 -, juris Rn. 23; *OLG Karlsruhe*, Beschluss v. 13.6.2014 - 18 UF 103/14 -, juris Rn. 19, 21 = NJW 2014, 3044 = FamRZ 2014, 1797; *OLG Frankfurt*, Beschluss v. 20.1.2014 - 1 UF 356/13 -, juris Rn. 16, FamRZ 2014, 852.

562 *Heilmann*, Die Reform des Sorgerechts nicht miteinander verheirateter Eltern - Das Ende eines Irrwegs? NJW 2013, 1473 (1476); *Fink/Bitter*, Eine unendliche Geschichte - kommt endlich die verfassungsgemäße Reform des Sorgerechts für nichteheliche Kinder? ZKJ 2012, 172 (173).

If the summary procedure is wrongfully applied, the case shall be referred back to the family court by the court of appeal upon application of proceeding participants according to § 69 I 3 *FamFG*.[563]

5.2.6 Another Type?

It has been suggested that it should be easier for the father of a child born out of wedlock to gain joint parental custody if joint parental custody serves the best interests of the child. Therefore, parents of a child born out of wedlock could be presumed to exercise joint parental custody automatically upon birth of the child, and they do not have to submit a joint declaration for joint parental custody, conclude a marriage or apply to the court for the joint parental custody.[564] Although such a presumption overturning § 1626a *BGB* completely contributes to further equality between fathers and mothers of a child born out of wedlock, it might lead to a nominal joint parental custody which will be generally inconsistent with the best interests of the child, especially when a father escapes from exercising parental custody jointly with the mother. However, § 1626a *BGB* could be slightly modified so that ways of the father to gain access to joint parental custody towards his child born out of wedlock could be expanded. As suggested by *Schumann* and *Löhnig*, the father who has run the same household with the mother from the time of birth of their joint child born out of wedlock could be presumed to exercise joint parental custody with the mother.[565] However, it is also criticised that living in the same household does not certainly indicate capability of the unwed parents in communication and cooperation.[566]

563 *OLG Frankfurt*, Beschluss v. 20.1.2014 - 1 UF 356/13 -, juris Rn. 19 = FamRZ 2014, 852 (853); *OLG Thüringen*, Beschluss v. 19.1.2015 - 1 UF 727/13 -, juris Rn. 14.

564 *Schmitt*, Das Sorgerecht nichtverheirateter Väter, P. 267.

565 *Schumann*, B 37; Löhnig, Lösungsmodelle für das Sorgerecht nicht miteinander verheirateter Eltern - Plädoyer für einen Perspektivenwechsel, in Reformbedarf im nichtehelichen Eltern-Kind-Verhältnis, 10. Göttinger Workshop zum Familienrecht 2011, P. 34.

566 *Ernst*, Gemeinsame Elternverantwortung nach Trennung und Scheidung, DRiZ 2018, 302 (304).

5.3 Rights of the Biological but Not the Legal Father

5.3.1 Introduction

The notion of 'family life' under Article 8 *ECHR* is not confined to marriage-based relationships and may encompass other de facto 'family' ties where the parties are living together out of wedlock.[567] However, the biological but not the legal father cannot justify his right to exercise parental rights towards his child born out of wedlock only by the mere biological relationship. In German law, although parents in Book 4 (Family Law) of the *BGB* only refer to legal parenthood defined in § 1591 and 1592 *BGB*, it cannot be concluded that Article 6 II 1 *GG* excludes the right of a biological (but not the legal) father to care for his child born out of wedlock. Neither can it be inferred from Article 6 II 1 *GG* that the legal fatherhood shall always prevail over the biological fatherhood, and legal rights of the legal father therefore should be protected with priority compared with the biological but not the legal father.

This chapter presents rights of the biological but not the legal father provided for in the *BGB* and studies possible conflicts between the biological but not the legal father and the legal father.

5.3.2 Right to Acknowledge Paternity and Apply for Determination of Paternity

The biological father can acknowledge the paternity of a child. Such an acknowledgement requires approval of the mother, or approval of the child if the mother is not entitled to parental custody (§ 1595 I, II *BGB*). However, the acknowledgement is not valid if the paternity of another man exists (§ 1594 I *BGB*). It has been put forward that approval of the mother is not necessary and might be replaced by genetic proof of paternity.[568] However, the law does not show a presumed biological father the way to obtain the genetic proof of paternity, as only the child and legal parents are entitled to the right under § 1598a *BGB* with respect to clarification of the genetic origin of the child.

If there is no paternity under § 1592 1 and 2 and § 1593 *BGB*, the biological father can apply to the court for determination of paternity (§ 1600d I *BGB*). In the proceedings for court determination of paternity, it is presumed that the

567 *ECtHR*, Case of Schneider v. Germany, Judgement on 15 September 2011, Application no. 17080/07, Rn. 79.

568 *Schmitt*, Das Sorgerecht nichtverheirateter Väter, P. 94.

legal father of a child is the man who had sexual intercourse with the mother in the period of conception[569] (§ 1600d II *BGB*). The presumption does not apply if there are serious doubts as to the paternity.

5.3.3 Right to Challenge Paternity

5.3.3.1 Historical Development

The *BVerfG* declared in its decision on 9 April 2003 that § 1600 *BGB* a.F was inconsistent with Article 6 II 1 *GG* insofar as the biological father was excluded from challenging paternity without exception.[570] Furthermore, it indicated that the right to challenge paternity should be granted to the biological father if the legal parents did not establish a social family relationship with the child that was under protection of Article 6 I 1 *GG*. However, it is since the entry into force of the *Act to Amend Rules Concerning the Challenge of Paternity and Contact Right of Related Person to the Child*[571] in 2004 that the biological father has been granted the right to challenge paternity on the condition that there is no social family relationship between the child and the legal father (§ 1600 II *BGB*).[572]

In order to prevent the abusive and improper acknowledgement of paternity, the *Law of Amendments on Right to Challenge Paternity*[573] expanded the right to challenge the paternity to authorities.[574] However, the right of authorities to challenge paternity was held to be against Article 6 I *GG* and other fundamental

569 The period of conception is deemed to be the time from the 300th to the 181st before the birth of the child, including 300th and 181st days. If it is certain that the child is conceived outside the period in Sentence 1, this deviating period of time will be deemed to be period of conception (§ 1600d III *BGB*).

570 *BVerfG*, Beschluss v. 9.4.2003 - 1 BvR 1493/96 -, juris Rn. 79 = *BVerfGE* 108, 82 = NJW 2003, 2151 = FamRZ 2003, 816 = FPR 2003, 471.

571 BGBl. I 2004, 598: *Act to Amend Rules Concerning the Challenge of Paternity and Contact Right of Persons Related to the Child, and on Registration of Advance Directive and Introduction of Using Paper Forms for Payment of Professional Guardians* (*Gesetz zur Änderung der Vorschriften über die Anfechtung der Vaterschaft und das Umgangsrecht von Bezugspersonen des Kindes, zur Registrierung von Vorsorgeverfügung und zur Einführung von Vordrucken für die Vergütung von Berufsbetreuern*).

572 *BGH*, Urteil v. 6.12.2006 - XII ZR 164/04 -, *BGHZ* 170, 161–175, juris Rn. 27 = NJW 2007, 1677 = FamRZ 2007, 538.

573 BGBl. I 2008, 313: *Law to Supplement Right to Challenge Paternity* (*Gesetz zur Ergänzung des Rechts zur Anfechtung der Vaterschaft*).

574 § 1600 I 5 and § 1600b 1a *BGB* (abolished).

rights and therefore was declared unconstitutional and void in the decision of the *BVerfG* on 17 December 2013.[575]

5.3.3.2 Reform Need in German Law

a) Impulse from Decisions of the ECtHR

The *ECtHR* deemed it a violation of Article 8 *ECHR* if application of the alleged biological father to challenge paternity was dismissed just because paternity had been acknowledged by another man.[576] However, Article 8 of the *ECHR* would not be violated if such an application of an alleged biological father had been dismissed because there was a social relationship between the child and its legal father.[577] Nevertheless, the *ECtHR* also emphasised that the social family relationship is only a conceivable criterion, and all the legal interests concerned (of the child and the mother) and particular circumstances in each individual case should be given sufficient consideration under guidance of the children's best interests.[578]

In addition, the *ECtHR* has interpreted the term 'social family relationship'. It is pointed out by the *ECtHR* that a social family relationship between a biological but not the legal father and his child should be based on the fact that the father has borne actual responsibility for the child at least for some time.[579] Furthermore, cohabitation is generally a requirement for establishment of a relationship in family law.[580] Conversely, the (presumed) biological father's wish to take over responsibility or to build up a social and family relationship with the child was not sufficient to attract protection of Article 6 I *GG* and Article 8 *ECHR*.

---

575 *BVerfG*, Beschluss v. 17.12.2013 - BvL 6/10 -, juris Rn. 27–28 = FamRZ 2014, 449 = NJW 2014, 1364.

576 *ECtHR*, Case of L. D. and P.K. v. Bulgary, Judgement on 8 December 2016, Application no. 7949/11 and 45522/13 = FamRZ 2017, 385.

577 *ECtHR*, Case of Ahrens v. Germany, Judgement on 22 March 2012, Application no. 45071/09 = FamRZ 2012, 691; *ECtHR*, Case of Kautzor v. Germany, Judgement on 22 March 2012, Application no. 23338/09 = FamRZ 2012, 691; *Hähnchen*, Vergangheit und Zukunft der Rechte des nichtehelichen Vaters, JZ 2015, 708 (712); FamRZ 2017, 387.

578 *ECtHR*, Case of Ahrens v. Germany, Judgement on 22 March 2012, Application no. 45071/09, Rn. 68 = FamRZ 2012, 691.

579 *ECtHR*, Case of Schneider v. Germany, Judgement on 15 September 2011, Application no. 17080/07, Rn. 26.

580 *ECtHR*, Case of Anayo v. Germany, Judgement on 21 December 2010, Application no. 20578/07, Rn. 56.

b) Advice on Legal Reform

Under § 1600 I *BGB*, mother, child and the man whose paternity exists under § 1592 Nr. 1, 2 *BGB* (the legal father), or who makes a statutory declaration that he had sexual intercourse with the child's mother during the period of conception (the biological, but not the legal father), are entitled to challenge paternity. However, the right of a biological but not the legal father to challenge the paternity can only be exercised if there is no social and family relationship between the legal father and the child (§ 1600 II *BGB*) or the social and family relationship between them only exists on paper.[581] A social and family relationship between the legal father and the child does not come into question if the legal father only undertakes the responsibility officially and financially.[582]

Apparently, the lawmakers only give regard to the social family relationship between the legal father and the child, but do not consider whether there is or has been a social family relationship between the biological father and the child and why the biological but not the legal father could and cannot establish a social family relationship with his child.[583] Therefore, it is suggested that § 1600 II *BGB* should be abolished[584] so that establishment of the social family relationship will not be a crucial criterion to exclude right of a biological but not the legal father to challenge paternity. Furthermore, it is suggested that the period limit for the biological father to contest paternity should be reduced to one year from two years in § 1600b I *BGB* in order to limit uncertainty burdened to a social family.[585]

---

581 *BGH*, Urteil v. 6.12.2006 - XII ZR 164/04 -, *BGHZ* 170, 161–175, juris Rn. 31 = NJW 2007, 1677 = FamRZ 2007, 538.

582 *OLG Hamm*, Beschluss v. 11.2.2016 - 12 UF 244/14 -, juris Rn. 24 = FamRZ 2016, 1187.

583 *ECtHR*, Case of L. D. and P.K./Bulgary, Judgement on 8 December 2016, Application no. 7949/11 and 45522/13 = FamRZ 2017, 386.

584 *Helms*, Rechtliche, biologische und soziale Elternschaft - Herausforderungen durch neue Familienformen, Gutachten F zum 71. Deutschen Juristentag 2016, F 50 = NJW-Beil 2016, 49 (51).

585 *Helms*, Rechtliche, biologische und soziale Elternschaft - Herausforderungen durch neue Familienformen, Gutachten F zum 71. Deutschen Juristentag 2016, F 50 = NJW-Beil 2016, 49 (51); *Heiderhoff*, Herausforderungen durch neue Familienformen - Zeit für ein Umdenken, NJW 2016, 2629 (2631).

5.3.3.3 *Two Fathers?*

The child should not be shared like a cake by the biological and legal father.[586] Two fathers might be better for the child if the biological father as well as the legal father who has established and maintains a social family relationship with the child are willing to undertake responsibilities to the child, which will not cause any damage to the child's interests.[587] There should be an agreement about how to divide father's responsibilities between the two fathers. Generally, compared with the legal father, the biological father should play a subsidiary role. However, legal acknowledgement of the paternity of the biological father by adopting the cumulative parentage should not lead to an extra burden on the child who only needs to pay support to legal parents, while the biological father just acquires the right to contest the paternity.[588]

5.3.4 Right of Contact and to Claim Information

5.3.4.1 *Introduction*

Unlike the legal parents who have been conferred the right to have contact with their child and claim information on personal circumstances of the child (§§ 1684, 1686 *BGB*),[589] it was not taken granted for the biological but not the legal father to claim such a right, as such a right of the biological but not the legal father had not been legally written down. However, the *BVerfG* held it was a violation of Article 6 I *GG* if the biological father who had established a social family relationship with the child was without exception deprived of the right to have contact with the child which serves the best interests of the child.[590] Therefore, the biological father who took or had taken responsibility (a social family relationship) for the child could claim contact with the child according to § 1685 II

586 *Heiderhoff*, Herausforderungen durch neue Familienformen - Zeit für ein Umdenken, NJW 2016, 2629 (2631).

587 Article 6 *GG* steht dem nicht entgegen; *BVerfG*, Urteil v. 19.2.2013 - 1 BvL 1/11 -, juris Rn. 51 = *BVerfGE* 133, 59 (78) = NJW 2013, 847 = FamRZ 2013, 521= FPR 2013, 278.

588 *Coester-Waltjen*, Statusrechtliche Folgen der Stärkung der Rechte der nichtehelichen Väter, FamRZ 2013, 1693 (1699).

589 *ECtHR*, Case of Schneider v. Germany, Judgement on 15 September 2011, Application no.17080/07, Rn. 34.

590 *BVerfG*, Beschluss v. 9.4.2003 - 1 BvR 1493/96 -, juris Rn. 88, 99 = *BVerfGE* 108, 82 = NJW 2003, 2151 = FamRZ 2003, 816, 824 = FPR 2003, 471; *BVerfG*, Nichtannahmeschluss v. 20.9.2006 - 1 BvR 1337/06 -, juris Rn.17 = FamRZ 2006, 1661.

BGB which requires the biological father to have or have had established a social family relationship with the child.[591] However, the lawmakers did not give consideration to the biological but not the legal fathers for whom it was impossible to have established a social family life with the child.

Not only legal loopholes mentioned above but also decisions of the *ECtHR* promoted legal reforms on the right of the biological but not the legal father to have contact with his child. The *ECtHR* held that it violated Article 8 of the *ECHR* if the biological father had been excluded the right to contact with his child only because there was no social family relationship between the biological father and the child, especially when the fact that a family life has not been established was not attributable to the biological father.[592] It was noted that whether a biological father should be granted the right to contact with his child should depend on whether such a contact is consistent with the best interests of the child.[593]

It is since entry into force of the *Act to Strengthen Rights of the Biological but not the Legal Father* which came into force in July 2013 that rights of the biological but not the legal father to have contact with the child and claim information about personal circumstances of the child from the other parent have been legally acknowledged in §1686a *BGB*. However, a biological father who has demonstrated a serious interest in the child can only claim the right in §1686a *BGB* if a father in the legal sense already exists. If the child does not have a legal father, the biological father must first invoke § 1600d I *BGB* for court determination of paternity.

5.3.4.2 Application Precondition

The biological but not the legal father is entitled to right of contact, only when he has a serious interest in establishing contact with the child and such a contact serves the best interests of the child (§ 1686a I 1 *BGB*). Therefore, the court should examine in each individual proceeding the foregoing aspects. For claim of the biological father for information on personal circumstances of the child,

591 *BGH*, Beschluss v. 9.2.2005 - XII ZB 40/02 -, juris Rn. 8, 9 = FamRZ 2005, 705; *BT-Drucks.* 15/2253, 5, 12.

592 *ECtHR*, Case of Anayo v. Germany, Judgement on 21 December 2010, Application no. 20578/07, Rn. 72; *ECtHR*, Case of Schneider v. Germany, Judgement on 15 September 2011, Application no. 17080/07, Rn. 104–105.

593 *ECtHR*, Case of Anayo v. Germany, Judgement on 21 March 2011, Application no. 20578/07, Rn. 70–72; *ECtHR*, Case of Schneider v. Germany, Judgement on 15 September 2011, Application no. 17080/07, Rn. 104.

there should be an extra examination of whether he has a justified interest (§ 1686a I 2 *BGB*).

a) Serious Interest

There are several criteria which can be followed to examine the serious interests of a biological father in his child. It is necessary to find out whether the biological father has accompanied the mother on regular medical examinations before birth, or during delivery of the child, whether the biological father has expressed his wishes to have contact with the child before or immediately after birth of the child, and how he has tried to realise his wishes.[594] However, these standards can only be applied if the biological father knows about the pregnancy of the mother, and the mother permits his participation in the development of the child.[595] Therefore, the court should also give regard to the biological father who has never got the chance to know about birth of the child but shown serious interest in the child immediately after finding out about the birth.

A serious interest cannot be deemed to exist if the biological father already knew of his biological fatherhood before birth of the child, but does not try to establish contact with the child until it has been seven years after he knew about the birth of that child, because the biological father is supposed to establish contact with the child in a short time after knowing that he might be the biological father.[596]

b) In the Best Interests of the Child

aa) Examination Criteria

Application of the biological father to establish contact with the child according to § 1686a I 1 *BGB* cannot be rejected just because the legal parents persistently refuse to allow the child to have contact with its biological father.[597] To examine whether contact of the biological father with his child is consistent with the best

---

594 *BT-Drucks.* 17/12163, 13.

595 *Peschel-Gutzeit*, Der doppelte Vater - Kritische Überlegung zum Gesetz zur Stärkung der Rechte des leiblichen, nicht rechtlichen Vaters, NJW 2013, 2465.

596 *OLG Bremen*, Beschluss v. 10.10.2014 - 5 UF 89/14 -, juris Rn.18 = FamRZ 2015, 267 = NJW 2015, 259; *ECtHR*, Case of Schneider v. Germany, Judgement on 15 September 2011, Application no. 17080/07, Rn. 81 = FamRZ 2011, 1641 = NJW 2012, 2781, 2784.

597 *BGH*, Beschluss v. 5.10.2016 - XII ZB 280/15 -, juris Rn. 35 = FamRZ 2016, 2082 = NJW 2017, 160–165.

interests of the child, the court should consider in each individual case the stability of a family, relationship between parents, resilience and age of the child, bond of the child with its legal parents and how long the biological father has known of the child's existence.[598] It would be inconsistent with the best interests of the child if the child gets trapped in conflict of loyalty or the social family relationship between the legal parents and the child has been injured because of contact with its biological father.

In consideration of the elements mentioned above, not only disadvantages, but also advantages brought about by contact between the biological father and the child should be taken into account. It will be in the best interests of the child if advantages clearly outweigh disadvantages.[599] In addition, the court also should give consideration to the risk that the wish of a biological father to establish or maintain contact with the child might break the peaceful life of the child and its legal parents.[600]

bb) Different Criteria Between § 1686a I 1 BGB *and § 1686a I 2* BGB

A biological but not the legal father who has shown serious interest in the child also has the right to demand information on personal circumstances of the child from the legal parents if he has justified interest and if it is not inconsistent with the best interests of the child (§ 1686a I 2 *BGB*). It has been held that a lower criterion standard should be set to examine claims of a biological father for information on personal circumstances of the child, compared with claims for contact with the child.[601] However, it is held that the different expressions in § 1686a I

---

598 *OLG Frankfurt*, Beschluss v. 20.7.2016 - 6 UF 98/16 -, juris Rn. 15 = FamRZ 2017, 308; *OLG Bremen*, Beschluss v. 10.10.2014 - 5 UF 89/14 -, juris Rn. 22 = FamRZ 2015, 267 = NJW 2015, 259–261; *BT-Drucks*. 17/12163, 13.

599 *OLG Frankfurt*, Beschluss v. 20.7.2016 - 6 UF 98/16 -, juris Rn. 17 = FamRZ 2017, 307; *OLG Bremen*, Beschluss v. 10.10.2014 - 5 UF 89/14 -, juris Rn. 22 = FamRZ 2015, 266 = NJW 2015, 259–261; *OLG Karlsruhe*, Beschluss v. 1.6.2015 - 20 UF 63/13 -, juris Rn. 31. = FamRZ 2015, 1624; *Palandt/Götz* (2018), § 1686a Rn. 5; *Johannsen/Henrich/Jaeger* (2015), § 1686a Rn. 5; *Staudinger/Rauscher* (2014), § 1686a Rn. 16; *BT-Drucks*. 17/12163, 13.

600 *OLG Frankfurt*, Beschluss v. 20.7.2016 - 6 UF 98/16 -, juris Rn. 16 = FamRZ 2017, 307; *OLG Bamberg*, Beschluss v. 20.12.2012 - 2 UF 210/11 -, juris Rn. 47 = FamRZ 2013, 710; *OLG Karlsruhe*, Beschluss v. 1.6.2015 - 20 UF 63/13 -, juris Rn. 37 = FamRZ 2015, 1624.

601 *Gottschalk*, in: *Heilmann*, Praxiskommentar Kindschaftsrecht, § 1686a *BGB* Rn. 30, § 1686 *BGB* Rn. 10.

1 *BGB* 1 'if the contact serves the best interests of the child' and in § 1686a I 2 *BGB* 'if the contact is not contradictory with the best interests of the child' do not imply a different examination criterion, and the court should take all the facts related to the child's best interests into account.

5.3.4.3 *Procedure According to § 167a I* FamFG

Applications for the grant of contact or information rights pursuant to § 1686a *BGB* shall only be permissible when the applicant submits a declaration in lieu of an oath that he engaged in sexual intercourse with the mother during the period of conception (§ 167a I *FamFG*). Besides, to the extent that clarification of the biological father is necessary in proceedings concerning rights of contact or information pursuant to § 1686a *BGB*, each person must acquiesce to examinations, particularly the drawing of blood samples, unless the person cannot reasonably be expected to undergo the examination (§ 167a II *FamFG*).

5.3.4.4 *Summary*

It is necessary to promote rights of the biological but not the legal father to establish contact with the child. However, it is noted that such a right might be misused, as § 1686a only emphasises the right of the biological father but not the legal father without imposing an equivalent obligation on him.[602] When determining whether the application of the biological father for contact with his child born out of wedlock should be granted, the court should examine not only the serious interests of the father but also if the contact is in the best interests of the child.

5.4 Right of the Child to Know Genetical Paternity

The right to know one's parentage has been acknowledged as part of general personal rights which should be under protection of the *GG* (Article 1 I and Article 2 I *GG*).[603] A child therefore has the right to know from whom it is descended. However, such a right might come into conflict with the basic right of others

602 *Hähnchen*, Vergangenheit und Zukunft der Rechte des nichtehelichen Vaters, JZ 2015, 708 (712).

603 *BVerfG*, Urteil 31.1.1989 - 1 BvL 17/87 -, juris Rn. 19, 44 = *BVerfGE* 79, 256 = NJW 1989, 891; *BVerfG*, Beschluss v. 26.4.1994 - 1 BvR 1299/89 -, juris Rn. 24 = *BVerfGE* 90, 263 = NJW 1994, 2475; *BVerfG*, Beschluss v. 18.8.2010 - 1 BvR 811/09 -, juris Rn. 14 = NJW 2010, 3772, 3773.

whom the claim for knowledge of parentage is brought against and therefore cannot be absolutely protected but restricted.[604]

Although a child can apply to the court for determination of its biological paternity according to § 1600d *BGB*, it is simply unrealistic to enforce this provision if the child has a legal father, because the child cannot be expected to terminate a secure relationship with its legal father in order to determine whether another man is its biological father.[605] However, the *BVerfG* holds that it does not infringe the general right of personality of a child if legal parenthood of a man whom the child claims to be its biological father but who is not the legal father of the child cannot be determined in separate proceedings, but can only be determined according to § 1600d *BGB*.[606] Therefore, the lawmakers should find a better solution to the existing problem for the child who has a legal father to know about its genetical paternity.

If a child doubts the genetic paternity of its legal father, it can, according to § 1598a *BGB* adopted into the *Law to Clarify the Paternity Independent of Proceedings of Paternity Contestation* on 26 March 2008,[607] require both parents to consent to a genetic paternity test and to acquiesce in taking a genetic sample appropriate for the test.

5.5 Conclusion

Although children born out of wedlock enjoy the same rights as children born in wedlock, provisions on parental custody towards them differ. Parents of a child born in wedlock exercise joint parental custody, whereas parents of a child born out of wedlock can acquire joint parental custody if conditions in § 1626a I *BGB* are satisfied, or the mother will be entitled to sole parental custody. Only when

---

604 *BVerfG*, Urteil v. 19.4.2016 - BvR 3309/13 -, juris Rn. 40 = *BVerfGE* 141, 186–220; *Löhnig* (Comment to *BGH*, Beschluss v. 29.10.2014 - XII ZB 20/14 -, juris Rn. 29), FamRZ 2015, 132; *Löhnig/Plattenberg/Runge-Rannow* (Comment to *BVerfG*, Urteil v. 19.4.2016 - BvR 3309/13), NZFam 2016, 400 (408); *Zimmermann* (Comment to *BVerfG*, Nichtannahmebeschluss v. 13.10.2008 - 1 BvR 1548/03), NJW 2009, 423 (425).

605 *Heiderhoff*, Anspruch des Kindes auf Klärung der genetischen Vaterschaft? NJW 2016, 1918 (1920).

606 *BVerfG*, Urteil v. 19.4.2016 - BvR 3309/13 -, juris Rn. 70 = *BVerfGE* 141, 186–220 = NJW 2016, 1939, Rn. 29.

607 BGBl. I 2008, 441: *Gesetz zur Klärung der Vaterschaft unabhängig vom Anfechtungsverfahren.*

types of parental custody are determined can it be found out how parental custody shall be exercised after separation of parents.

Not only legal parents but also the biological but not the legal father might get involved in parental custody towards a child born out of wedlock. Legal rights of the biological but not the legal father who, however, does not enjoy the same rights as the legal father have been greatly extended in the last few decades, but there is still room for the lawmakers to work on further promotion of rights of the biological but not the legal father. However, the enhancement of legal status of the biological father should not be at expense of the best interests of the child.[608] In addition, rights of the child should also be expanded along with the expansion of rights of the biological but not the legal father. For instance, the child's right to claim contact with its biological father should also be written down in § 1686a *BGB*.

608 *Lack*, Anmerkung zum *BGH*, Beschluss v. 15.6.2016 - XII ZB 419/15 = FamRZ 2016, 1446.

6 Involvement of State Authorities

6.1 Justification of Involvement of State Authorities

6.1.1 Autonomy of Parents and Supervision and Assistance of State Authorities

To care for and bring up the child is not only a natural right of parents, but also a duty primarily incumbent upon them (Article 6 II 1 *GG*, § 1 II *SGB VIII*, § 1 II *KKG*). Parents can decide how they fulfil their parental responsibility as they wish, which nevertheless should be under the guidance of the principle of the best interests of the child.[609] However, overemphasised autonomy of parents might lead to abuse of parental rights.[610] It is therefore necessary for state authorities to supervise the exercise of parental custody (Article 6 II 2 *GG*), which can support and supplement tasks of parents in caring for and educating the child[611] and protect the best interests of the child from being endangered.[612] On the other hand, parents under supervision of state authorities have the right to demand support from the state if the parents cannot guarantee the best interests of the child and the support is appropriate and necessary for the development of the child (§ 27 I *SGB VIII*).

6.1.2 Fundamental Rights of the Child

The *GG* sees no difference in fundamental rights between children and adults. Instead, children who are less capable to protect themselves need special

---

609 *BVerfG*, Beschluss v. 17.2.1982 - 1 BvR 188/80 -, juris Rn. 51 = *BVerfGE* 60, 79 = NJW 1982, 1379 = FamRZ 1982, 567 = JZ 1982, 416; *Mortsiefer*, Die Gefährdungsmitteilung des Jugendamts an das Familiengericht, NJW 2014, 3543.

610 *Röthel*, Authonomie im Familienrecht der Gegenwart, JZ 2017, 123.

611 *BVerfG*, Urteil v. 19.2.2013 - 1 BvL 1/11 -, juris Rn. 42 = *BVerfGE* 133, 59 (74) = NJW 2013, 847 = FamRZ 2013, 521= FPR 2013, 278; *Britz*, Kinderschutz - aktuelle verfassungsrechtliche Leitlinien, NZFam 2016, 1113 (1114); *Rauscher*, Familienrecht, S. 828 Rn. 953; *Schwab*, Familie und Staat, FamRZ 2007, 1 (4); *Coester*, Elternautonomie und Staatsverantwortung bei der Pflege und Erziehung von Kindern, FamRZ 1996, 1181 ff.

612 *Gernhuber/Coester-Waltjen*, Familienrecht, § 1 Rn. 22–23.

protection from the state.[613] Therefore, the child, according to Article 2 I, II *GG* in connection with Article 6 II 2 *GG*, has the right to claim protection from the state if its parents cannot provide to it the protection and help which it needs to grow up healthily and develop an independent personality.[614] Such an obligation of protection grants the state the right to separate the child from its parents if physical, mental or spiritual interests of the child are lastingly endangered.[615] Furthermore, children have the right to ask the state to help their parents as much as possible to stay suitable as parents.

6.1.3 Roles of State Authorities

Regulations on the involvement of state authorities in matters regarding parental custody are scattered not only in substantive laws (*BGB*[616], *SGB VIII*[617]) but also in procedural laws (*FamFG*[618]). The main task in supervision on exercise of

613 *BVerfG*, Urteil v. 19.2.2013 - 1 BvL 1/11 -, *BVerfGE* 133, 59 (74), juris Rn. 42 = NJW 2013, 847 = FamRZ 2013, 521= FPR 2013, 278; *Britz*, Kinderschutz - aktuelle verfassungsrechtliche Leitlinien, NZFam 2016, 1113.

614 *BVerfG*, Beschluss v. 3.2.3017 - 1 BvR 2569/16 -, juris Rn. 38 = FamRZ 2017, 527; *Fröschle*, Sorge und Umgang in der Rechtspraxis, S.10 Rn. 41.

615 *BVerfG*, Beschluss v. 3.2.3017 - 1 BvR 2569/16 -, juris Rn. 44 = FamRZ 2017, 527.

616 Relevant rules can mainly be found in: § 1628 *BGB* (Court decisions in the case of disagreement between parents), § 1631b *BGB* (Accommodation associated with deprivation of liberty), § 1666 *BGB* (Court measures in the case of endangerment of the best interests of the child), § 1666a *BGB* (Principle of proportionality; Priority of public support), § 1667 *BGB* (Court measures in the case of endangerment of the property of the child), § 1693 *BGB* (Courts measures where parents are prevented from exercising parental custody), § 1696 *BGB* (Amendment of judicial decisions and of court-approved settlement) and § 1697a *BGB* (Principle of the best interests of the child).

617 Relevant rules can mainly be found in: § 8a (Protection in case of endangerment of the best interests of the child), § 8b (Professional advice and support to protect the child and youth), § 16 (General promotion of education in the family), § 17 (Consultation on partnership, separation and divorce), § 18 (Consultation and support in exercise of care for the person of the child and contact right), § 42 (Taking into custody of the child und youth), § 50 (Participation in proceedings before the family court), and § 52a (Consultation and support in determination of paternity and assertion of claim for maintenance).

618 Relevant rules can mainly be found in: § 26 (Inquiry *ex officio*), § 34 (In-person hearing), § 49 (Interlocutory order), § 155 (Principles of priority and expediting proceedings), § 155a (Proceedings of transfer of joint parental custody), § 156 (Facilitation of agreement), § 157 (Discussion of endangerment of the best interests of the

parental right falls to the family court and the *Youth Welfare Office*.[619] Compared with the *Youth Welfare Office* which mainly provides consultation and support to parents and children, the involvement of the family court in supervising parental custody after separation or divorce is characterised by interference to parents' rights.

To supervise parents' performance in exercising parental custody is not to make sure that the child will be provided with the best development conditions by the parents, but to prevent the child's fundamental rights in Article 1, 2 *GG* from being infringed, such as human dignity, physical, mental and spiritual integrity, and the right to develop to be a responsible and socially capable adult.[620] Therefore, the state authorities generally should not force parents to accept their own perception on the best way to educate or care for the child.[621] Meanwhile, it is not a duty for state authorities to provide the best possible support to the child while performing their function as watchdogs over parents.[622]

6.2 Family Court

6.2.1 Introduction

The family court which was established as a division of the *Local Court* by the *First Act of Marriage and Family Law* (*1. EheRG*) of 1976[623] had jurisdiction over disputes concerning parental authority towards children born in wedlock.[624] The

child; interlocutory order), § 158 (Guardian ad litem for minors), § 159 (In-person hearing of the child), § 160 (Hearing of parents), § 165 (Conciliation procedure), and § 166 (Amendment and review to court decisions and court-approved settlement).

619 *Willutzki*, Der Schutzauftrag des Jugendamtes im neuen Recht, FPR 2008, 488; *Kaufmann*, Eltern, Kinder und Fachkräfte der Jugendämter im familiengerichtlichen Verfahren zur Regelung der elterlichen Sorge bei Trennung und Scheidung, FamRZ 2001, 7.

620 *Coester*, Kinderschutz - Übersicht zu den typischen Gefährdungslagen und aktuellen Probleme, FPR 2009, 549.

621 *BVerfG*, Beschluss v. 19.11.2014 - 1 BvR 1178/14 -, juris Rn. 29 = NJW 2015, 223 = FamRZ 2015, 112, Rn. 29.

622 *BVerfG*, Beschluss v. 19.11.2014 - 1 BvR 1178/14 -, juris Rn. 29 = NJW 2015, 223 = FamRZ 2015, 112, Rn. 23, 38; Further comment from *Heiß*, Höchste Anforderungen an Feststellungen zur Kindeswohlgefährdung bei Sorgerechtsentziehung, NZFam 2015, 86.

623 BGBl. I 1976, 1443.

624 *BGH*, Beschluss v. 3.5.1978 - IV ARZ 26/78 -, juris Rn. 9 = *BGHZ* 71, 264 = NJW 1978, 1531; *Staudinger/Peschel-Gutzeit* (2015), Vorbemerkungen zu §§ 1626 ff., Rn. 85.

KindRG in 1998[625] and the *FGG-ReformG* in 2009 expanded the jurisdiction of the family court over family matters, which only left a few family matters under the jurisdiction of the *Guardianship Court*[626]. Applicable procedural rules concerning parental custody which used to be scattered in the *ZPO* and *FGG* have been incorporated into the *FamFG* by *FGG-ReformG*. It is stipulated in the substantive law whether the family court has jurisdiction over a subject matter.[627] According to § 111 *FamFG*, the relationship between parents and children as a family issue is subject to jurisdiction of the family court.

Generally, the family court, in the district of which the child resides habitually, has exclusive jurisdiction over matters between parents and the child (§ 152 II *FamFG*), unless such matters depend on a pending marital matter (§ 152 I *FamFG*). In a case where more than one court has local jurisdiction, the court which was first involved with this matter has jurisdiction. There is always only one judge making the decision of the trial on the family matters. Decisions made by a family court can be appealed in the civil senate of its *Higher Regional Court* (*OLG*).

Proceedings, discussions and hearings on family matters and non-contentious matters shall not be public. The court may only allow the above-mentioned procedure to be held in public if it is not against the will of either participant. The complaint hearing may be public only when the interests of any participant in non-public discussion do not outweigh the ones in public discussion (§ 170 of *the German Court Constitution Act*).[628]

6.2.2 Involvement of the Court from the Perspective of Substantive Law

6.2.2.1 Court Decision in §§ 1628 and 1631 BGB

The family court shall provide support in case parents turn to it for help in exercising the right to care for the person of the child (§ 1631 III *BGB*), but only

625 BGBl. I 1997, 2951.

626 The guardianship court has been replaced by the Adult Guardianship Court (Betreuungsgericht) which has jurisdiction on adult guardianship matters, placement matters and matters relating to adult guardianship appointments since the *FGG-ReformG* came into force.

627 *Staudinger/Peschel-Gutzeit* (2015), Vorbemerkungen zu §§ 1626 ff., Rn. 85; *BGH*, Beschluss v. 17.9.1980 - Ivb ARZ 543/80 -, juris Rn. 7 = *BGHZ* 78, 108 = NJW 1981, 126 = FamRZ 1980, 1107.

628 § 170 of the *German Court Constitution Act* which came into force on 1 September 2009.

upon application of the parents can the family court take action. In cases of disagreement between parents on the issues which are of significant importance to the child, each parent may apply to the family court (§ 1628 *BGB*). However, the court can only transfer decision-making power to one parent, rather than adjudicating on the merits of the issue in dispute.[629]

6.2.2.2 *Court Measures upon Endangerment of the Best Interests of the Child in § 1666* BGB

The family court is obliged to take necessary measures to avert the danger if the physical, mental or spiritual best interests of the child or its property are endangered or jeopardised and the parents do not wish or are not able to avert such a danger (§ 1666 I *BGB*). The court, by undertaking measures according to § 1666 *BGB*, aims primarily at safeguarding or restoring the best interests of the child to fulfil its obligation to protect the child in Article 6 II 2 *GG*, rather than only interfering right of parents to exercise parental custody from the *GG*.[630]

It is noted that only endangerment of the best interests of the child can justify involvement of the family court, and there is no need to find out whether parents' misconduct has contributed to such an endangerment.[631] *Heiß* and *Castellanos* listed the common cases where the best interests of the child are endangered by exercise of parental custody, among which there are physical and mental ill-treatment; sexual abuse; neglect of the child; alcohol, drug and gambling addiction of the parent exercising parental custody; thwarting contact of the child with the other parent, etc.[632] Court measures which have been brought into § 1666 *BGB* by the *Act to Facilitate Court Measures in Case of Endangerment to the Best Interests of the Child*[633] include in particular (§ 1666 III *BGB*):

1. instructions to seek public assistance, such as from the child and youth welfare and healthcare associations,
2. instructions to ensure that the obligation to attend school is complied with,

629 *OLG Dresden*, Beschluss v. 31.3.2016 - 20 UF 165/16 -, juris Rn. 6 = FamRZ 2017, 39.

630 *MüKo/Olzen* (2017), § 1666 Rn. 1; *Staudinger/Coester* (2016), § 1666 Rn. 62; *Britz*, Kinderschutz - aktuelle verfassungsrechtliche Leitlinien, NZFam 2016, 1113 (1114).

631 *BT-Drucks*. 16/6815, 10, 14; *Müko/Olzen* (2017), § 1666 Rn. 37.

632 *Heiß/Castellanos*, Gemeinsame Sorge und Kindeswohl nach neuem Recht, Rn. 319–358.

633 BGBl. I 2008, 1188: *Gesetz zur Erleichterung familiengerichtlicher Maßnahmen bei Gefährdung des Kindeswohls*. This law aims at enhancing protection to the child in case of endangerment of the child's welfare.

3. prohibitions to use the family home or another dwelling temporarily or for an indefinite period, to be within a certain radius of the home or to visit certain other places where the child regularly spends time,
4. prohibitions to establish contact with the child or to bring about a meeting with the child,
5. substitution of declarations of the person with parental custody,
6. part or complete removal of parental custody.

The list of requirement and prohibition from the family court in § 1666 III *BGB* should not be definite so that the other ways to avert the endangerment will not be excluded. Before one parent is deprived of the right to parental custody in order to prevent and eliminate endangerment of the child' best interests, all of the other possible more lenient measures in § 1666 III *BGB* shall have been undertaken.

In the proceedings connected to § 1666 and § 1666a *BGB*, the court should discuss with the parents and in certain cases with the child as well how endangerment of the welfare of the child can be handled, particularly through public associations and the possible consequences of not accepting necessary assistance (§ 157 I *FamFG*). The *Youth Welfare Office* shall be included as a participant in proceedings pursuant to § 1666 and § 1666a *BGB* (§ 162 II *FamFG*). If the court does not view a measure pursuant to § 1666 *BGB* as necessary, it shall review its decision at reasonable intervals (generally after three months) in order to make sure that the best interests of the child will not be endangered (§ 166 III *FamFG*).

a) Precondition of Application

aa) Determination of Endangerment

The best interests of a child shall include not only the basic and indispensable necessities of life (health, food, clothes, accommodation and minimal expense for personal care of a child) but also self-development interests guaranteed by education, adequate social contacts, educational and vocational training, etc.[634] Not every error or neglect of parents will lead the family court to withdraw right of parents to care for and educate the child.[635] The best interests of a child will not be endangered either if its parents are not able to provide it with the best caring

---

634 *Schwab*, Familienrecht, P. 391 Rn. 889.

635 *BVerfG*, Beschluss v. 20.1.2016 - 1 BvR 2742/15 -, juris Rn. 12 = FamRZ 2016, 441; *Fahl*, Die Verantwortungsgemeinschaft von Familiengerichten und Jugendämtern in Kindschaftsverfahren, NZFam 2015, 247 (248).

or education and talents of the child cannot be encouraged at the best level.[636] Therefore, the court cannot withdraw parental custody from parents only because there are other persons or institutions which are more suitable to educate and promote the child[637] or the child refuses to reside with its parents.[638] *Coester* listed the typical cases where the state authorities should interfere, among which child abuse, child neglect and impairment of psychosocial relationship of the child to parents are common.[639] Endangerment occurs not only when parents punish the child corporally, but also when the child is neglected or negatively influenced. The best interests of a child might be endangered in case parents are not capable of dealing with conflicts with each other and often get their joint child involved in their conflicts so that spiritual and mental development of the child has been seriously damaged.[640]

A lasting endangerment of the welfare of the child in § 1666 I *BGB* is present if a danger has been found out which will to a sufficient degree of probability cause significant damage to the mental and physical interests of the child.[641] The sufficient degree of probability is proved if the damaging process has begun and

636 *BVerfG*, Beschluss v. 19.11.2014 - 1 BvR 1178/14 -, juris Rn. 29 = NJW 2015, 223 = FamRZ 2015, 112; *BVerfG*, Beschluss v. 19.12.2007 - 1 BvR 2681/07 -, juris Rn. 18 = FamRZ 2008, 492; *BVerfG*, Beschluss v. 18.6.1986 - 1 BvR 857/85 -, juris Rn. 57 = *BVerfGE* 72, 122 = FamRZ 1986, 871 = NJW 1986, 3129, 3131; *BVerfG*, Beschluss v. 17.2.1982 - 1 BvR 188/80 -, juris Rn. 51 = *BVerfGE* 60, 79 = FamRZ 1982, 567 = NJW 1982, 1379, 1381; *OLG Hamm*, Beschluss v. 21.2.2013 - II-2 UF 246/12 -, juris Rn. 23 = FamRZ 2013, 1989; *OLG Hamm*, Beschluss v. 23.11.2009 - II-11 UF 99/09 -, juris Rn. 30 = FamRZ 2010, 1091; *OLG Hamm*, Beschluss v. 2.4.2009 - II-11 UF 232/08 -, juris Rn. 80 = FamRZ 2009, 1753; *Palandt/Götz* (2018), § 1666 Rn. 7.

637 *OLG Hamm*, Beschluss v. 10.9.2003 - 8 UF 32/03 -, juris Rn. 17 = FamRZ 2004, 1664 (1665).

638 *OLG Hamm*, Beschluss v. 22.6.2015 - 4 UF 16/15 -, juris Rn. 31 = FamRZ 2015, 1909.

639 *Coester*, Kindesschutz - Übersicht zu den typischen Gefährdungslagen und aktuellen Problemen, FPR 2009, 550–552.

640 *OLG Köln*, Beschluss v. 22.3.2011 - 4 UF 29/11 -, juris Rn. 4 = FamRZ 2011, 1307.

641 *BVerfG*, Beschluss v. 20.1.2016 - 1 BvR 2742/15 -, juris Rn. 12, 23 = FamRZ 2016, 439; *BVerfG*, Beschluss v. 29.9.2015 - 1 BvR 1292/15 -, juris Rn. 17 = FamRZ 2016, 22; *KG Berlin*, Beschluss v. 28.4.2015 - 16 UF 244/14 -, juris Rn. 27 = FamRZ 2015, 1906; *BVerfG*, Beschluss v. 19.11.2014 - 1 BvR 1178/14 -, juris Rn. 23 = NJW 2015, 223 = FamRZ 2015, 112; FamRZ 2014, 1005; *BVerfG*, Beschluss v. 7.4.2014 - 1 BvR 3121/13 -, juris Rn. 18 = FamRZ 2014, 907; *BVerfG*, Beschluss v. 19.12.2007 - 1 BvR 2681/07 -, juris Rn. 18–19 = FamRZ 2008, 492; *BGH*, Beschluss v. 15.12.2004 - XII ZB 166/03 -, juris Rn. 11, 19 = FamRZ 2005, 344.

cannot be halted at a later stage.[642] A lasting endangerment of the welfare of the child which leads to withdrawal of parental custody occurs if parents are unable to recognise needs of the child, the damage incurred to the best interests of the child and any measure made to improve the situation has been unsuccessful.[643] However, a mother will not be definitely deprived of the right to exercise parental custody if she is suspected to suffer from a post-traumatic stress disorder, which might negatively influence relationship with the child.[644]

bb) Non-conduct of the Parents

After an endangerment of the best interests of the child has been found out, the family court, according to the subsidiarity clause of interference of state authorities, generally cannot take measures without checking whether parents are willing to and capable of averting the existing danger.[645] No court measures should generally be undertaken if parents who have violated their obligation are willing and capable of removing endangerment caused to the best interests of the child. It is suggested that the courts, to determine the will and capability of parents to take action against the endangerment, should rely on opinions of the *Youth Welfare Office* and experts, not just on the statement of parents, especially in the cases where causes of endangerment might probably occur repeatedly.[646]

b) Principle of Proportionality

All court measures to avert endangerment of the welfare of the child pursuant to § 1666 III *BGB* should follow the principle of proportionality.[647] Whether the state authorities can undertake measures and which measures should be taken depends on what kind and how serious the endangerment to the best interests of the child is. Any measure can only be taken when it is suitable and necessary.[648]

---

642 *OLG Brandenburg*, Beschluss v. 4.12.2015 - 13 UF 95/15 -, juris Rn. 35 = FamRZ 2016, 1180.

643 *KG Berlin*, Beschluss v. 28.4.2015 - 16 UF 244/14 -, juris Rn. 33 = FamRZ 2015, 1906.

644 *OLG Naumburg* (*OLG Naumburg*, Beschluss v. 28.7.2015 - 3 UF 139/15) and *AG Burg* (*AG Burg*, Beschluss v. 15.6.2015 - 5 F 811/14 UG) held it necessary to withdraw the right of parental custody from the mother, while the *BVerfG* (Beschluss v. 20.12016 - 1 BvR 2742/15) dismissed their decisions.

645 *Müko/Olzen* (2017), § 1666 Rn. 117; *Staudingert/Coester* (2017), § 1666 Rn. 169.

646 *Kindler*, Kinderschutz im *BGB*, FPR 2012, 426.

647 *Müko/Olzen* (2017), § 1666 Rn. 7, 164.

648 *BVerfG*, Beschluss v. 27.8.2014, - 1 BvR 1822/14 -, juris Rn. 24–25 = FamRZ 2014, 1772; *BVerfG*, Beschluss v. 17.3.2014 - 1 BvR 2695/13 -, juris Rn. 27 = FamRZ 2014, 1177.

To examine whether a measure is proportionate, not only interests of the child but also the ones of parents should be taken into account.[649] A child can only be separated from its parents when its interests are endangered by misconduct of the parents, and there are no less stringent measures to avert such an endangerment.

aa) Suitability

A court measure is not suitable if it cannot remove the endangerment and improve the situation of the child,[650] or if it might bring adverse effects to the welfare of the child which are as serious as or more serious than the endangerment they can remove.[651] It is required by the *BVerfG* to take possible adverse consequences brought about by court measures in § 1666 *BGB* into consideration when weighing whether these measures are proportionate.[652] In addition, to measure the suitability of a court measure, attention should be given to how serious the endangerment would be and to which degree of probability it would occur. A partial or complete withdrawal of parental custody is proportionate if there is an increased risk that the endangerment is with reasonable certainty to take place.[653] However, the *BVerfG*[654] dismissed some court decisions which have unconstitutionally jeopardised the fundamental right of parents in Article 6 II 1 *GG*.

---

649 *Müko/Olzen* (2017), § 1666 Rn. 154.

650 *BVerfG*, Beschluss v. 27.8.2014 - 1 BvR 1822/14 -, juris Rn. 35 = NJW 2015, 48.

651 *OLG Nürnberg*, Beschluss v. 18.11.2016 - 9 UF 551/16 -, juris Rn. 32 = FamRZ 2017, 455; *BVerfG*, Beschluss v. 22.9.2014 - 1 BvR 2108/14 -, juris Rn. 15–17 = FamRZ 2015, 208; *BVerfG*, Beschluss v. 17.3.2014 - 1 BvR 2695/13 -, juris Rn. 30 = FamRZ 2014, 1177; *BGH*, Beschluss v. 26.10.2011 - XII ZB 247/11 -, juris Rn. 29 = FamRZ 2012, 99–103 = NJW 2012, 151 (153); *BGH*, Beschluss v. 11.7.1984 - Ivb ZB 73/83 -, juris Rn. 21 = FamRZ 1985, 169–172.

652 *BVerfG*, Beschluss v. 28.2.2012 - 1 BvR 3116/11 -, juris Rn. 25–27 = FamRZ 2012, 1127 = ZKJ 2012, 186; *BVerfG*, Beschluss v. 24.3.2014 - 1 BvR 160/14 -, juris Rn. 38 = FamRZ 2014, 1005 = ZKJ 2014, 242.

653 *BGH*, Beschluss v. 23.11.2016 - XII ZB 149/16 -, juris Rn. 27 = FamRZ 2017, 285.

654 *BVerfG*, Beschluss v. 17.3.2014 - 1 BvR 2695/13 -, juris Rn. 41 = FamRZ 2014, 1177; *BVerfG*, Beschluss v. 24.3.2014 - 1 BvR 160/14 -, juris Rn. 24, 27 = FamRZ 2014, 1005 = ZKJ 2014, 242; *BVerfG*, Beschluss v. 7.4.2014 - 1 BvR 3121/13 -, juris Rn. 15 = FamRZ 2014, 907 = ZKJ 2014, 281; *BVerfG*, Beschluss v. 22.5.2014 - 1 BvR 2882/13 -, juris Rn. 27 = FamRZ 2014, 1266; *BVerfG*, Beschluss v. 22.5.2014 - 1 BvR 3190/13 -, juris Rn. 18 = FamRZ 2014, 1270; *BVerfG*, Beschluss v. 14.6.2014 - 1 BvR 725/14 -, juris Rn. 21 = NJW 2014, 2936.

bb) Principle of Necessity

A necessary measure should cause the least damage to the protected legal interests of every participant.[655] A court measure will not be deemed necessary if there is another measure less stringent to avert endangerment of the child. Accordingly, before a child is separated from its parents or the right to exercise parental custody is withdrawn from the parents (partially or completely), the court should check if there is a less stringent measure, for instance, if parents have claimed public assistance from the *Youth Welfare Office* according to § 1666 III 1 *BGB*.[656] A complete withdrawal of the right to exercise parental custody shall be the last resort to avert endangerment of the best interests of a child.[657]

The family court, which should not just rely on the assessment of the *Youth Welfare Office*, is obliged to carry out an investigation on its own (§ 26 *FamFG*) to find out whether a less stringent measure in the form of ambulatory assistance is sufficient to remove the endangerment.[658] However, it is not indicated where the boundary of the public assistance is.[659] Another problem arising out of the priority of public assistance from § 1666a I *BGB* is that the family court cannot force the *Youth Welfare Office* to implement a less stringent measure, which makes § 1666a I *BGB* meaningless.[660]

Refusal of a court to separate the child from its parents should be subject to stricter constitutional control if there are grounds indicating that the best interests of the child will be lastingly endangered.[661] If a court insists that a child should stay with its parents regardless of evaluation of an expert or guardian ad litem who has indicated a lasting endangerment of the child's best interests, the court should provide another reliable basis and detailed justification.[662]

---

655 *Britz*, Kinderschutz - aktuelle verfassungsrechtliche Leitlinien, NZFam 2016, 1113 (1116).

656 *BVerfG*, Beschluss v. 24.3.2014 - 1 BvR 160/14 -, juris Rn. 41 = FuR 2014, 724 = BeckRS 2014, 49403 Rn. 41.

657 *OLG Köln*, Beschluss v. 22.3.2011 - 4 UF 29/11 -, juris Rn. 2–3 = FamRZ 2011, 1307.

658 *BVerfG*, Beschluss v. 24.3.2014 - 1 BvR 160/14 -, juris Rn. 47, 49 = FuR 2014, 724 = BeckRS 2014, 49403.

659 *BVerfG*, Beschluss v. 22.5.2014 - 1 BvR 2882/13 -, juris Rn. 35 = FamRZ 2014, 1266 = BeckRS 2014, 15448 Rn. 34.

660 *Fahl*, Die Verantwortungsgemeinschaft von Familiengerichten und Jugendämtern in Kindschaftsverfahren, NZFam 2015, 247 (250).

661 *BVerfG*, Beschluss v. 3.2.3017 - 1 BvR 2569/16, -, juris Rn. 37 = FamRZ 2017, 526 Rn. 37.

662 *BVerfG*, Beschluss v. 3.2.3017 - 1 BvR 2569/16, -, juris Rn. 49 = FamRZ 2017, 526 Rn. 58.

c) *Study on Court Decisions Concerning Partial Withdrawal of Parental Custody*

The court can withdraw a part of the right to exercise parental custody, for instance, the right to decide the residence of the child if the parents do not allow their child to receive a school education and there is no other less severe measure to guarantee compulsory schooling of the child.[663] However, in a case where parents in favour of home education refuse to let their unmarried child receive school education, the *Court of Appeal* dismissed the appeal of the *Youth Welfare Office* and held that complete withdrawal of parental custody in order to guarantee school attendance of the child according to § 1666 III *BGB* is neither proper nor necessary, as withdrawal of parental custody will bring more adverse consequences than home schooling.[664] The argument that the child receiving home education will fall behind the other children of the same age in levels of knowledge and cognitive competence cannot justify the home education of the child, because the child is expected not only to gain knowledge but also grow up in a community of society to become a person who is responsible by attending school.[665]

6.2.2.3 *§ 1696 I* BGB *Amendment of Judicial Decisions and of Court-Approved Settlement*

The court decision or the court-approved settlement on parental custody or right of contact should be amended if it is appropriate for sound reasons which affect the interests of the child lastingly (§ 1696 I 1 *BGB*). It is pointed out that § 1696 I *BGB* cannot be invoked to amend parental custody which is determined statutorily, for instance, the sole parental custody according to § 1626a *BGB*.[666] Moreover, application of § 1696 I *BGB* is limited by other provisions to amend court decisions concerning parental custody. For instance, § 1671 I *BGB* shall be applied with priority if one parent applies for termination of the joint parental custody ordered by the court according to § 1626a II *BGB* (§ 1696 I 2 *BGB*).

663 *OLG Nürnberg*, Beschluss v. 15.9.2015 - 9 UF 542/15 -, juris Rn. 13 = FamRZ 2016, 564
664 *OLG Nürnberg*, Beschluss v. 18.11.2016 - 9 UF 551/16 -, juris Rn. 32–33 = FamRZ 2017, 454–458.
665 *OLG Frankfurt*, Beschluss v. 15.8.2014 - 6 UF 30/14 -, juris Rn. 14 = FamRZ 2014, 1857; *BVerfG*, Nichtannahmebeschluss v. 31.5.2006 - 2 BvR 1693/04 -, juris Rn. 16 = FamRZ 2006, 1094.
666 *OLG Brandenburg*, Beschluss v. 11.4.2014 - 3 UF 50/13 -, juris Rn. 45 = FamRZ 2014, 1861.

However, it is unclear whether § 1671 I *BGB* and § 1696 I 1 *BGB* shall apply to a new application after the one for transfer of sole parental custody according to § 1671 I *BGB* has been dismissed.

a) Sound Reasons

A court decision can only be amended when there are sound reasons for it. Both legal rules and legal facts can lead to the amendment of court decisions. If legal rules and facts which the previous decision was based on have not changed, there is generally no need to amend the previous decision. The court decisions can be amended if legal rules have been modified, which can be seen from the fact that more applications of the father for joint parental custody have been received by courts after entry into force of § 1626a II *BGB*.[667] In addition, a court decision can also be amended if the legal facts have changed.[668] For instance, measures under §§ 1666, 1667 *BGB* which should be taken if it is necessary to avert a danger to the child's best interests or which should be withdrawn if such endangerment has disappeared and the measure is no longer necessary (§ 1696 II *BGB*). To decide whether an amendment is justified, the court should consider not only the new legal facts and situation, but also the best interests of the child in every individual case.[669] Therefore, the court shall determine whether those sound reasons mentioned above will affect the best interests of the child lastingly.

b) Criteria

The criteria on amendment of court decision according to § 1696 *BGB* are stricter than the ones in §§ 1626a II, 1671 II 2 *BGB*.[670] The amendment to a previous court decision concerning parental custody cannot be justified only if parents have reached agreement on the amendment and the new court decision is in the best interests of the child. Instead, advantages of the new decision should substantially overweigh disadvantages created by the amendment.[671]

667 *Schwab*, Handbuch des Scheidungsrechts (2013), P. 641 Rn. 193; *OLG Brandenburg*, Beschluss v. 23.3.2015 - 13 UF 240/14 -, juris Rn. 22.

668 *Staudinger/Coester* (2014), § 1696 Rn. 56.

669 *Staudinger/Coester* (2014), § 1696 Rn. 60–66.

670 *Palandt/Götz* (2018), § 1696 Rn. 9; *Heilmann*, Die Reform des Sorgerechts nicht miteinander verheirateter Eltern - Das Ende eines Irrwegs? NJW 2013, 1473 (1478).

671 *Palandt/Götz* (2018), § 1696 Rn. 9; *OLG Nürnberg*, Beschluss v. 30.11.2016 - 7 UF 1309/16 -, juris Rn. 70 = NZFam 2017, 185.

c) *Proceedings*

Proceedings concerning amendments to court decisions according to § 1696 I 1 *BGB* are generally initiated by the courts,[672] while a court-approved settlement can only be amended upon application of parents according to dominant opinion[673]. It is to point out that § 1696 II *BGB* does not apply to summary proceedings, and decisions made in summary proceedings shall be amended according to § 54 *FamFG*.[674]

Proceedings according to § 1696 *BGB* are not extension of the first proceedings, but completely new and independent proceedings with new facts and their own decision-making criteria.[675] Therefore, the court amending the decision of another court is not bound to the previous decision and should make a different decision according to new legal facts and principle of the best interests of the child.[676]

While § 1696 *BGB* justifies and regulates the substantial legal authority and obligation of the family court to amend decisions concerning the legal relationship between children and parents, § 166 *FamFG* complements the corresponding procedural authority and obligation of the family court to § 1696 *BGB*.[677] According to § 166 II *FamFG*,[678] the court is required to review measures of a longer duration undertaken to protect the child by law at reasonable intervals. However, it is not indicated by the law how long the interval should be. Generally, if the court does not deem a measure pursuant to §§ 1666, 1667 *BGB* necessary, it shall review its decision at an interval of three months (§ 166 II *FamFG*).

---

672 *Staudinger/Coester* (2014), § 1696 Rn. 43; *Palandt/Götz* (2018), § 1696 Rn. 14.

673 *Staudinger/Coester* (2014), § 1696 Rn. 136; *MüKo/Olzen* (2017), § 1696 Rn. 22.

674 *Staudinger/Coester* (2014), § 1696 Rn. 33; *BVerfG*, Beschluss v. 27.8.2014 - 1 BvR 1822/14 -, juris Rn. 29 = NJW 2015, 48.

675 *Staudinger/Coester* (2014), § 1696 Rn. 8; *Palandt/Götz* (2018), § 1696 Rn. 14.

676 *OLG Bamberg*, Beschluss v. 20.3.1990 - 2 UF 49/90 -, juris Rn. 7 = FamRZ 1990, 1135; *BVerfG*, Beschluss v. 27.8.2014 - 1 BvR 1822/14 -, juris Rn. 27 = NJW 2015, 48.

677 *Staudinger/Coester* (2014), § 1696 Rn. 10.

678 § 48 *FamFG* as *lex generalis* is displaced by § 166 *FamFG*. § 48 I *FamFG*: The court of first instance may rescind or modify a permanent final and binding decision if the factual or legal circumstances at the basis of the decision have thereafter significantly changed. In proceedings that may only be commenced by the filing of an application, rescindment or modification shall also occur only upon an application therefor.

6.2.3 From the Perspective of Procedural Law

6.2.3.1 *Interlocutory Orders*

The family court may impose temporary measures by way of interlocutory order insofar as it is justified in accordance with the relevant provisions concerning the legal relationship and there is an urgent need for immediate action (§ 49 I *FamFG*). These temporary measures could compel a participant to perform or refrain from performing an act, which can secure or temporarily regulate existing circumstances (§ 49 II *FamFG*).

The interlocutory order is an independent proceeding, even if the main action is pending (§ 51 III *FamFG*). Generally, decisions in proceedings of interlocutory orders in family matters shall not be repealed, unless the court in the first instance reached a decision based upon an oral discussion concerning parental custody or surrender of a child to the other parent, etc. (§ 57 *FamFG*). Transfer of joint parental custody can only be ordered by means of interlocutory order in case of special urgency and endangerment of the best interests of the child.[679]

6.2.3.2 *Principle of Priority and Summary Procedure*

Parents and child matters concerning the residence of a child, right of contact, or surrender of the child, as well as proceedings based upon endangerment of the welfare of the child, shall have priority and the proceedings shall be handled in an expedited manner (§ 155 I *FamFG*). The court should arrange an appointment where the court discusses the case with participants at the latest one month after start of the procedure (§ 155 II 1 and 2 *FamFG*). However, § 155 *FamFG* is not an obligatory provision, and there are no concrete rules on sanction if the time limit is violated.[680]

6.2.3.3 *Guardian ad Litem in § 158* FamFG

To guarantee the interests of minors in proceedings which involve the person of the minors, § 50 *FGG* a.F (abolished) was introduced in the reform in 1998[681], according to which the child could apply for appointment of a procedural curator

679 *OLG München*, Beschluss v. 4.11.2015 - 12 UF 1302/15 -, juris Rn. 18 = FamRZ 2016, 245.

680 *Brilla*, Comment to case 'Kuppinger v. Germany', *ECtHR* Judgement on 15 January 2015, Application no. 62198/11 = jM 2015, 184.

681 BGBl. I 1998, 2958.

(Verfahrenspfleger) to represent them in proceedings. Legislature in 2009 carried on the spirit of § 50 *FGG* and confirmed in § 158 *FamFG* the necessity to appoint a suitable guardian ad litem (Verfahrensbeistand) for minor children in the parent and child matters concerning the person of the child if it is necessary to protect its interests. However, if the interests of the child can be reasonably represented by an attorney or another suitable authorised representative, there is no need to make such an appointment or the appointment made before shall be rescinded (§ 158 V *FamFG*). The court shall specify the form and scope of the appointment and explain the reasons for such an appointment.

a) Legal Prerequisite

In the following situations, a guardian ad litem shall be appointed (§ 158 II *FamFG*): 1) when the interests of the child are significantly at odds with those of its legal representative; 2) in proceedings connected to § 1666 and 1666a *BGB*, when there is consideration of withdrawal of care of the person of the child in whole or in part; 3) when separation of the child from the person currently caring for him will occur; 4) in proceedings which involves the surrender of the child or an order for the child to remain where he currently is; or 5) if exclusion or significant limitation of contact is under consideration. The guardian ad litem for minors shall be appointed as early as possible (§ 158 III 1 *FamFG*), and he or she shall become a participant in the proceedings upon the appointment (§ 158 III 2 *FamFG*).

b) Responsibility of Guardian ad Litem

The guardian ad litem shall determine and assert the interests of the child in court proceedings (§ 158 IV 1 *FamFG*), and shall inform the child of the object, course and potential result of the proceedings in a suitable manner (§ 158 IV 2 *FamFG*). Not only risks but also chances should be pointed out by the guardian ad litem.[682] If required by the circumstances of the individual matter, the court may assign additional duties to the guardian ad litem for minors to conduct interviews with the parents and other persons whom the child trusts and to participate in facilitating an agreed settlement over issues in dispute (§ 158 IV 3 *FamFG*). To perform its duties to represent the child's will and promote the child's interests better, it is suggested that the guardian ad litem should be present during the hearing of the child.[683] Otherwise, it will be hardly conceivable that

---

682 *Büchner/Mach-Hour*, Verfahrensbeistandschaft bei Kindeswohlgefährdung, NZFam 2016, 597.

683 *BGH*, Beschluss v. 18.7.2012 - XII ZB 661/11 -, juris Rn. 14 = FamRZ 2012, 1556.

the guardian ad litem can perform his or her duties meaningfully and present his or her opinions comprehensively.[684]

To avoid that parental rights are interfered by the guardian ad litem,[685] it is emphasised that the guardian ad litem is not the legal representative of the child (§ 158 IV 6 *FamFG*). However, the guardian ad litem may lodge appeals in the interest of the child (§ 158 IV 5 *FamFG*). In addition, the guardian ad litem can file a constitutional complaint and make claim with rights of the child in its own name.[686]

Regarding the scope of duties of a guardian ad litem, there are different views. It has been confirmed in a court decision that one of the duties of a guardian ad litem is to objectively investigate the best interests of the child through exploration and conversation with parties to proceedings,[687] while the opposite opinion insists that duties of a guardian ad litem should be restricted to representation of interests of the child and investigate true will of the child.[688] It is held the latter opinion is more convincing and duties of the guardian ad litem should not be expanded, as it is duties of the court to evaluate the best interests of the child according to objective facts.

c) *Selection of Guardian ad Litem*

It is expected by the lawmakers that a guardian ad litem shall be a person who is appropriate from both personal and professional aspects to determine interests of the child and bring them before the court.[689] Although a guardian ad litem is not legally required to have a legal educational background, he or she should at least have knowledge in family law, *SGB VIII* and the relevant family procedural law. In addition, a qualified guardian ad litem should have basic knowledge in psychology or pedagogy. Guardians ad litem should receive relevant training in order to perform their duties, which is better for the minor's interests.[690] Apart from professional knowledge, inner will and ability to mediate parties to proceedings (if necessary according to § 158 IV 3 *FamFG*) of guardian ad litem is

---

684 *BGH*, Beschluss v. 28.4.2010 - XII ZB 81/09 -, juris Rn. 48 = *BGHE* 185, 272.

685 *Salgo*, Aktuelle Tendenzen der Verfahrensbeistandschaft, ZKJ 2013, 349 (351); *BT-Drucks.* 17/10490, 27.

686 *BVerfG*, Beschluss v. 3.2.3017 - 1 BvR 2569/16 -, juris Rn. 1 = FamRZ 2017, 526 Rn. 35.

687 *OLG Zweibrücken*, Beschluss v. 7.5.2001 - 6 WF 51/01 -, juris Rn. 7 = FamRZ 2002, 627.

688 *MüKo/Tillmanns* (2017), § 1666 Rn. 215.

689 *BT-Drucks.* 16/6308, 238.

690 *Mayer*, Die Bestellung eines Verfahrensbeistands, jM 2016, 272 (274); *Burschel*, Anforderungen an die Arbeit eines Verfahrensbeistandes NZFam 2014, 565.

also an important criterion for the court to make the selection.[691] Furthermore, it is suggested that wishes of the child should also be taken into account in selecting a guardian ad litem in certain circumstances where, for instance, the child has established a trustworthy relationship with a guardian ad litem appointed in previous proceedings.[692]

6.2.3.4 Facilitation of Agreement in § 156 FamFG

In matters concerning parental custody upon separation or divorce, the residence of the child, rights of contact and surrender of the child, the court shall facilitate agreement of the participants at every phase of the proceedings if it is not inconsistent with the best interests of the child (§ 156 I 1 *FamFG*). To help the parents reach an agreement on how to exercise parental custody and parental responsibility, the court may consult with the *Youth Welfare Office* (§ 156 I 2 *FamFG*).

If participants reach agreement regarding contact or surrender of the child, the agreement shall be recorded as a settlement when it has been approved by the court (court-approved settlement). The court shall approve an agreement regarding contact with the child when it is not contrary to the best interests of the child (§ 156 II *FamFG*).

If an agreement cannot be reached at a court hearing within the period pursuant to § 155 II *FamFG* in parents and child matters concerning residence of the child, right of contact or the surrender of the child, the court shall discuss issuance of an interlocutory order with participants and the *Youth Welfare Office* (§ 156 III 1 *FamFG*).

6.2.3.5 Investigation of the Court

a) Hearing

The right of the child to be heard before a court according to Article 103 I *GG* has already been confirmed by the *BVerfG*.[693] In proceedings concerning parent and child matters (§ 151 *FamFG*), the courts shall conduct an in-person hearing of the child who has reached the age of 14 (§ 159 I *FamFG*). If the child has not reached the age of 14, it shall be heard in-person when the preferences,

---

691 *Bergmann*, Verfahrensbeistand - Ein Beitrag zum Kindeswohl, ZKJ 2016, 288 (289).

692 *Bergmann*, Verfahrensbeistand - Ein Beitrag zum Kindeswohl, ZKJ 2016, 288, 290.

693 *BVerfG*, Beschluss v. 14.4.1987 - 1 BvR 332/86 -, juris Rn. 46 = *BVerfGE* 75, 201, 215 = NJW 1988, 125 = FamRZ 1987, 786.

relationships or the desires of the child are significant to the decision or when an in-person hearing is otherwise indicated (§ 159 II *FamFG*).[694] The child should be informed of the object, course and potential result of the proceedings in a suitable manner corresponding to its age to the extent that there is no negative impact on its development, education or health. It shall be given the opportunity to make a statement. If the court appointed a guardian ad litem for the minor child pursuant to § 158 *FamFG*, the in-person hearing shall take place in presence of the guardian ad litem (§ 159 IV 3 *FamFG*). Otherwise, the format of the in-person hearing may be determined within the discretion of the court (§ 159 IV 4 *FamFG*).

It cannot be denied that the court could better get to know attitude, wishes and emotional connection to parents of the child by means of a hearing. However, a great many children do not feel comfortable during the hearing, even if the hearing is held in a way suitable for them.[695] The family court, under guidance of the principle of the best interests of the child, generally should not cancel an in-person hearing with the child unless the child is too young or there are substantial grounds (for instance, the child suffers psychically from the hearing) (§ 159 III *FamFG*).[696] *Krumm* analysed important problems in the practice of in-person hearing of the child and listed the situations in which opinions of the child cannot be heard.[697] Not only opinions of the child but also opinions of parents shall be heard by court. For instance, in proceedings pursuant to §§ 1666 and 1666a *BGB* an in-person hearing with the parents shall be conducted (§ 160 I *FamFG*).

---

694 *Staudinger/Coester* (2016), § 1671 Rn. 238; *KG Berlin*, Beschluss v. 26.8.1983 - 17 WF 1325/83, FamRZ 1983, 1159, 1161 (aged 3 and above); *OLG Brandenburg*, Beschluss v. 24.2.2012 - 10 UF 360/11 -, juris Rn. 41 = ZKJ 2012, 308, 311 (children aged about 4 and above); *BVerfG*, Beschluss v. 28.4.2010 - XII ZB 81/09 -, juris Rn. 47 = FamRZ 2010, 1060, Rn. 31, 49 (children aged 7 and above); *BGH*, Beschluss v. 6.12.1989 - IVb ZB 66/88 -, juris Rn. 9 = FamRZ 1990, 392 (smaller children are under the age of 10).

695 *Arntzen*, Elterliche Sorge und Umgang mit Kindern: ein Grundriss der forensischen Familienpsychologie, P. 63.

696 *BGH*, Beschluss v. 15. Juni 2016 - XII ZB 419/15 -, juris Rn. 44 = NJW 2016, 2497–2502 = FamRZ 2016, 1439 = BeckRS 2016, 12735 Rn. 46 (Different as in *OLG Karlsruhe*, Beschluss v. 2.4.2015 - 18 UF 253/14 -, Juris Rn. 44, FamRZ 2015 2168, *BGH* holds that hearing of the child under 14 should not be generally excluded).

697 *Krumm*, Die wichtigsten Praxisprobleme der persönlichen Kindesanhörung nach § 159 *FamFG*, FamFR 2013, 265–268.

If the in-person hearing required by law is not conducted, it is substantial violation of procedural rules, which might lead to a repeal or referral of a trial or a retrial.[698]

b) Assessment of Expert Opinion

aa) Appointment of an Expert

Generally, it is at the due discretion of the court to decide whether to collect opinions of an expert and how to select an expert.[699] The court is not obliged to grant every application for obtaining expert opinions,[700] especially when it can obtain reliable basis or criteria to make decisions in another way, for instance, by determining the will of the child.[701] However, it should be noted that the court might misuse its discretion and violate its obligation to conduct the judicial investigation if it cannot justify its decision against obtaining expert opinions.[702]

bb) Qualification of an Expert

With the *Law of Amendment of Expert Witness Act, the FamFG and Other Laws*[703], the lawmakers aimed at improving the quality of expert opinions.[704] The new provision imposes stricter and more specific requirements to the qualification

---

698 *OLG Zweibrücken*, Beschluss v. 20.11.1997 - 5 UF 53/97 -, juris Rn. 7 = FamRZ 1998, 960; *BayObLG*, Beschluss v. 5.9.1986 - Breg 1 Z 41/86, FamRZ 1987, 87, 88; *BGH*, Beschluss v. 12.7.1984 - IVb ZB 95/83 -, juris Rn. 16 = FamRZ 1984, 1084; *Bayerische Oberstes Landesgericht*, Beschluss v. 1.7.1983 - Breg 1 Z 37/83 -, juris Rn. 24 = FamRZ 1984, 205, 207; *OLG Hamburg*, Beschluss v. 10.2.1983 - 15 UF 32/83 S, FamRZ 1983, 527; *BayObLG*, Beschluss v. 21.7.1980 - Breg 1 Z 56/80 -, juris Rn. 12 = FamRZ 1980, 1152; *Sommer*, Die Rechtsstellung des Kindes im familiengerichtlichen Verfahren, FPR 2012, 376.

699 *BayObLG*, Beschluss v. 30.4.1993 - 1 Z BR 104/92 -, juris Rn. 4, 22 = FamRZ 1993, 1350 (1351).

700 *BVerfG*, Nichtannahmebeschluss v. 22.8.2000 - 1 BvR 2006/98 -, juris Rn. 17 = FamRZ 2000, 1489 (1490).

701 *BVerfG*, Nichtannahmebeschluss v. 22.9.2014 - 1 BvR 2102/14 -, juris Rn. 13 = FamRZ 2015, 210, 211.

702 *Heiß/Castellanos*, Gemeinsame Sorge und Kindeswohl nach neuem Recht, P. 181 Rn. 424.

703 *Gesetz zur Änderung des Sachverständigenrechts und zur weiteren Änderung des FamFG und anderer Gesetze.* Details about this law see BGBl. I 2016, 2223; *BT-Drucks.* 18/9092; *BT-Drucks.* 18/6985; *BR-Drucks.* 438/15; *BR-Drucks.* 465/16; *Weber*, Die Entwicklung des Familienrechts seit Mitte 2015, NJW 2016, 3076.

704 *Lüblinghoff*, Das Gesetz zur Änderung des Sachverständigenrechts, NJW 2016, 3329.

of an appropriate expert. According to the modified § 163 I *FamFG*, an expert should have obtained at least one professional qualification in psychology, psychological therapy, psychiatry for children and youth, medicine, pedagogy or social pedagogy. In addition, it is suggested that experts appointed for children-parents-issues should have knowledge about relevant procedural and substantive laws, and they should keep up to date with judicial decisions and changes in legislation which affect their work.[705]

cc) Duties of an Expert

The experts are expected to investigate legal facts and provide a professional evaluation. Furthermore, they can also be required by the court to facilitate an agreement between the participants in proceedings concerning the person of the child (§ 163 II *FamFG*).[706] To conduct the work mentioned above, experts generally need to communicate with not only parents and children but also other persons who might help to explore legal facts, for instance, the legal guardian ad litem and lawyers. Key legal questions for which expert opinions are collected in proceedings concerning exercise of parental custody after separation and divorce of parents, right of contact, whether the physical, spiritual and mental interests of the child are endangered, whether the transfer of parental custody (or part of it) is most consistent with the best interests of the child, whether restriction or exclusion of the right of one parent to maintain contact with the child is necessary.[707] In addition, certain psychological questions might also be raised by experts, for instance, about the family relationship and connection, competence and capability of parents to care for the child and cooperate with each other, needs and will of the child, etc.

Experts used to be required to submit their reports within the time limit set by the courts (§ 163 I a.F *FamFG*)[708], which has been abolished by the *Law of*

---

705 *Arbeitsgruppe Familienrechtliche Gutachten 2015*, Mindestanforderungen an die Qualität von Sachverständigengutachten im Kindschaftsrecht, FamRZ 2015, 2027.

706 *Balloff*, Die Beauftragung des Sachverständigen in Kindschaftssachen, FPR 2011, 12, Rn. 14.

707 *Lüblinghoff*, Gutachten in Kindschaftssachen, NZFam 2015, 579.

708 § 163 *FamFG* a.F before 15 October 2016: (1) if a written expert opinion is ordered, the court shall concurrently set a deadline for the expert within which the expert report shall be submitted. (2) In proceedings that concern the person of the child, the court may order that the expert should also attempt to facilitate an agreement between the participants during the preparation of his report. (3) The child shall not be interrogated as a witness.

Amendment of Expert Opinions Act in 2016. The experts should put the court in the position to review their factual findings, application of scientific knowledge and conclusions and to form its own opinions. The results or evaluation of the experts to legal questions can be presented in the form of a written report or oral hearing. Expert opinions which might be crucial to a court decision should be objective and transparent.[709]

dd) Participation of Parties Involved

Although every party of a proceeding shall participate to clarify the facts (§ 27 I *FamFG*) at court, they are not obliged to participate in any investigation conducted by experts out of court, which means that experts cannot force parents to participate in the investigation.[710] If parents do not allow experts to make an assessment on the child's physical, mental, spiritual health or its true will, the court can replace the necessary declaration of parents or withdraw their right to exercise parental custody during the assessment for the purpose of expert assessment. It is noted that in the assessment of expert opinions, no burden shall be imposed on the child and the conflict between the participants should not be aggravated because of the expert opinions.[711] Therefore, the child shall not be interrogated as a witness or participant (§ 163a *FamFG*).

To improve the quality of expert opinions in legal matters concerning parents and child, a work group made up of lawyers, judges, educators, psychologists and doctors gave advice on the minimum requirements to quality as an expert opinion.[712] A reliable report of expert opinion depends not only on the professional practice and experience of an expert, but also on the collaboration between experts, lawyers and the court and the participation of psychologists, psychiatrists, educators and sociologists, without whom it would be difficult to find out what the best children's interests are in every individual case.[713] In addition, investigation of an expert may involve the representative of *Youth Welfare Office*, family helper, guardian ad litem.

---

709 *Fichtner/Salzgeber*, Die Kommunikation des Sachverständigen mit den Verfahrensbeteiligten und dem Familiengericht, FPR 2013, 478.

710 *BVerfG*, Nichtannahmebeschluss v. 2.4.2009 - 1 BvR 683/09 -, juris Rn. 11 = FamRZ 2009, 944.

711 *Staudinger/Peschel-Gutzeit* (2015), Vorbemerkungen zu §§ 1626 ff., Rn. 100.

712 Arbeitsgruppe Familienrechtliche Gutachten 2015: Mindestanforderung an die Qualität von Sachverständigengutachten im Kindschaftsrecht, NZFam 2015, 937.

713 *Häfele*, Seelische erkrankte Eltern und Kindeswohlgefährdung, FPR 2003, 307 (312).

6.3 Youth Welfare Office

6.3.1 Carriers of Youth Welfare Service

There are two kinds of associations providing youth welfare service, namely the voluntary and public youth welfare associations (freie und öffentliche Träger der Jugendhilfe, § 3 II 1 *SGB VIII*). Responsibilities imposed by the *SGB VIII* are only addressed to the latter (§ 3 II 2 *SGB VIII*). To perform such responsibilities, the *Youth Welfare Office* is established as the local carrier and the *State Youth Welfare Office* is established as the supra-regional carrier of youth welfare services (§ 69 II 3 *SGB VIII*).

6.3.2 Evolvement of the Role of the Youth Welfare Office

The *SGB VIII* (as the first Article of the *Reform Act on Child and Youth Welfare Law*[714]) which replaced the *Youth Welfare Act*[715] and came into force on 1 January 1991 laid down specific rules concerning the promotion of welfare of the child and youth. Although the *Youth Welfare Office* was obliged to protect against the endangerment of the best interests of the child (§ 1 III 3 *SGB VIII*), it was more characterised by its role to support parents in fulfilling their responsibilities. In order to balance the role of the *Youth Welfare Office* between support and protection, the lawmakers have added § 8a and § 42 to *SGB VIII* in the *Act of Further Development of Child and Youth Welfare*[716] (*KICK*) to strengthen and concretise the task of the *Youth Welfare Office* to protect children whose interests are endangered. Since then, rather than just only providing support and assistance, the *Youth Welfare Office* shall evaluate the risks of the endangerment of children's interests and undertake appropriate and necessary measures to avert the risks and protect children, even without consent of parents.

To strengthen the active protection of the children and youth, the *Act of Further Development of Welfare of the Child and Youth* (*KKG*[717]), aiming at promoting a better physical, mental and spiritual development of the children and youth, emphasises the shared responsibility of state authorities in supporting parents in exercising the right and fulfilling the duty to care for and bring up the

---

714 BGBl. I 1990, 1163: *Das Gesetz zur Neuordnung des Kinder- und Jugendhilferechts.*

715 BGBl. I 1977, 633: *Gesetz für Jugendwohlfahrt.* This law put the role of the *Youth Welfare Office* to intervene with family issues in the central place.

716 BGBl. I 2005, 2729: *Gesetz zur Weiterentwicklung der Kinder- und Jugendhilfe* (*KICK*).

717 BGBl. I 2011, 2975: *Gesetz zur Stärkung eines aktiven Schutzes von Kindern und Jugendlichen* (*KKG*).

child so that risks in development of the child can be detected earlier and further endangerment and damage of the best interests of the child can be prevented (§ 1 III *KKG*).

6.3.3 Involvement of the Youth Welfare Office in Issues Concerning Parental Custody After Separation or Divorce

The *SGB VIII* recognises the priority of parents' right to care for and bring up their children as a general principle (§ 1 II *SGB VIII*), yet it grants the *Youth Welfare Office* the right to get involved in the exercise of parental custody by providing consultation, support or taking necessary measures.[718]

6.3.3.1 Consultation and Support

According to § 1 III *SGB VIII*, the youth welfare agencies are obliged to provide consultation and support to parents and to protect children from any endangerment. Therefore, not only parents but also children have right to claim services from youth welfare agencies.

Parents in case of separation or divorce can consult with the youth welfare agencies which should help parents to develop a consensual concept about how to exercise parental custody and fulfil responsibilities (§ 17 II *SGB VIII*). Besides, a parent who exercises sole parental custody towards the child or factually cares for the child alone has the right to consult with the youth welfare agencies or demand them to provide support if he or she has problem in the exercise of care for the person of the child or maintenance claims (§ 18 I *SGB VIII*). In addition, parents of the child born out of wedlock can demand a consultation about submitting a declaration of joint parental custody and the possibility of the transfer of joint parental custody by court decision (§ 18 II *SGB VIII*).[719] According to § 52a *SGB VIII*, the *Youth Welfare Office* should provide consultation and support to the mother of a child born out of wedlock without delay after birth of the child, especially when paternity needs to be determined and a claim for maintenance is to be made.

The child should participate in all decisions made by the *Youth Welfare Office* according to the level of its development (§ 8 I *SGB VIII*). It can turn to the *Youth Welfare Office* for help on all the issues involving education and development (§ 8 II *SGB VIII*). Only in certain circumstances listed in § 8 III *SGB VIII*) can the

---

718 *Staudinger/Peschel-Gutzeit* (2015), Vorbemerkungen zu §§ 1626 ff., Rn. 61.
719 *MüKo/Tillmanns* (2017), § 18 *SGB VIII* Rn. 6.

child consult with the *Youth Welfare Office* without the caring parents knowing about it. In case of separation or divorce of parents, the child can participate in consultation of its parents with the *Youth Welfare Office* on exercise of parental custody (§ 17 II *SGB VIII*). In addition, the child has the right to claim consultation and support on the exercise of the right of contact (§ 18 III *SGB VIII*).

The consultation and support from youth welfare agencies plays an important role in alleviating or resolving conflicts between parents. As indicated in §§ 156, 165 III 3 *FamFG*, parents who have disputes in the exercise of parental custody are first encouraged to reach an agreement out of court. However, a prior consultation with the youth welfare agencies is not a precondition to initiating a proceeding.[720]

6.3.3.2 Protection in Case of Endangerment Pursuant to § 8a SGB *VIII*

In case there is conclusive evidence indicating endangerment of the best interests of the child, the *Youth Welfare Office* shall assess the risk of the endangerment and inform the family court to take action if necessary (§ 8a II *SGB VIII*). If prevention of such an endangerment needs actions from different authorities, the *Youth Welfare Office* should urge parents to make claims or can directly inform the responsible authorities that it is necessary to take measures (§ 8a II *SGB VIII*).

6.3.3.3 Participation in Proceedings Before the Court

The *Youth Welfare Office* is obliged to participate in family proceedings.[721] According to § 50 I *SGB VIII*, the *Youth Welfare Office* shall support the family court in dealing with matters concerning the person of the child and youth, inform the court whether a family conflict have been eased, then the court will decide whether further measures shall be taken. In addition, its opinions should be heard in proceedings concerning the transfer of parental custody (§ 155a IV *FamFG*) and endangerment of the child's best interests (§ 162 *FamFG*). Though being obliged to participate in proceedings, the *Youth Welfare Office* is an independent authority which is not subordinate to the family court. Such a participation obligation is only a kind of administrative assistance from an expert

---

720 *MüKo/Tillmanns* (2017), § 18 *SGB VIII* Rn. 7.

721 *Willutzki*, Familiengericht and Jugendamt - neue Formen der Zusammenarbeit, ZfJ 1994, 202.

authority.[722] Moreover, the *Youth Welfare Office* is entitled to the right to appeal in proceedings concerning the person of the child (§§ 59 III, 162 II 2 *FamFG*).

6.4 Conclusion

The family court and the *Youth Welfare Office* as two independent authorities play different roles in supervising and supporting parents in exercising parental custody. Such an involvement of these two authorities is especially of importance in case of separation or divorce of the parents. Compared with the family court which can interfere with parents' right to exercise parental custody, the *Youth Welfare Office* has priority to provide assistance and support to parents and children before interference of the state. It is noted that the *Youth Welfare Office* which shall participate in proceedings concerning parental custody is not subordinate to the family court.[723] On the contrary, they should cooperate with each other to guarantee the best interests of the child in case of separation or divorce of its parents.

722 *Ballof*, Das *KJHG* - Noch einmal: Zum Spannungsverhältnis von Beratung und Familiengerichtshilfe nach §§ 17 und 50 *KJHG*, ZfJ 1992, P. 455.

723 *Wabnitz*, Mitwirkung der Jugendhilfe im familiengerichtlichen Verfahren - Rechtsgrundlagen, Aufgaben und Selbstverständnis, ZfJ 2000, 336.

7 Parental Custody in Chinese Law

7.1 Legal Historical Development on 'Parental Custody'

7.1.1 Before and in the Feudal Dynasties

7.1.1.1 'Li' (Rites) and Confucianism

a) 'Li' (Rites)

'Li' which originated in the primitive society and was first a religious ceremony held for sacrifice and worship was later changed into standards for marriages, blood relationships, social status and even for behaviours for rulers and ministers in the *Xia* (2070 B.C.-1600 B.C.) and *Shang Dynasty* (1600 B.C.-1046 B.C.).[724] It was in the *Western Zhou Dynasty* (1046 B.C.-771 B.C.) that 'Li' had been systemised and standardised. The major function of 'Li' was to mark the distinction between the noble and the humble, the superior and the inferior and to establish a hierarchical system of rites in which honour should be paid to the honourable, affection should be shown to kin, the elderly should be respected, and social status should be differentiated between males and females.[725]

b) Legalisation of Confucianism

In the *Eastern Zhou Dynasty*[726] (771 B.C.-221 B.C.), there were hundreds of Schools of thoughts, among which the Confucian School started by Confucius was the one which has exerted significant influence on Chinese legal culture. During the reign of Emperor *Wu* of the *Western Han Dynasty* (202 B.C.-A.D. 26), Confucian thoughts which advocated the recovery of 'Li' were accepted as the dominating ideology for the imperial government.[727] Since then, Confucian classics were used to settle lawsuits for more than 700 years.[728] During this time, the principle of 'Li' was applied if no relevant legal rules existed, and 'Li' should prevail if laws were in conflict with 'Li'. The Confucianisation of the traditional Chinese laws which began in the *Han Dynasty* was fully developed in the *Sui*

724 *Zhang*, The tradition and modern transition of Chinese law, P. 3–4.

725 *Zhang*, The tradition and modern transition of Chinese law, P. 7.

726 The *Eastern Zhou Dynasty* is made up of two parts, the *Spring and Autumn Period* (771 B.C.- 476 B.C.) and the Warring States (475 B.C.-221 B.C.).

727 *Ebrey*, Confucianism and family ritual in Imperial China, P. 34.

728 *Zhang*, The tradition and modern transition of Chinese law P. 28.

(A.D. 581 AD-A.D. 618) and *Tang* (A.D. 618-A.D. 907) *Dynasties*.[729] The penal code[730] of the *Tang Dynasty* is the final product of 'Confucianisation of the law'. In the *Song* (A.D. 960-A.D. 1279), *Ming* (A.D. 1368-A.D. 1644) and *Qing* (A.D. 1636-A.D. 1912) *Dynasties*, Confucianism in a somewhat revised form (Neo-Confucianism) continued to be the state orthodoxy. Although challenged by other schools of thoughts, the predominance of Confucianism had survived in Imperial China[731] since the *Han Dynasty*. That is the reason why fundamental changes was not seen in the provisions concerning kinship which were based on the notion of hierarchy and filial piety in Confucianism.[732]

7.1.1.2 Penetration of Confucianism in Kinship

a) Hierarchical Family Structure and Parental Authority

The notion of hierarchy is implicit in the Confucian conception of family, under which each family member in a family could always be classified as the senior and the junior. Patriarchal families as essential units of feudal society were important to society stabilisation and consolidation of political power. Therefore, the patriarchs were granted extraordinary power to decide for and control the family's members.[733]

The authority of the senior of a family was supposed to contribute to stability of the state by ruling his family members. According to Confucius, a society made up of thousands of families only functions properly when its members including the parents and children behave in accordance with the roles that they occupy within it, and a family should first be put in order so that a state can be well administered.[734] The senior owed kindness, affection, and protection to the inferior, whereas the inferior owed gratitude, submission, and respect to the superior. However, it was the latter aspect of the relationship that received the

---

729 *Ch'u, T'ung-tsu*, Law and society in traditional China, P. 280.

730 One of the characteristics of the Chinese traditional law is that the part of criminal law and civil law were mingled together in a code.

731 The imperial period of China refers to the period from the *Qin Dynasty* (221 B.C.-206 B.C.) to the *Qing Dynasty* (A.D. 1644-A.D. 1912).

732 *MacCormack*, The spirit of traditional Chinese law, Preface P. XV.

733 *Zhang*, The tradition and modern transition of Chinese law, P. 188.

734 See chapter 12.11 of the Analects of Confucius: Duke Jing of Qi asked Confucius about governance. Confucius replied, 'Let the ruler be ruler, ministers be ministers, fathers be fathers, sons be sons'; *Ebrey*, Confucianism and family ritual in Imperial China, P. 26.

greater prominence in legislation of the following feudal dynasties, which was marked, on the one hand, by the fact that offences committed by juniors against seniors were always treated more seriously than offenses committed by seniors against juniors and, on the other hand, by the fact that the duty of filial piety of the juniors was given a very wide legal definition.[735]

In a traditional Chinese family characterised by patriarchy, the grandfather or father as the senior was the ruling head and had absolute authority over all the members of the family. During the reign of Emperor *Gaozu* of the *Han Dynasty*, parents were free to sell their children in order to provide clothing and food for the families.[736] Although the seniors had absolute power to control and punish their children, their right to kill their children was restricted. However, if parents in the *Yuan*, *Ming* and *Qing Dynasties* who punished their child in accordance with the law for violation of moral ethics killed the child accidentally, the parents should be exempted from criminal punishments.[737] A father could decide the marriage of his children without taking the children's will into consideration.[738] Apart from authority towards person of the juniors, the seniors also exercised supreme authority over the property of them.

b) *Filial Piety*

It is emphasised in chapter 1.2 of *the Analects of Confucius*[739] that filial piety and respect to the elders is the root of benevolence. Confucius equated filial piety with no disobedience.[740] Filial piety came to be exalted in the *Han Dynasty* in which mourning austerities became the most widely used measure of filial piety (202 B.C.-A.D. 220).[741] However, offences against filial piety which was legally written down in the legal code at the early stage of feudal dynasties were only limited to not attending upon the parents or not fulfilling the obligation to mourn the death of the parents at the beginning of the feudal dynasties.[742]

---

735 *MacCormack*, The spirit of traditional Chinese law, P. 10.

736 *Zhang*, The tradition and modern transition of Chinese law, P. 198; 'Shi Huo Zhi' (Records of Food and Commerce) in *Han Shu* (The History of *Former Han Dynasty*).

737 *Zhang*, The tradition and modern transition of Chinese law, P. 199.

738 *Ch'u, T'ung-tsu*, Law and society in traditional China, P. 30.

739 *Yang*, Interpretation of the Analects of Confucius, P. 2.

740 See chapter 2.5 of the Analects of Confucius.

741 *Ebrey*, Confucianism and family ritual in Imperial China, P. 31–32.

742 It was in the *Jin Dynasty* (A.D. 265-A.D. 420) that Wufu system was for the first time codified. Such a system refers to mourning rules according to which the punishment of an offence between family members could be decided. In case of death of parents, the

It was from the *Northern Qi Dynasty* (A.D. 550-A.D. 577) till the *Qing Dynasty* (A.D. 1644-A.D. 1912) that 'Bu Xiao' (being unfilial) was regarded as one of the ten most abhorrent crimes.[743] The range of offences was expanded in *Ming and Qing Dynasties* which were influenced by Neo-Confucianism.[744] Offences listed in the code at that time were beating, cursing, or accusing a parent before the court; maintaining a separate household during the lifetime of parents; marrying during mourning for parents or while they are in prison; generally failing to carry out the mourning rites properly, etc.[745]

If the children were not filial or disobedient to a proper order of the parents, the parents could punish the children or ask the authorities to prosecute the children according to the traditional laws. A guilty sentence towards the accusation of 'disobeying the instructions' might be made by the authority without demanding the father to submit any evidence or even without a trial.[746] Under *Tang* and *Song* laws, if parents killed their child who was disobedient, the punishment was one degree less than that imposed for killing with intent. However, the parents had to prove that their order which the child disobeyed was a proper one and could have been obeyed.[747] Offences against the obligation of filial piety might lead to severe punishment including imprisonment, exile or beheading.

7.1.1.3 Conclusion

Although traditional legal culture was influenced by Confucianism, little emphasis was laid on reciprocity of obligation between parents and children in the penal codes of the imperial period, especially those of the *Ming and Qing Dynasties*. Contrarily, it was the obligation of respect and submission resting on the children that was highly stressed. The character of this legislation on the parent-children-relationship was attributed to increasing moral puritanism

---

child should mourn its parents at least for three years, whereas parents just mourned their child for one year.

743 § 6 of Tang lü shu yi (*Commentary on Criminal Law of Tang Dynasty*, issued in the year of A.D. 653); § 2 of Da qing lü li (*Great Qing Legal Code*, issued in the year of A.D. 1644); *Zhang*, The tradition and modern transition of Chinese law, P. 208.

744 *MacCormack*, The spirit of traditional Chinese law, P. 77.

745 *MacCormack*, The spirit of traditional Chinese law, P. 84.

746 *Ch'u, T'ung-tsu*, Law and society in traditional China, P. 28.

747 *Tang lv shu yi*; *Song xing tong*; *Ch'u, T'ung-tsu*, Law and society in traditional China, P. 23.

of Neo-Confucian thought, which placed the greatest weight on the value of filial piety and argued that the child must in all circumstances be obedient and respectful.[748]

7.1.2 During the Transition Period

7.1.2.1 Late Qing Dynasty and the Republic of China (1912–1949)

a) Legal Modernisation

The modernisation of Chinese laws at the end of *Qing Dynasty* and during the *Republic of China* began with the adoption of the modern western legal system, particularly the German one. Legal modernisers chose the selected appropriations with consideration of Chinese culture and legal tradition.[749] Although there were still lots of disjunctions between the modernised laws and actual legal practice, this period is marked as a transitional period of great significance in the development of Chinese legal history.

During the modernisation of traditional Chinese law, the *New Culture Movement*[750] played an important role in the transition of rules on parental custody, as authoritarianism, hierarchy and family organisation were criticised in this movement. For instance, the traditional patriarchal family was blamed for sacrificing youth on the altar of filial obligation. It was further believed that rise of the West was attributed to the western conjugal family which encouraged productivity, independence, and civic virtue and China, therefore, could only be restored by dismissing the traditional family values and rebuilding them according to Western blueprints.[751]

---

748 *Gardner, Daniel K: Chu His and the Ta-hsüeh,* Neo-Confucian reflection on the Confucian canon, P. 110: For example, Zhu Xi emphasised 'parental kindness' as well as 'filial piety' and 'fraternal respect' as the essential requirements for the management of the family and state. Also see *MacCormack*: The spirit of traditional Chinese law, P. 77.

749 *Huang, Philip C.C.*, Code, custom, and legal practice in China, P. 209: 'The West-facing legal modernizers realised that a civil code could not disregard the cultural and social context in which it was to operate. Therefore, they tried to adapt the law to Chinese custom and came to espouse a syncretic vision for China's reformed legal system – to combine what they considered the individualist emphasis of the West with the familial emphasis of Chinese tradition, into something new that was "social" in its emphasis.'

750 The beginning of the New Culture Movement was signalled by Chen Duxiu's famous essay 'Call to Youth', which appeared on the magazine *New Youth* in September 1915. The debate in 1923 on role of science in solving China's problems marked the end of the movement.

751 *Glosser*, Chinese visions of family and State, 1915–1953, P. 3.

b) Civil Law of the Republic of China in 1930

The Civil Law of Republic of China which has been invalid in mainland of China since foundation of the People's Republic of China is, after three modifications, nowadays still applicable in Taiwan. The Civil Law of Republic of China categorised the children who used to be divided into children born by the legal wife, the concubines and illegitimate children into the child born out of wedlock and in wedlock. However, the substantial equality between the child born out of wedlock and in wedlock was not acknowledged in this law. Although having followed a modern legislative technique, the Civil Law of the Republic of China still carried features of feudalism, which can be shown by the domination of paternal authority. According to this law, the fathers had right to determine the family name (§ 1059 a.F) and residence (§ 1060 a.F) of the child. In addition, the fathers should be the custodian parent for the child after divorce of parents (§ 1051 a.F).

7.1.2.2 Marriage Regulation and Law of the Chinese Soviet Republic

At the same time in this period, the Chinese Communist Party issued *Marriage Regulation* and *Marriage Law*, respectively, in 1931 and 1934, which later provided theoretical basis and practical experience for legislation of the *Marriage Law of 1950*.

The fourth chapter (Articles 11–16) of the *Marriage Regulation of 1931* dealt with the care and custody of the children after divorce, according to which the father, who was generally the economically stronger party, should be awarded parental custody of the child after divorce of parents. However, the principle of tender years was worshipped by this regulation, according to which infants should be cared for by the mother following the divorce (Articles 11–12).

Significant change took place in the *Marriage Law of 1934* according to which the mother should generally be the parent who exercised physical parental custody towards the children after divorce (Article 16). Such a change reflected to a certain extent a rising social status of the women who were credited with more independence. Parasitism of the divorced woman was also lessened by the provision that the man should support her only if she lacked the capacity to work and could not support herself, and the man was excused if he lacked that capacity.[752]

752 *Buxbaum* (editor), Chinese family law and social change in historical and comparative perspective, P. 444–445.

7.1.3 Early Stage After Foundation of the People's Republic of China

7.1.3.1 Marriage Law of 1950

The *Marriage Law of 1950* is the first law to regulate family relationship after the foundation of the People's Republic of China. The Communist Party which had overturned rule of the Nationalist Party tried to abolish all the traditions and rules contrary to its propositions. Therefore, freedom of marriage, monogamy, equality between women and men, and protection of legitimate interests of the woman and child were enshrined as fundamental principles of the Chinese *Marriage Law*.[753]

As to the relationship between children and parents, this law deemed it an obligation of parents to raise and educate their children (Article 13 I of *Marriage Law of 1950*). In accordance with the *Marriage Law of 1950*, the blood relationship between biological parents and their children should not be eliminated by divorce, and the parents should continue to raise and educate their children after divorce, no matter with whom the children lived (Article 20 I, II of *Marriage Law of 1950*). Generally, the child being breast-fed should live with the mother after divorce of its parents (Article 20 III of *Marriage Law of 1950*). If parents could not make an agreement on with whom the child should live, the court should render a decision in accordance with the interests of the child. However, interpretation of 'interests' of the child at that time was influenced by politics and was generally made on the basis of the ideological correctness of the parents.[754]

The parent with whom the child did not live after divorce was obliged to pay all or part of child support necessary for the living expenses and education of the child. Different from the *Marriage Law of 1980*, the *Marriage Law of 1950* allowed the payment of child support in kind or with labour (Article 21 I 2 of *Marriage Law of 1950*). In addition, the *Marriage Law of 1950* acknowledged the same rights of the child born out of wedlock as the child born in wedlock. The biological father should pay all or part of child support needed for living expenses and education of the child born out of wedlock until the child reached the age of 18.[755]

753 Article 1 II of *Marriage Law of 1950* and Article 2 II of *Marriage Law of 1980* a.F.

754 *Buxbaum* (editor): Chinese family law and social change in historical and comparative perspective, P. 467

755 According to *Marriage Law of 1950*, the biological father should pay child support until the child reached the age of 18, while according to *Marriage Law of 1980*, the biological father should pay child support until the child could make a living independently.

7.1.3.2 Historical Influence

Compared with the *Marriage Law of 1930 and 1934*, the first Marriage Law in 1950 of the People's Republic of China made bigger progress not only in legislative skills but also in content. Although implementation of this law was strongly characterised by political ideology, it laid a solid foundation for the subsequent legal reforms in marriage law by separating individuals from the patriarchal clan and promoting new marriage under the principle of equality between men and women.[756]

7.1.4 Summary

In traditional Chinese law, there was no boundary between civil law and criminal law, which always mingled in the same code. It was the obligation of children to parents and authority of fathers over their children that were emphasised in the legislation concerning the relationship between parents and children in traditional Chinese law. Although modernisation of traditional Chinese law from the beginning of the 20th century challenged patriarchy, legislation on parental custody during the Republic of China and Chinese Soviet Republic was characterised by inequality between mothers and fathers and subordination of the child to paternal authority. It was in the first *Marriage Law* of the Chinese Republic of China in 1950 that equality between parents in exercise of parental care and equality between children born out of wedlock and in wedlock was nominally realised. However, it is noted that the child should not always be an object in the legal relationship between parents and children, and rights of the child with respect to parental custody should be further promoted.

7.2 Current Legal Basis

7.2.1 Domestic Laws

7.2.1.1 Constitution

It is a constitutional duty of parents to bring up and educate their minor children (Article 49 III), which implies that neither of the parents who have separated or got divorced can escape from caring for their joint minor child. Meanwhile, the duty of children who come of age to support their parents is to the same degree emphasised. It should be pointed out that neither the right of parents towards

756 *Jin*, Modern and contemporary transition of Chinese law of domestic relation, P. 49.

children nor the right of children towards parents has been acknowledged in writing by the Chinese *Constitution*. Furthermore, it is stressed in the *Constitution* that the state should protect marriage, the family, mother and child (Article 49 I) and foster the comprehensive (moral, intellectual and physical) development of youth, teenagers and children (Article 46), which can provide a legal basis for state interference in case of endangerment of the child's welfare.

7.2.1.2 General Rules of Civil Law *and Opinions of the Supreme People's Court on Its Implementation*

a) From General Principles of Civil Law to General Rules of Civil Law

The *General Principles of Civil Law* (hereinafter referred to as *GPCL 1987*) which became effective on 1 January 1987 was amended in 2009. However, no significant changes of rules concerning the relationship between parents and children were made in the amendment. The *GPCL 1987* does not adopt the legal terminology 'parental custody' but introduces guardianship, under which a guardian shall fulfil his or her duty and protect the person, property and other lawful rights and interests of his or her wards (Article 18 of *GPCL 1987*). Parents of a minor child shall generally be its legal guardians (Article 15 of *GPCL 1987*).[757] However, guardianship is not exclusively designed for minor children, but for all without or with limited capacity for civil law acts. Furthermore, the *GPCL 1987* explicitly highlights the importance of protecting children (Article 104 of *GPCL 1987*) and also the equality between women and men in enjoying civil rights (Article 105 of *GPCL 1987*).

It was on 1 October 2017 that *General Rules of Civil Law* (*GRCL 2017*) which replaced the *GPCL 1987* came into effect, which is considered an important milestone for China in codifying its own civil code. In this law, the constitutional duty of parents to raise, educate and protect their minor child has been added in Article 26 as the first Article in section 2 (Guardianship) of chapter 2 (Natural Person). Furthermore, the *GRCL 2017* emphasises that guardians should perform their duties under the principle of the best interests of the wards (Article 35 I). The guardian of a minor shall, in the performance of the duty of guardianship, respect the ward's true will when making decisions related to the ward's interests according to the ward's age and intelligence (Article 35 II). To protect interests

757 In case that the parents are dead or lack the competence to be guardian, the grandparents or elder brothers and sisters, or any other closely related relatives or friends can act as guardians of the child.

of the wards better, the *GRCL 2017* lists certain circumstances where the courts can upon application of individuals or organisations, disqualify guardians and arrange necessary provisional guardianship measures (Article 36)[758]. Although disqualification of guardianship was provided for in Article 18 III of the *GPCL of 1987*, it was seldom practised. The main reason was that the provision was too abstract and vague to be enforced and did not provide a solution to the problem that who was to take over the guardianship after disqualification of parents' guardianship.

b) *Opinions of the Supreme People's Court on Several Issues Concerning the Implementation of* GPCL 1987

Opinions of the Supreme Court, regarded as the interpretation of the Supreme Court, also have legal force. In Article 10 of the *Opinions of the Supreme Court on Several Issues Concerning the Implementation of GPCL 1987* (shortened as *Opinions GPCL 1987*), duties of the guardian are listed. According to Article 10, the guardians shall protect the personal health of their wards, take care of the life of the wards, manage and protect the property of their wards, take charge of and educate the wards, and act as agent of the wards to conduct civil activities and to file litigation in case the legal rights and interests of wards are infringed or the ward has any dispute with any other person. A guardian may entrust a part of or all the duties under guardianship to the others (Article 22), from which

758 Article 36: where a guardian falls under any of the following circumstances, the People's Court shall, upon application of the relevant individual or organisation, disqualify the guardian, arrange necessary provisional guardianship measures, and designate another guardian in accordance with the law under the principle of most benefiting the ward: (1) Acting seriously to the detriment of the ward's physical and mental health. (2) Being slack in performing the duty under guardianship or being incapable of performing the duty of guardianship but refusing to delegate part or all of the duty of guardianship to another person, which causes distress of the ward. (3) Otherwise seriously infringing upon the ward's lawful rights and interests. For the purposes of this article, the relevant individuals and organisations include but are not limited to: any other person legally qualified for guardianship, an urban residents' committee, a villagers' committee, a school, a medical institution, a women's federation, a disabled persons' federation, an organisation for the protection of minors, an organisation legally formed for seniors and a civil affairs department. Where the individuals and organisations except the civil affairs department as prescribed in the preceding paragraph fail to apply for the disqualification of the guardian to the People's Court in a timely manner, the civil affairs department shall file such an application with the People's Court.

it can be concluded that the guardianship a parent has towards his or her child is different from parental custody which cannot be transferred. The *Opinions GPCL 1987* also acknowledge the equality between parents in exercising rights as legal guardians of the child after divorce, by noting that one parent with whom the child resides after divorce has no right to deprive guardianship of the other parent, unless it is deemed reasonable by the court (Article 21).

7.2.1.3 Marriage Law

a) Marriage Law of 1980

The *Marriage Law of 1980* followed the guidance of the *Marriage Law of 1950.* Both the *Marriage Law of 1950 and* the *Marriage Law of 1980*[759] set equality between women and men, and protection of legitimate interests of the child as fundamental principles of Chinese *Marriage Law.*[760] In addition, they both deemed it an obligation of parents to raise and educate their children.[761] Article 23 of the *Marriage Law of 1980* has stressed that it is not only a right but also an obligation for parents to protect and educate their minor children and that the parents shall bear civil liability for the damages caused by the children to others.

The *Marriage Law of 1980,* sticking to the general principle that divorce does not change joint parental custody[762], only made tiny modifications to the provisions concerning parental custody after divorce in the *Marriage Law of 1950.* For instance, if parents cannot make an agreement on physical parental custody towards the child who has been weaned, the court should render a decision by taking both interests of the child and specific situations of the parents into consideration, instead of just considering interests of the child.[763] In addition, the

---

759 Adopted at the Third Session of the Fifth *National People's Congress* on 10 September 1980 and promulgated by Order no. 9 of the Chairman of the *Standing Committee of the National People's Congress* on 10 September 1980; and amended in accordance with the *Decision on Amending the Marriage Law of the People's Republic of China,* adopted at the 21st Meeting of the *Standing Committee of the Ninth National People's Congress* on 28 April 2001.

760 Article 1 II of *Marriage Law of 1950* and Article 2 II of *Marriage Law of 1980* a.F.

761 Article 13 I of *Marriage Law of 1950* and Article 15 I of *Marriage Law of 1980* a.F (Article 21 of Revision on *Marriage Law of 1980* in 2001).

762 Article 20 I, II of *Marriage Law of 1950* and Article 29 I, II of *Marriage Law of 1980* a.F (Article 36 I, II of *Revision of Marriage Law* of 1980 in 2001).

763 Article 20 III of Marriage Law of 1950 and Article 29 III of Marriage Law of 1980 a.F (Article 36 III of Revision of Marriage Law of 1980 in 2001).

Marriage Law of 1980 has removed the specification of payment of child support in kind or labour provided for in Article 21 I of *Marriage Law of 1950*. Furthermore, the biological father according to the *Marriage Law of 1980* should pay child support to his child born out of wedlock until the child can make a living independently.[764]

b) Revision of the Marriage Law of 1980 in 2001

The most significant change made to the *Marriage Law of 1980* by Revision in 2001 is the acknowledgement of the contact right of one parent with whom the child does not reside habitually after divorce of parents (Article 38 I of *Marriage Law*).[765] However, only the right but not the obligation of the non-resident parent to have contact with the child is emphasised here. Meanwhile, the resident parent is obliged to assist the non-resident parent in exercising the contact right. If parents fail to reach agreement on ways and time to exercise the contact right, the People's Court shall make the decision (Article 38 II of *Marriage Law*).

Besides, for the child born out of wedlock, it is no longer only the father[766], but the parent who does not care for the child directly[767] who should pay for child support, which indicates that the mother could also be obliged to pay child support including living and educational expenses.

c) Interpretations of the Supreme People's Court on Marriage Law

To deal with the emerging new conflicts between family members, the *Supreme People's Court* issued three interpretations[768] on several issues about the application of *Marriage Law of 1980*, respectively, in 2001, 2003 and 2011. The *Interpretations* of the *Supreme People's Court* specified rules on the right of contact (Article 24–26 of *Interpretation I* of 2001). It is also explicitly indicated that the courts can only take coercive measures by means of imposing fines or detention to enforce a court decision on right of contact, and the child should not be

764 According to *Marriage Law of 1950*, the biological father should pay child support until the child reached the age of eighteen, while according to *Marriage Law of 1980*, the biological father should pay child support until the child can make a living independently.

765 Article 38 of *Revision of Marriage Law* of 1980 in 2001.

766 Article 19 II of *Marriage Law of 1980*.

767 Article 25 II of *Revision of Marriage Law* of 1980 in 2001.

768 Interpretations of the Supreme People's Court have the full legal force (Article 5 of Provisions of the Supreme People's Court on the Judicial Interpretation Work).

forced to establish contact with parents. Furthermore, the *Interpretations* have also established proceedings to verify the existence of parenthood, which enable parents of a child born either in wedlock or out of wedlock or even the presumed biological father to contest parenthood (Article 2 of *Interpretation III of the Marriage Law*). In the proceedings concerning verification of parenthood, the court can presume the existence or non-existence of the parenthood if one party provides necessary evidence, and the other party fails to provide any contrary evidence and refuses a paternity test (Article 2 of *Interpretation III*).

7.2.1.4 Rules Protecting the Minors' Rights and Interests

a) Law on the Protection of Minors

The *Law on the Protection of Minors*[769] is a comprehensive law for the protection of children in China.[770] To fulfil its obligations as a contracting State of the *Convention on the Rights of the Child* which require that the best interests of the child should be taken into consideration in all the matters involving the child, the *Law on the Protection of Minors* has adopted the fundamental principle that minors should be protected with priority (Article 3). According to this law, it is a joint responsibility of state authorities, armed forces, political parties, public organisations, enterprises and institutions, self-governing organisations of a mass character at grass-roots level in urban and rural areas, guardians of minors and other adult citizens to protect minors under the principle stipulated in Article 5.[771]

To strengthen protection from the family, parents are required to create a good and harmonious environment for minors to live in (Article 10), to avoid any domestic violence against minors, to pay close attention to the minors' physiological or psychological conditions (Article 11), to gain knowledge on how to bring up and educate the minors (Article 12), to ensure that school-age minors receive and complete the compulsory education (Article 13), and to inform the

769 The *Law on the Protection of Minors* came into force on 1 January 1992 and was revised in 2006 and 2012.

770 Response of the Chinese Government to Questions Concerning the Combined 3rd and 4th Periodic Reports on the Implementation of the Convention on the Rights of the Child.

771 Article 6 of the *Law on the Protection of Minors*; Article 5: in the protection of minors the following principles shall be followed: (1) respecting the personal dignity of minors, (2) following the laws which govern the minors' physical and mental development and the characteristics of such development and (3) combining education with protection.

minors of their decisions and hear the opinions of minors on the basis of the minor's age and intellectual development (Article 14).

In this law, not only the roles of the family, but also the ones played by school, society and judicial organs are listed respectively. However, most of the rules on these roles just function as abstract guidelines from which more concrete rules are expected. Despite this, this law has raised the awareness of the whole society to protect children.[772]

b) *Opinions on Legally Handling Several Issues on Guardian's Infringement upon the Rights and Interests of Minors*

Considering that the applicable law could not provide minors whose interests are seriously infringed by parents with concrete protection[773], the *Supreme People's Court*, the *Supreme People's Procuratorate*, the *Ministry of Public Security*, and the *Ministry of Civil Affairs* jointly promulgated *Opinions on Legally Handling Several Issues on Guardian's Infringement upon the Rights and Interests of Minors* (hereinafter referred to as *Opinions of four authorities*) in November 2014, according to which not only individuals and organisations, but also state authorities (namely the Civil Affairs Bureau) can apply to the court for disqualification of guardianship. The first application submitted by the Civil Affairs Bureau was granted by the *People's Court of Tongshan* in Jiangsu on 4 February 2015[774] after entry into force of the joint *Opinions of four authorities*. The *GRCL* 2017 has responded to the *Opinions of four authorities* positively by specifying the subject scope of applicants and preconditions of guardianship disqualification. Furthermore, minors' relief and protection institutions should be established by the Civil Affairs Bureau (Article 3 II of *Opinions of four authorities*).

---

772 Response of the Chinese Government to Questions Concerning the Combined 3rd and 4th Periodic Reports on the Implementation of the *Convention on the Rights of the Child*, Section One, Part 1, Question 2.

773 Legal protection to minor children came to be discussed again after the sensational tragedy in Nanjing in 2013 where two children starved because the mother did not fulfil her responsibilities as legal guardian to care for the child.

774 The People's Court of Tongshan in Xuzhou, (2015) tong min te zi No. 00001.

7.2.1.5 *Opinions of the Supreme People's Court on the Matter of Parental Custody in Divorce Trials*

The *Opinions of the Supreme People's Court on the Matter of Parental Custody in the Divorce Trial*[775] (hereinafter referred as *Opinions on Divorce Trials*) which have full legal effect (Article 5, 6 of Provisions of the Supreme People's Court on Judicial Interpretation Work) should be followed by the People's Courts in all the instances when they make any decision on parental custody/care in divorce proceedings. In the *Opinions on Divorce Trials*, the *Supreme People's Court* has given instruction to regional courts on how to decide the habitual residence of the child (from Article 1 to 6) and payment of child support (from Article 7 to 12, 18, 19) if parents cannot reach an agreement on these issues. Furthermore, it is regulated that either parent can apply for change of direct/physical parental custody under certain circumstances (from Article 15 to 17).

7.2.1.6 *Civil Procedure Law*

There is no special law like the *FamFG* in Germany which is only applied in proceedings involving family issues. Therefore, the *Civil Procedure Law* and its interpretation shall apply in any proceeding related to parental custody.

In cases where there are only disputes over the amount, time and ways of payment of child support and no dispute over personal relationships, the small claims procedure which was introduced in 2015 by the *Supreme People's Court* (Article 274 II of *Judicial Interpretation of the Supreme People's Court on Application of Civil Procedure Law*)[776] shall apply (foreign-related civil disputes are excluded).[777] In the small claims procedure, the trial has to be completed within three months after the case is filed (Article 161 of *Civil Procedure Law*) and adjudication of the court of first instance shall be final (Article 162 of *Civil Procedure Law* and Article 271 of *Judicial Interpretation of the Supreme People's Court on Application of Civil Procedure Law*).

---

775 Adopted in the 603rd session of the Judicial Committee of the *Supreme People's Court* on 3 November 1993.

776 No. 5 (2015) of the *Supreme People's Court* which was issued on 30 January 2015 and came into force on 4 February 2015.

777 The People's Court of Huangpu in Shanghai, (2016) hu 0101 min chu No. 5985.

7.2.2 International Conventions

7.2.2.1 Convention on the Rights of the Child

The 7th Standing Committee of the National People's Congress of China approved the *CRC* on 29 December 1991 but made a reservation to Article 6[778] of *CRC* by declaring that it would fulfil the obligation under this Article on the condition that Article 25[779] of the Chinese Constitution concerning family planning would not be violated. The authority responsible for the overall coordination of the implementation of the Convention across sectors is the *National Working Committee on Children and Women* under the State Council (NWCCW). Although provisions in the *CRC* cannot be directly invoked by a Chinese court, they are exerting important influence on Chinese legislation and judicature, because China has been trying to promote reforms on domestic laws related to children under guidance of the *CRC*, and provisions in this Convention (except those with reservations) are being incorporated into domestic laws gradually.

7.2.2.2 Conventions of HCCH

Although China has become a member state of Hague Conference since 1987, it is not a contracting member of the *Convention of the Civil Aspects of International Child Abduction* of 1980 and the *Convention on Jurisdiction, Applicable Law, Recognition, Enforcement and Co-operation in Respect of Parental Responsibility and Measures for the Protection of Children* of 1996.[780] Even if necessity and feasibility of joining the preceding conventions have been analysed and elaborated by scholars, these conventions have not been ratified. The reason might lie in the lack of confidence in dealing with the potential family conflicts with foreign elements which are characterised by the culture, history and mentality of one nation.

---

778 Article 6 of *CRC*: I. States Parties recognise that every child has the inherent right to life. II. States Parties shall ensure to the maximum extent possible the survival and development of the child.

779 Article 25 of Chinese *Constitution of 1982*: The State promotes family planning so that population growth may fit the plans for economic and social development.

780 China is only bound to *Convention on the service abroad of judicial and extra judicial documents in civil or commercial matters* of 1965, *Convention on the taking of evidence abroad in civil or commercial matter* of 1970, and *Convention on protection of children and co-operation in respect of intercountry adoption* of 1993.

7.2.3 Summary

The constitutional duty of parents to raise, educate and protect their minor children is not only emphasised in the *GRCL 2017* but also in the *Marriage Law*. However, the *GRCL 2017* covers the relationship between parents and children from the perspective of legal guardians of the first order and wards, while such a relationship is regulated in the *Marriage Law* from the perspective of parental custody. Apart from general rules provided by the *GRCL* 2017 and the *Marriage Law*, the *Interpretations* and *Opinions* of the *Supreme People's Court* which have the same legal force as laws provide concrete rules in dealing with issues concerning parental custody after separation or divorce.

7.3 Parental Custody After Separation or Divorce in China

If both parents desire divorce, they can apply for divorce with the *Marriage Registration Office*. The *Marriage Registration Office* shall issue divorce certificates provided that both of the couple are willing to divorce, and they have made appropriate arrangement on care of children and disposition of property (Article 31 of *Marriage Law*). However, in case only one parent desires divorce, he or she can directly file a divorce lawsuit with the Basic People's Court. A divorce can only be granted by the court if the mediation as a necessary prior procedure in divorce proceedings fails because there is no mutual affection between the couple (Article 31 of *Marriage Law*).

Since divorce does not change the legal relationship between parents and children, both parents shall continue to exercise parental custody jointly. However, given that parents generally do not live together any more after divorce, it must be decided which parent should exercise physical/direct custody, namely with whom the child resides habitually. The non-resident parent should pay child support and has the right to visit the child (§ 38 of *Marriage Law*).

7.3.1 Domination of Joint Parental Custody

Parents should exercise parental custody jointly towards their child either born in wedlock or out of wedlock upon birth of the child, which will not be changed by separation or divorce of the parents. After divorce, the parent with whom the child habitually resides exercises physical parental custody and cares for the child directly, while the non-resident parent cares for the child indirectly by maintaining contact with the child and paying child support. It is noted that there is no provision concerning transfer of sole parental custody after their separation or divorce in Chinese law. However, the non-resident parent can apply to the court for transfer of physical parental custody to become the resident parent according to opinions of the *Supreme People's Court* (Article 15 of *Opinions on Divorce Trials*).

7.3.2 Criteria to Determine Habitual Residence of the Child After Divorce of Parents

7.3.2.1 Applicable Rules

In a divorce proceeding, parents usually cannot reach an agreement on the division of matrimonial property or the habitual residence of the child (physical care). To determine the habitual residence of a child after divorce, namely which parent shall exercise physical care of the child, the court is required to take into consideration the principle of tender years. Generally, the child under the age of 2 shall live with the mother[781], unless the parents have otherwise agreed, or the mother is not suitable to be living with the child because she suffers from contagious or other serious illnesses or does not fulfil her obligations (Article 1 of the *Opinions on Divorce Trials*). As to the habitual residence of the child over the age of 2 after divorce of parents, the parent should be granted the priority to live with the child if he or she lost fertility, or the child has lived with her/him for such a long time that changing the living environment is not good for its growth[782], or the child is the only child that he has while the other party has other children (Article 3 I, II, III of the *Opinions on Divorce Trials*). It can be concluded that sufficient regard has been given to the 'weak' parents, which could lead to neglect and infringement of the best interests of the child. Although the will of the child above ten years should be considered in case of disputes between parents over the habitual residence of the child (Article 5 of the *Opinions on Divorce Trials*),[783]

---

781 The People's Court of Huairou District in Beijing, (2015) huai min chu zi No. 05164 (The child is one and a half years old and the child support is paid twice a year, specifically on 1 January and 1 July); The No. 3 Intermediate People's Court of Beijing, (2015) san zhong min zhong No. 04708 (The child born out wedlock is one year and seven months old).

782 The Intermediate People's Court of Haikou in Hainan, (2000) hai zhong fa min zhong No. 131 (The child was born on 4 November 1993); The No. 1 Intermediate People's Court of Shanghai, (2001) hu yi zhong min Zhong zi No. 2752 (The child born in December 1986 was raised most of the time by his mother and was willing to be raised by his mother).

783 The People's Court of Huairou District in Beijing, (2015) huai min chu zi No. 04921 (In this case, will of the girl at the age of 12 should be considered as long as it is not detrimental to her best interests).

it is not the crucial criterion. Therefore, the court could disregard the will of the child in the case where a mother applied for transfer of right to determine habitual residence of the child, but the father was infertile.[784]

Not only the age and will, but also capability and qualification of parents are taken into consideration in determination of the habitual residence of the child. Generally, the court will dismiss application of one parent to live with the child after divorce if he does not have a fixed residence and regular income.[785] In case both parents who are equally suitable to raise the child apply to live with the child, the application of the parent whose parents (grandparents of the child) having lived with the child for many years request to and are capable to care for the child might be considered with priority (Article 4 of the *Opinions on Divorce Trials*). In addition, a parent will not be granted priority to reside with the child if he or she suffers from a contagious or other serious illness which exerts a bad influence on the development of the child while it is beneficial to the child to reside with the other parent (Article 3 IV of the *Opinions on Divorce Trials*).

As long as the best interests of the child are guaranteed, parents are allowed to care for the child by turns (Article 6 of the *Opinions on Divorce Trials*), which is considered the legal basis for the switching model (hereinafter referred to as the Wechselmodell in this chapter).

7.3.2.2 Case-Law

In the research in which three hundred court decisions were studied, it was found that the status of primary care giver before divorce is the most-cited criterion by the court in determining habitual residence of the child after divorce.[786] By granting the primary care giver the priority to exercise physical parental custody after divorce, the court has given much attention to the principle of stability according to which the living situation of the child should be maximally maintained. In addition, unknown whereabouts of one parent, will of the child, the principle of tender years and capability of parents can also play a crucial role in determining the habitual residence of the child after divorce.

784 The Intermediate People's Court of Guangzhou in Guangdong, (2015) sui zhong fa shao min zhong zi No. 175.

785 The Intermediate People's Court of Qingyang in Gansu, (2014) qing zhong min zhong zi No. 653.

786 *Chen*, Study of legal system on kinship after divorce, China Social Science Publishing House, 2011, P. 89.

7.3.3 Exercise of Contact Right

7.3.3.1 Applicable Rules

It is provided for in Article 38 of the *Marriage Law* that the parent who does not exercise physical parental custody of the child after divorce has the right to visit the child, and the resident parent shall have the duty to assist the non-resident parent in exercise of such a right. Parents can reach an agreement on how to exercise contact rights, specifically on the time and place of the visits. In case the parents fail to reach an agreement, the courts shall decide on it (Article 38 II of *Marriage Law*). However, there are no concrete provisions indicating ways of exercise of contact. Therefore, it is suggested that the common ways (for instance, personal meeting, communication by letters, emails, short message, phone or video) to exercise the contact right should be listed in the *Interpretation* of *Marriage Law*. Although such a list cannot cover all the ways to exercise contact rights, it can at least provide guidance to parents and courts in dealing with issues concerning right of contact.

If exercise of contact right of the non-resident parent is not conducive to the physical or mental health of the child, the court shall suspend the right of the non-resident parent to visit the child (Article 38 III of *Marriage Law*). However, neither legislature nor the *Supreme People's Court* has specified circumstances where the contact right should be suspended.

7.3.3.2 Case-Law

In cases where parents cannot reach an agreement on the exercise of contact right, the court shall decide on frequency, way, time and place of contact after giving consideration to age, will of the child and relationship between the child and the non-resident parent and living conditions of the non-resident parent. A visit every two weeks is normally preferred by the court,[787] as a more frequent visit would disturb the life of the child with the resident parent, while a more infrequent visit cannot meet the needs of both the child and the resident parent.

---

787 The Intermediate People's Court of Dandong in Liaoning, (2017) liao 06 min zhong No. 1919; The Intermediate People's Court of Huanggang in Hubei, (2017) e 11 min zhong No. 1662; The Intermediate People's Court of Shenyang in Liaoning, (2017) liao 01 min zhong No. 3336; The Intermediate People's Court of Fuyang in Anhui, (2017) wan 12 min zhong No. 412; The No. 2 Intermediate People's Court of Shanghai, (2016) hu 02 min zhong No. 5895; The Intermediate People's Court of Cangzhou in Hebei, (2016) ji 09 min zhong No. 4358.

Contact rights can be exercised by visiting the child at school or at home of the resident parent or taking the child out and spending time alone with the child for a fixed time. In the latter case, the non-resident parent could stay overnight if it is not inconsistent with the best interests of the child. Generally, the court rules in favour of overnight stay with the non-resident parent if the child is above the age of 6[788], while dismissing the claim of the non-resident parent for overnight stay of the child who is younger than six years.[789] Not only the age, but also the will of the child play a crucial role in a court decision on contact rights. In the case where children aged twelve and seven were strongly unwilling to be visited, the court only granted the non-resident a visit to his or her children every three months.[790] To the claims of non-resident parents for stay with their children during summer or winter vacation, there are different opinions in judicature. Those courts who deem that a long-term stay (for instance, half of summer and winter holidays) is no more an issue of contacts rights but of parental custody generally dismiss such a claim, while some courts granted the non-resident parents the right to spend several days together with the child during the holidays.[791]

---

788 The People's Court of Shunyi District in Beijing, (2015) shun shao min chu zi No. 12575 (the child is 5 years and 10 months old); The People's Court of Fangshan District in Beijing, (2015) fang shao min chu zi No. 13037 (the child is 6 years and 9 months old); Exception: The People's Court of Shunyi District in Beijing, (2015) shun shao min chu zi No. 12969 (the child at the age of 6 years and 5 months); The No. 1 Intermediate People's Court of Beijing, (2015) yi zhong shao min zhong zi No. 4107 (the child at the age of 6 years and 8 months).

789 The People's Court of Dongcheng District in Beijing, (2015) dong shao min chu zi No. 8204 (the child is 3 years old); The People's Court of Xicheng District in Beijing, (2015) xi shao min chu zi No. 12657 (the child is 3 years old); The No. 1 Intermediate People's Court of Beijing, (2015) yi zhong shao min zhong zi No. 8595 (the child is 5 years old); The People's Court of Shijingshan District in Beijing, (2015) shi shao min chu zi No. 5135 (the child is 3 years and 4 months old); The People's Court of Xicheng District in Beijing, (2015) xi shao min chu zi No. 20705 (the child is 3 years old); Exception in the case where claim of the non-resident parent to stay with the child under the age of 3 overnight has been approved by the court: The People's Court of Shunyi District in Beijing, (2015) shun shao min chu zi No. 10061 (the child is 2 years and 10 months old); The People's Court of Huairou District in Beijing, (2015) huai min chu zi No. 05143 (the child is 2 years and 8 months old).

790 The Intermediate People's Court of Handan in Hebei, (2017) ji 04 min zhong No. 5130.

791 Such a claim has been dismissed by: The Intermediate People's Court of Dandong in Liaoning, (2017) liao 06 min zhong No. 1919 (the child is 2 years old); The Intermediate People's Court of Longyan in Fujian, (2017) min 08 min zhong No. 967; The Intermediate People's Court of Fuyang in Anhui, (2017) wan 12 min zhong No. 412;

In case the resident parent institutes proceedings to suspend or terminate the right of the non-resident to visit the child, he shall provide evidence to prove that the child's interests (physical, mental, moral or emotional) have been endangered by the contact.[792] The fact that the non-resident parent cannot afford to pay the child support or pay it regularly should not lead to suspension of the exercise of contact right.[793] The non-resident parent who has recovered from mental illness (e.g., bipolar disorder) can continue contact with the child.[794]

Although only the right of the non-resident parent to contact with the child after divorce is legally written down, the claim of a parent to maintain contact with his or her child born in wedlock during separation or such a claim of a parent to his or her child born out of wedlock is also generally approved by the court if it is not inconsistent with the best interests of the child.[795]

The Intermediate People's Court of Liaoyang in Liaoning, (2016) liao 10 min zhong No. 781; The No. 1 Intermediate People's Court of Beijing, (2015) yi zhong shao min zhong zi No. 4584; The No. 1 Intermediate People's Court of Beijing, (2015) yi zhong shao min zhong zi No. 8595 (the child is 5 years old).
Such a claim has been granted by The Intermediate People's Court of Huanggang in Hubei, (2017) e 11 min zhong No. 1662; The People's Court of Wuxi in Jiangsu, (2016) su 02 min zhong No. 3495; The No. 3 Intermediate People's Court of Beijing, (2015) san zhong min zhong No. 06017; The No. 1 Intermediate People's Court of Beijing, (2015) yi zhong shao min zhong zi No. 3639; The People's Court of Fangshan District in Beijing, (2015) fang shao min chu zi No. 13037 (the child is 6 years and 9 months old).

792 The People's Court of Pudong in Shanghai, (2013) pu shao min chu zi No. 433.

793 The Intermediate People's Court of Liaoyuan in Jilin, (2017) ji 04 min zhong No. 443.

794 The No. 3 Intermediate People's Court of Beijing, (2015) san zhong min zhong No. 11377.

795 The Intermediate People's Court of Xi'an in Shanxi, (2011) xi min yi zhong zi No. 01149.

8 Legal Comparison and Reform Discussion

8.1 Legal Comparison

8.1.1 From the Perspective of Substantive Law

8.1.1.1 General Rules Concerning Parental Custody

a) Position of Parental Custody in the Legal System

Since the codification of the Chinese Civil Code is still under discussion, substantial legal rules related to parental custody after divorce are scattered between the *General Rules of Civil Law*, *Marriage Law* and *Interpretations* or *Opinions* of the *Supreme People's Court*,[796] whereas legislation on parental custody in Germany is primarily located in Title 5 (Parental custody) of Section 2 (Relationship) in Book 4 (Family Law) of the *BGB*. According to Chinese law, parents not only exercise parental custody but also are legal guardians to their minor children, while parental custody and guardianship for the minors who do not have parents or whose parents are not entitled to parental custody are two totally different legal terms under German law. Duties of parents under parental custody (elterliche Sorge) in German law are similar to the duties under guardianship towards the minors in Chinese law.

b) Principle of the Best Interests of the Child

As mentioned in section 7.3.2, the principle of the best interests of the child is not enshrined as principle guideline for the courts when deciding on parental custody in China. Nevertheless, the principle of the best interests of the child is applied in practice. However, in most Chinese court decisions where the principle of the best interests of the child were mentioned, criteria of determining what was in the best interests of the child were not systematically analysed, whereas the principle of the best interests of the child, anchored in § 1697a of the *BGB*, is followed by the court in deciding on any issue concerning relationship between parents and children regulated in Title 5 of Section 2 of Book 4 of the *BGB* in Germany. In addition, key elements in determination of the best interests

796 *Bergmann/Ferid/Henrich*, Internationales Ehe- und Kindschaftsrecht, Ordner IV Volksrepublik China, P. 29.

of the child are studied not only in literature but also in judicature in Germany, among which there are capability of parents to care for and educate the child, connection between the child and parents, will of the child and continuity of living environments of the child, etc.

Despite the difference in practising the best interests of the child illustrated above, it is noted that the principle of the best interests of the child is playing more and more important role in dealing with relationship between parents and children both in Germany and China.

8.1.1.2 Concrete Rules Concerning Parental Custody After Divorce or Separation

a) For the Child Born in Wedlock

Both in China and in Germany, parents of the child born in wedlock generally exercise joint legal custody after divorce, which means both parents make major decisions regarding the child jointly. The parent with whom the child resides, exercises physical and direct custody of the child. Compared with the Chinese law, the German law provides more concrete rules on exercise of joint legal custody (in § 1628 and § 1687 *BGB*) and preconditions of transfer of sole parental custody (in § 1671 *BGB*). Although parents are still legal guardians of the child and entitled to joint parental custody following divorce in China, they only exercise a nominal joint custody towards their child, because the non-resident parents seldomly participate in decision-making of issues which are important to the child. Unlike the non-resident parent in China, the non-resident parent in Germany can decide upon significant matters of the child jointly with the resident parent.

b) For the Child Born Out of Wedlock

As for the child born out of wedlock, both legal systems acknowledge equality of legal status between children born in and out of wedlock. However, neither of these legal systems provides the child born out of wedlock routes to determine its biological paternity. The presumed biological (not the legal) father in Germany can challenge the legal paternity and apply to the court for determination of the legal paternity under certain conditions, and they even have the right to contact their children born out of wedlock or demand information about personal circumstances of them if it is consistent with the best interests of the child. On the contrary, the biological but not the legal father has never been mentioned in the Chinese laws, regulations or interpretations, and opinions of the *Supreme People's Court* in China, let alone increasing promotion of the legal interests of the biological but not the legal father of the child born out of wedlock. Considering legislative changes to parental custody of children born out of wedlock should also align with the best interests of the child, it is therefore suggested both of the legal systems should take steps to legally acknowledge double paternity.

c) *Right of Contact*

Right of contact in the Chinese legal system is categorised under divorce, while such a right in the German law is a natural right and obligation independent from divorce. Not only the legal parents, but also other related persons, for instance, the biological but not the legal father, grandparents are entitled to such a right according to the *BGB*. Furthermore, right of the child to have contact with its parents is explicitly written down in the *BGB*, whereas such a right of the child, though acknowledged in practice, is not legally provided for in the Chinese law.

Compared with the German courts, most of the Chinese courts which mention the right of the non-resident parent to maintain contact with the child in their verdicts do not specify methods, times and locations to exercise this right after separation or divorce. In addition, they do not fulfil their duties to review agreements between parents on right of contact and make modification if it is necessary.

d) *The Wechselmodell*

Although the Wechselmodell, an alternative caring model of parental custody to enable a shared physical care after divorce or separation, is legally possible, it is seldom practised in China. On the contrary, the Wechselmodell is thoroughly discussed in both literature and judicature in Germany, though not acknowledged by law. The *BGH* has made statements relating to the questions whether the court can order the Wechselmodell *ex officio* and whether the Wechselmodell can only be ordered in proceedings concerning parental custody or contact right.

Despite the emerging trend of shared care in two-parent families, the sole physical custody still remains intact in many states.[797] However, to promote a meaningful exercise of joint parental custody after separation or divorce which has been adopted as the general rule by both China and Germany, it is suggested joint physical parental custody in the form of the Wechselmodell should

797 *Kruk*, Child Custody – Access and parental responsibilities, The University of British Columbia 2008, P. 52.

be presumed legally in a litigated case if it is not contradictory to the best interests of the child.

8.1.2 From the Perspective of Procedural Law

According to the Chinese law, a couple can apply for divorce either with the Civil Affairs Bureau or the People's Court. However, neither of these two authorities before making the decision on whether to grant the divorce will conduct a substantial review on whether parents have reached an agreement on exercise of parental custody after divorce and whether the agreement is in the best interests of the child. In Germany, only the court can decide whether a divorce should be granted, and the German law sees it necessary to combine divorce proceedings with related proceedings including proceedings of parent custody and right of contact. Furthermore, the court in Germany is obliged to conduct investigation *ex officio* if necessary to find out whether the agreement between parents is consistent with the best interests of the child.

There is no specific procedural law for proceedings of family issues in Chinese laws and therefore, the Chinese *Civil Procedure Law* applies to all civil proceedings, whereas procedure rules concerning family matters in Germany have been separated from the *ZPO* and integrated into the *FamFG*. The specialised family procedural law provides more concrete procedural rules to proceedings related to parental custody so that the child's best interests are better guaranteed. It demands that proceedings related to relationship between parents and children, for instance, the determination of habitual residence, contact right, surrender of the child and transfer of parental custody according to § 1626a II *BGB*, should be expedited and carried out primarily. Furthermore, parties participating in the proceedings are expanded. Not only the *Youth Welfare Office*, but also the guardians ad litem and experts from different fields (educators, psychologists, etc.) are required to take part in proceedings concerning personal care of the child.

8.1.3 From the Perspective of Specialised Authority

In Germany, the *Youth Welfare Office* is particularly established to benefit the young people and families (§ 2 I *SGB VIII*), whereas mass associations and governmental authorities work together to carry out policies and laws related to minors in China. With roles to promote and protect minors being divided between different associations and authorities in China, it might lead to overlaps of functions and inefficiency of implementation of their duties. Therefore, it is suggested that a specialised authority or at least a department should be established to promote welfare of minors and families.

Duties of the *Youth Welfare Office* are explicitly listed in the *SGB VIII* (§ 2 II). The *Youth Welfare Office* provides not only protection, but also consultation and assistance to parents and children. In addition, it is obliged to participate in family proceedings. Compared with the *Youth Welfare Office* in Germany, duties of competent Chinese authorities and associations focusing on protection to minors are generally too abstract and therefore need to be illustrated concretely. Although role of state authorities in protecting interests of minors from being seriously endangered by their legal guardians has been strengthened in China, their duties should not be limited to providing protection but be extended to providing consultation and assistance and participation in family proceedings so that the best interests of the child, especially for the one whose parents get divorced or separated, can be guaranteed and promoted.

8.2 Reform Discussion on Parental Custody After Separation in Germany

8.2.1 From Parental Custody to Parental Responsibility

Considering that the term 'parental responsibility' has predominated in certain conventions (for instance, *Brussels IIa* and *HCCH*) and that legal status of the child has been promoted, it has been suggested that parental responsibility should de lege ferenda be given priority over parental custody by law to describe legal relationship between parents and children.[798] Introduction of the legal concept of parental responsibility which can be more widely interpreted than the legal term 'parental custody' and emphasises responsibilities of parents towards the child could protect the interests of the child better.

Parental responsibility could be a generic term into which parental custody, right of contact and payment of child support should be categorized. Therefore, § 1626 *BGB* (parental responsibilities and general rules) could define parental responsibility by listing what it contains as follows: Parents are obliged to care for, educate and contact the minor child (parental responsibilities). In case of separation or divorce of parents, the non-resident parent shall pay child support.

798 *Ernst*, Gemeinsame Elternverantwortung nach Trennung und Scheidung, DRiZ 2018, 302 (303).

8.2.2 Exercise of Parental Responsibility After Separation of Parents

8.2.2.1 Further Promotion of Joint Parental Responsibility

It is generally acknowledged that parental responsibility should not be restricted or changed by separation of parents.[799] Therefore, parents should generally exercise parental custody jointly after their separation or divorce. It is suggested by *Schumann* that preconditions for transfer of sole parental custody according to § 1671 I 2 *BGB* should be restricted and reestablishment of joint parental custody according to § 1696 I 1 *BGB* should be facilitated.[800]

According to § 1671 I 2 (1) *BGB*, the application of one parent for sole parental custody should be granted if the other parent consents to it unless the child who has reached the age of 14 objects such a transfer. It is questioned that the easy access to sole parental custody here diverges to some extent from the guiding principle of joint parental custody.[801] Therefore, there should be stricter requirement for withdrawal of joint parental custody in § 1671 I 2 (1) *BGB*, which requires not only consensus between parents but also grounds lastly affecting the best interests of the child.[802]

8.2.2.2 From Residenzmodell to Wechselmodell (Shared Care)

§ 1687 *BGB* regulating exercise of joint parental custody after separation of parents implies the habitual residence with one parent as a general rule by emphasising the sole right of the parent with whom the child habitually resides to decide on issues of daily life for the child (§ 1687 I 2 *BGB*). However, separation or divorce of parents does not inevitably lead the child to habitually reside with one parent.

Compared to the traditional residence model which generally indicates that the child lives with one parent habitually after separation or divorce of parents, the Wechselmodell distributes parental caring responsibility equally between parents. Resident and non-resident parents who are generally fixed in the

---

799 *Schumann*, B 13; *Dethloff*, Familienrecht in Europa – Quo vadis? NJW 1–2/2018, S. 28; *BVerfGE* 61, 358 (374); *BT-Drucks.* 13/4899, 99 zur Elternverantwortung nach Trennung und Scheidung.

800 *Ernst*, Gemeinsame Elternverantwortung nach Trennung und Scheidung, DRiZ 2018, 302 (304); *Schumann*, B 33 and B 37.

801 *Schumann*, B 33.

802 Ibid.

Residenzmodell switch frequently in Wechselmodell. It was already called for on the parliamentary assembly of the Council of Europe on 2 October 2015[803] that double residences of the child after separation of its parents should be regulated by law as a principle by the member states and the time distribution between parents should be orientated towards the needs and interests of the child.

Although it is not absolutely necessary to adopt the Wechselmodell into § 1687 *BGB*, it is suggested that the legislature should avoid any provision which favours the Residenzmodell and 'gewöhnlich (habitually)' in § 1687 I 2 *BGB* could be deleted. However, there is no need to define the Wechselmodell by following the criterion whether the co-caring parent has taken over more than 30 % of the parental responsibilities suggested by scholars[804].

8.2.3 Balance Between Parental Autonomy and Interference of State Authorities

Family autonomy is expected to play the primary role to care for and educate the child and deal with family conflicts, which is manifest from Article 6 II *GG* and § 1627 *BGB*. Therefore, parents should be encouraged and assisted to reach an agreement on the ways to exercise of parental custody after divorce or separation (§ 17 II *SGB VIII*),[805] and the public authorities can only step in a family conflict when it cannot be resolved within the family,[806] or the best interests of the child are or are to be endangered (§ 1666 *BGB*). For instance, the court can order the Wechselmodell which is in the best interests of the child against consensus of the parents or the court can decide on right of contact beyond agreement of parents (§ 1684 III and IV *BGB*).

However, rights of the family court to undertake measures *ex officio* should be properly restricted, while autonomy of parents to suspend or institute proceedings should be promoted. It has been criticised that the threshold of the order of a contact supervisor should not be the violation of cooperative obligation of parents in § 1684 II *BGB* but the endangerment of the best interests of the child in § 1666 *BGB*.[807] In addition, only upon application of one parent could a contact

803 Parliamentary Assembly, Resolution 2079 (2015).

804 *Schumann*, B63.

805 *Ernst*, Gemeinsame Elternverantwortung nach Trennung und Scheidung, DRiZ 2018, 302 (305).

806 *Frösche*, Sorge und Umgang in der Rechtspraxis, P. 142 Rn. 643; *Boele-Woelki/Ferrand/González Beilfuss*, Principles of European family law regarding parental responsibilities, 92 f., 102, 133.

807 *Schumann*, B 75–76.

supervisor or a accompanied contact be ordered if it is in the best interests of the child.[808] It is held that the precondition of interference of public authorities should be the best interests of the child which make sure that procedures instituted by the court could conform to the *GG* and to which the parental autonomy should be subordinated.

8.2.4 On Parental Custody of Child Born Out of Wedlock

8.2.4.1 Joint Parental Custody as Guiding Principle for Parents of the Child Born Out of Wedlock

Although the father of a child born out of wedlock has been provided another way to joint parental custody since entry into force of the *Reform of Act of Parental Custody of the Unmarried Parents* in 2013, it has been discussed whether there could be an easier way to joint parental custody for parents of a child born out of wedlock in certain circumstances. *Schumann* suggests that the father of a child born out of wedlock should obtain joint parental custody automatically by law if he has joint place of residence with the mother and the child at the time of acknowledgement of paternity.[809] In this way, there would be no extra administrative burden for the parents to submit application for joint custody according to § 1626a I 1 *BGB*.[810]

Considering the increasing equality in partnership and the fact that it is generally in the best interests of the child for the child to have or keep both of its parents as contact persons,[811] joint parental custody should be a guiding principle not only for children born in wedlock but out of wedlock in case of separation of their parents. Therefore, § 1626a *BGB* could list the precondition of withdrawal of joint parental custody, rather than list the ways to joint parental custody for parents of a child born out of wedlock.

8.2.4.2 Promotion of Rights of the Biological but Not the Legal Father and Multiple Parenthood for Child Born Out of Wedlock

Although rights of the biological but not the legal fathers have been promoted, their constitutional right to care for and educate the child cannot be exercised in certain circumstances due to existence of the legal fathers. The biological father

808 *Schumann*, B 77.
809 *Schumann*, B 37.
810 *Schumann*, B 35.
811 *Dethloff*, Familienrecht in Europa - Quo vadis? NJW 1–2/2018, 23 (28).

who has given birth to a child cannot acknowledge the paternity (§ 1594 II *BGB*) or apply to the court for court determination of the paternity (§ 1600d I *BGB*) if the legal father of the child exists. Extension of legal rights of the biological but not the legal father has caught attention of the German legislators but should be further discussed.

It can be concluded from § 1600 II *BGB* that the German legislature has given sufficient regard to the social family relationship between the legal father and the child. However, it has not taken into consideration whether there is or has been a social family relationship between the biological father and the child and why the biological but not the legal father could and cannot establish a social family relationship with his child. Therefore, it is suggested that § 1600 II *BGB* should be abolished[812] so that establishment of the social family relationship between the child and its legal father will not be a crucial criterion to exclude right of a biological but not the legal father to challenge paternity. To guarantee the best interests of the child, the parental rights and responsibilities, especially parental custody, should in certain circumstances be separated from legal parenthood.[813] Therefore, parental custody should no longer be only connected to legal parenthood and multiple parenthood could be legally acknowledged and protected.

8.3 Advice on Further Reform on Parental Custody After Separation of Parents in China

8.3.1 Draft of Book of Family Law of the Chinese Civil Code

Almost two yeSars after the approval of the *GRCL 2017*, draft of specific provisions of the Chinese Civil Code was submitted for the second review on the 11th session of the standing committee of the 13th National People's Congress on 25 June 2019.[814] It is required in the draft that parents in case of consensual divorce should reach a written agreement on parental custody, matrimonial property, etc., and then apply to *Marriage Registration Office* for divorce (§ 853 II).

812 *Helms*, Rechtliche, biologische und soziale Elternschaft - Herausforderungen durch neue Familienformen, Gutachten F zum 71. Deutschen Juristentag 2016, F 50 = NJW-Beil 2016, 49 (51).

813 *Dethloff/Timmermann*: Multiple Elternschaft – Familienrecht und Familienleben im Spannungsverhältnis, P. 188–189 in 'Familien mit multipler Elternschaft: Entstehungszusammenhänge, Herausforderungen und Potenziale', Verlag Barbara Budrich, Opladen Berlin Toronto 2017.

814 It was submitted for the first review on 27 August 2018.

However, the *Marriage Registration Office* has still not imposed the obligation to review whether agreement of parents on parental custody after divorce is in the best interests of the child. For the criterions on redistribution of parental custody of the courts, the draft still follows the principle of tender years and insists that the mother should generally exercise physical parental custody to the child under the age of 2 after divorce of parents, while parental custody of the child above the age of 2 shall be decided according to the best interests of the minors by the courts having considered concrete situations of the parents (§ 861 III).

As to the legal rights of the child born out of Wedlock, the draft does not provide more concrete rules but only stresses that the child born out of wedlock enjoys the same rights as the child born in wedlock and any organization and person should not discriminate or injure the right of the child born out of wedlock (§ 848 I).

8.3.2 From the Perspective of Substantive Law

8.3.2.1 Systematic Modification of Legal Rules Concerning Relationship Between Parents and Children

As summarised at the end of section 7.2, the relationship between parents and children is regulated both in the *GRCL 2017* and in the *Marriage Law*. The overlapping part between guardianship in the *GRCL 2017* and parental custody in the *Marriage Law* might cause confusion regarding the accuracy of legal expression regarding parental responsibilities. It is therefore suggested that guardianship of the parents towards their children should be removed from the *GRCL 2017* and only the general rules concerning guardianship should remain in the *GRCL*, as guardianship in the Chinese law is designed for any individual who does have capability for civil conduct or has limited capability for civil conduct. In addition, the relationship between parents and children as one of the important relationships in a family should be specifically regulated in the *Marriage Law*.

8.3.2.2 Principle of the Child's Best Interests

According to Article 35 of the *GRCL 2017*, guardians shall fulfil their obligations under guidance of the principle of most benefiting the ward. Since parents are the legal guardians of the first order of a minor child, they should also follow such a principle in exercising parental custody. When making decisions for minors, parents as guardians shall consider the age and intelligence of the children and respect their true will (Article 35 II). However, it is not explicitly stipulated that the court in proceedings concerning parental custody shall make decisions which are most conducive to the best interests of the child, as it is provided for in § 1697 *BGB* in the German law. Instead, in certain circumstances, for instance, where the parent has lost fertility, the lawmakers give priority to parents over the child's interests. It is therefore suggested that the principle of the best interests of the child should be adopted as a guideline for the courts to deal with issues concerning parental custody.

8.3.2.3 Parental Custody After Divorce

a) Determination of the Habitual Residence of the Children After Divorce

By determining the habitual residence of a child after divorce of parents, the court decides which parent shall exercise physical custody and care for the child directly. To decide which parent is suitable to exercise physical custody to the child after divorce, the court should follow the principle of the best interests of the child, which requires the court to abandon prioritization of interests of parents in certain circumstances and to strictly review application of the principle of tender years preference in Article 36 III of the *Marriage Law* and Article I of *Opinions on Divorce Trials*. It is suggested that the *Supreme People's Court* should introduce guidelines on key criteria to determine habitual residence of the child for reference of the courts.

Even if the habitual residence of the child after divorce has been determined, parents might have conflict in other issues, for instance, exercise of joint parental custody, contact right and payment of child support.

b) Exercise of Parental Custody

Although parents according to the Chinese law exercise joint parental custody after divorce, the laws do not indicate parents how to exercise it, which has led to the consequence that the non-resident parent is even unaware of his or her rights under joint parental custody and takes for granted that the resident parent is the only person who can decide on all issues concerning the child after divorce. It is suggested that specific rules on authority to make decisions for the child should be written down to remind the non-resident parent of his or her rights and obligations as legal custodian after divorce and avoid unnecessary conflicts between parents, which can guarantee not only the right of the non-resident parent to co-exercise parental custody after divorce but also a decision to be made in the best interests of the child.

c) Right of Contact

To maintain contact with the child after divorce should be not only a right, but also an obligation for the non-resident parent. However, the *Marriage Law* only highlights such a right without laying any emphasis on obligation of non-resident parents to keep contact with the child (Article 38 I of *Marriage Law*). If such an obligation was legally provided for, there would not have been a discussion about whether the non-resident parent could waive the right of contact.[815] Right to contact should not be a right or an obligation of parents derived from separation or divorce but a part of parental custody which can be neither waived nor transferred. Consequently, not only the non-resident but also the resident parent is entitled to right of contact. Although the right of the child to claim contact with the non-resident parent is generally acknowledged in judicature, there should be a legal provision for the child to invoke in dispute with its non-resident parent who does not exercise the contact right as agreed between parents or decided by the court. Therefore, Article 38 should be drafted as follows: the child has the right to contact with each parent, and parents are entitled and obliged to maintain contact with the child.

Furthermore, it is suggested legal grounds to suspend or terminate contact of the non-resident parent should be listed by means of judicial interpretation. Those grounds should include but not be limited to severe illness of the non-resident parent which might injure the health of the child; crimes such as domestic violence, abuse or sexual assault committed by the non-resident parent; alcoholic or drug addiction or severe mental health problems; and alienation behaviours of the non-resident parent.[816] In addition, coercive measures taken by the courts to enforce a court decision should be specified. There should be a minimal or maximal limitation either for the sum of the fine or the duration of detention.

8.3.2.4 Legal Protection of the Child Born Out of Wedlock and the Biological but Not the Legal Father

a) Parental Custody of the Child Born Out of Wedlock

Although it is explicitly provided for in the *Marriage Law* that the child born out of wedlock shall enjoy the same rights as the child born in wedlock (Article 25 II), the child born out of wedlock is not treated equally in practice. For instance,

---

815 *Chen*, Study of legal system on kinship after divorce, P. 146–148.

816 Ibid, P. 194.

parents of a child born out of wedlock must pay a social support fee whose sum depends on the local economic development standard in order to register residence to acquire citizen status for the child,[817] while parents of the child born in wedlock who have got a pregnancy permit do not need to pay it. In some regions, there is even no possibility to pay the social support fee, because paternity of the child born out of wedlock cannot be determined because of disappearance of one parent after its birth.

In addition, the child born out of wedlock does not have the right to initiate a proceeding for verification of parenthood. Instead, only parents of the child born in wedlock have such a right according to Article 2 of *Interpretation III of Marriage Law*. Although it is explicitly demonstrated in Article 2 that either of a couple as wife and husband can apply to the courts for verification of biological parenthood, Article 2 could be analogically applied in the case of the child born out of wedlock. For instance, if a presumed biological father of a child born out of wedlock who doubts parenthood of the child refuses to pay child support, the court may presume that the parenthood exists if the mother has provided the necessary evidence[818] and the presumed father does not provide samples for a paternity test.

After paternity has been determined, the child born out of wedlock has the same right as the child born in wedlock to claim maintenance from the parent who does not exercise physical parental custody or care for him or her directly.[819] If the non-resident parent does not pay child maintenance regularly as agreed by parents or ordered in the court decisions, the child born out of wedlock can institute proceedings to claim it.

b) Biological but Not the Legal Father

aa) Determination of Biological and Legal Paternity

There is no legal definition of the legal father in Chinese law. Provisions concerning paternity acknowledgement of a biological father, right to apply to court for determination of legal paternity and ways to gain joint parental custody of a presumed biological father cannot be found either.

---

817 Article 3 of *Regulation on Collection of Social Support Fee*.

818 For instance, an agreement between the mother and the presumed father in which the child has been acknowledged as their joint child in the case of No. 1 Intermediate People's Court of Beijing, (2015) yi zhong min zai zhong zi No. 06320.

819 The No. 1 Intermediate People's Court of Beijing, (2015) yi zhong shao min zhong zi No. 7858 (The child was born on 1 August 2009).

Two ways could be legally provided for the biological father to become the legal father of his child born out of wedlock. He could acknowledge his paternity towards the child if the mother consents to it, or he could apply to the court for determination of paternity if the legal father of the child born out of wedlock does not exist. It is therefore suggested that right holders in Article 2 of *Interpretation III of Marriage Law* should not be only limited to married parents but should be expanded to parents who are presumed to be the biological parents of the child. Article 2 could be drafted as following: I. Either parent or the presumed parent can apply to the court for determination of biological parenthood. II. One party shall be presumed not to be the biological parent if he or she refuses to take part in the paternity test and cannot present evidence which is contrary to the evidence presented by the other party.

bb) Contact Right of the Biological but Not the Legal Father

After paternity of a biological father is verified according to Article 2 of *Interpretation III of Marriage Law*, it is clearly indicated by law that the biological father becomes the legal father automatically and is awarded with the right to exercise joint parental custody if the legal father does not exist.

According to the current Chinese laws, the biological but not the legal father whose legal paternity cannot be determined does not have standing to apply for contact with his child either as a parent or as a third party, as the law provides a right of contact only to legal parents or relatives. However, the right of the biological father to establish contact with his child born out of wedlock should be guaranteed if there is proof of special affection between them or the biological father has lived with the child in the same household for a long period, and exercise of the right of contact of the biological father is consistent with the best interests of the child, even if legal paternity of the child already existed.

8.3.3 From the Perspective of Procedural Law

8.3.3.1 Substantial Review of Agreement on Parental Custody by Marriage Registration Office

In Chinese *Marriage Law*, there is no legal definition of separation as in § 1567 *BGB*. The courts, after failure of mediation, shall grant divorce to a couple who has separated from each other for more than two years because of lack of mutual affection (Article 32 III 4 of Chinese *Marriage Law*).

If both parents wish to get divorced and they have reached agreement on child upbringing, matrimonial property and debts, the *Marriage Registration Office* shall issue them a certificate of divorce after examining the certificate of marriage and other documents presented by applicants (§ 13 of *Regulation on Marriage Registration*). However, the examination is only formally conducted, because the *Marriage Registration Office* is not required to find out whether the agreement between parents on parental custody is in the best interests of the child. With no substantial supervision of divorce agreement, interests of the child might be put in danger. Therefore, it is suggested that the *Marriage Registration Office* should conduct both formal and substantial reviews of the agreement between parents before granting them a divorce certificate. Only an agreement which reflects the true willingness of parents and is best for the child can avoid unnecessary conflicts later.

The perspective that parental autonomy in exercise of parental custody is not boundless and shall be put under supervision or even intervention of state authorities could provide a legal basis for the *Marriage Registration Office* to substantially review divorce agreement between parents.

8.3.3.2 Reform on Family Trial

a) Combination of Divorce Proceedings and Proceedings Connected to Divorce

In a divorce proceeding, the court generally decides not only on the granting of divorce, but also on other relevant issues, for instance, the exercise of parental custody, child support and right of contact after divorce, although it is not regulated by law[820]. Considering that one parent could bring a separate lawsuit concerning right of contact if a legally effective divorce judgement does not involve exercise of contact right after divorce (Article 24 of *Interpretation I*), it is suggested the court should *ex officio* combine proceedings of the divorce and other relevant issues which are of significant importance for the child so that unnecessary or repeated litigation between parents could be avoided. The parents should be required to submit their agreement on exercise of parental custody, child support and right of contact to the court for review even though such claims have not been mentioned in the plaint.

820 Exception in Article 329 of *Interpretation of Civil Procedure Law* where the People's Court of second instance may, on the principle of free wills of parties, mediate in divorce together with issues of child upbringing and matrimonial property if it holds the judgement of first instance which disapproves a divorce should be dismissed.

b) Establishment of Summary Procedure

According to the current Chinese laws, a People's Court of first instance should complete the trial under the normal procedure within six months after the case is docketed (Article 149 of *Civil Procedure Law*), while the trial in appeal proceedings should be completed within three months after the appeal is docketed (Article 176 of *Civil Procedure Law*). A summary procedure which should be finished within three months after docket of the case (Article 161 of *Civil Procedure law*) can only apply in cases where facts, rights and obligations in this case are clear and disputes are minor, and over which the basic People's Court and its detached tribunal have jurisdiction (Article 157 of *Civil Procedure law*). However, in a divorce proceeding where parents cannot generally reach an agreement on matrimonial property, parental custody or the exercise of contact right, the court shall investigate facts and redistribute rights and obligations between parents. The normal procedure instead of the summary procedure shall therefore apply.

Considering that the faster disputes over parental custody are resolved, the better it is for reestablishment of a steady living environment for the child, it is therefore necessary to set a time limit by introducing a summary procedure to proceedings related to parental custody after separation or divorce of parents where the time limit of submitting written statement of defence and presenting evidence should be set. The *Interpretation of Civil Procedure Law* issued by the *Supreme People's Court* and having come into force on 4 February 2015 has established a small claims procedure which can apply in cases where the personal relationship is clear and there are only disputes over the amount, time and means of the child support payment (Article 274 of *Interpretation of Civil Procedure Law*). Adjudication of the People's Court to the small claim procedure shall be final (Article 271 of *Interpretation of Civil Procedure Law*). Similar reforms can also be made in the cases where there are disputes over the exercise of parental custody and contact rights.

c) On Court Investigation

aa) Expert Opinions

To make a decision most consistent with the best interests of the child, the court should investigate legal facts which are not clear. The court, when applying key criteria in evaluation of the best interests of the child, can rely on the opinions of experts who can provide professional opinions on criteria such as capability of the parents, will of the child, stability of living environment of the child, etc. In 2017, the Intermediate People's Court of Guangzhou introduced for the first time a 'social ombudsman' system for the proceeding concerning recovery of child support. The ombudsmen should submit an investigation report after having interviewed the child and parents. School visits were also part of the investigation. However, there should be concrete rules on the qualification, appointment and obligations of experts in court investigation so that experts can play their roles better and interests of the child can be better guaranteed.[821]

bb) Hearing

It is a compulsory obligation for the court to hear opinions of children having ability to express their will when dealing with parental custody issues in a divorce proceeding (Article 52 of the *Law on Protection to Minors*). In addition, the *Opinions on Divorce Trials* requires the court to hear opinions of the child above the age of 10 in disputes between parents on the habitual residence of the child after divorce (Article 5 of *Opinions on Divorce Trials*). However, hearing of opinions of the child should not only be conducted in determination of habitual residence of the child after divorce of parents but be extended to other procedures concerning relationship between parents and children. In addition, there should be specific procedural rules on how the hearing is conducted.

d) Special Trial Concerning Custody Disputes

The *Supreme People's Court* has called for a reform on the mode and working mechanism of family trials by conducting a pilot program in around 100 basic-level People's Courts and intermediate People's Courts from 1 June 2016.[822] Family proceedings under the pilot program include divorce and cases incidental thereto such as parental custody, child support after divorce as well as the upbringing of 'illegitimate children'.[823]

---

821 No. 98 of the 3rd and 4th periodic report of China on implementation of *CRC* due in 2009, 6 June 2010, *CRC/C/CHN/3–4*.

822 'Opinions of the Supreme People's Court on conducting the pilot program of the reform of the mode and working mechanism of the family trial', issued on 21 April 2016 by the Supreme People's Court with the document no. 128 (2016).

823 The scope of cases under the pilot program: 'family cases' means cases involving the determination of identity relationships and the family disputes arising out of identity relationships, mainly including: (1) marital cases and cases incidental thereto, such as divorce, marriage invalidation, and marriage revocation, and cases incidental thereto include guardianship, child support, and division of property upon divorce; (2) cases about upbringing, maintenance and support disputes; (3) parental relationship cases such as confirmation and denial of parental relationships; (4) cases about adoptive relationship disputes; (5) cases about cohabitation relationship disputes, including the

Having considered the similarity between juvenile and family trials, all the courts participating in the pilot program are required either to combine these two trials or to conduct them separately. However, in my view, there is little similarity or commonality between juvenile and family trials. Therefore, reforms on family trials and juvenile trials should better be conducted separately. In the reform on family trials, the establishment of a professional tribunal for the trial of family disputes should be put on the agenda.

It is believed that reform on the mode and working mechanism of family trial will promote legislation of procedure rules concerning family disputes. In addition, cooperation and assistance of personnel from the fields of psychology, sociology, etc., in trials of family cases will be enhanced, as it is suggested by the *Supreme People's Court* that various methods such as family investigators, social workers and child psychologists should be introduced to improve working mechanism of family trials.

8.3.4 Establishment of a Specialised Public Authority for Welfare of Children and Youth

8.3.4.1 Background

a) Working Committees at Central Levels

In China, legislative, judicial and governmental departments and social organisations work together to promote, carry out and oversee the protection of children's rights and interests. The *Internal Affairs and Judiciary Committee of the National People's Congress* has set up an ad hoc group of professionals working on the protection of women and children. Its main responsibilities are to deal with proposals concerning the protection of women's and children's lawful rights and interests delivered by the National People's Congress and its Standing Committee, to offer opinions on proposed legislation, to investigate enforcement of the laws related to women and children, and to investigate matters affecting women and children and make recommendations to the Committee. The *Chinese People's Political Consultative Conference* has also set up a committee, whose main responsibilities are to oversee and promote compliance with State laws and regulations in so far as they concern women, young people and children, to

division of property during cohabitation and the upbringing of illegitimate children; and (6) cases about disputes over the succession and separation of family property, among others.

make recommendations to the State legislative and administrative departments on matters and circumstances affecting women and children, and to improve the work of those departments. At the Central Government level, the body responsible for coordinating children's issues is the *State Council Working Committee on Women and Children*[824], which is composed of 33-member associations, including 27 government departments and six social organisations.

b) At Local Levels

At local levels, public authorities such as the People's Court, People's Procuratorate, Public Security Bureau, and Civil Affairs Bureau with the cooperation from mass organisations (Communist Youth League, Women's Federation and Working Committee of Caring for the Next Generation) play different roles to provide children with protection. In case of serious infringement of interests of the minors, neighbourhood or village committee of the minors, employer of their parents, mass organisations mentioned above, schools and the Civil Affairs Bureau can apply to the court for guardianship disqualification of the legal guardians (Article 27 III of *Opinions on Issues of Legally Handling Infringement from Legal Guardians to Minors*). It can be concluded that the only public authority obliged to participate in protection to minors at local levels except judicial authorities is the Civil Affairs Bureau, whose main responsibilities, however, do not include the protection or promotion of the children's best interests,[825] let alone special protection or assistance to the child whose parents get separated or divorced.

---

824 Retrieved from http://www.nwccw.gov.cn/node_2660.htm on 12 September 2019. Its functions are as follows: coordinating and promoting the work of government departments to safeguard the rights and interests of women and children; coordinating and promoting the formulation and implementation of women's and children's development programs of government departments, and providing the necessary human, financial and material resources to carry out work related to women and children; directing, supervising and inspecting the work of working committees on women and children in people's governments at the provincial, autonomous regional and municipal levels.

825 See main responsibilities of the *Civil Affair Bureau* on the homepage of the *Ministry of Civil Affairs*, retrieved from http://www.mca.gov.cn/article/jg/zyzz/ on 12 September 2019.

8.3.4.2 Need to Establish a Public Authority for the Child

Although the authorities mentioned above work closely together to protect lawful interests of the child and the *Law on Protection to Minors* has specified protection which should be provided by schools, society and judicial authorities, it is still expected that a specific authority should be established to particularly protect and promote the welfare of the child and youth. Such a public authority should not only provide children and youth protection in case of endangerment of their best interests, but also promote their development and provide parents with assistance and consultation in raising and educating their children. In case parents get divorced, the authority could help parents to reach an agreement on the exercise of parental custody, contact rights, payment of child support, etc. Such an authority can be an authority independent to the Civil Affairs Bureau or an apartment subordinate to the Civil Affairs Bureau.

8.3.5 Unification and Standardisation of Wordings in Verdicts or Literature

Wordings in many decrees and literature with the statement that it should be first determined which parent shall care for the child or should be the custodian parent after divorce might lead to neglect of the non-resident parent in fulfilling his or her obligation towards the child. As divorce does not change the fact that both parents are legal custodians or guardians of the child (Article 36 I, II of Chinese *Marriage Law*), it is therefore suggested such expressions should be avoided or formulated as 'it should be first determined which parent shall exercise direct/ physical parental custody to the child after divorce'.

Appendix

1. Extracts of Relevant Provisions in German Law

1.1 Basic Law

Article 1 I

Human dignity shall be inviolable. To respect and protect it shall be duty of all state authority.

Article 2

(1) Every person shall have the right to free development of his or her personality insofar as he does not violate the rights of others or offend against the constitutional order of the moral law.
(2) Every person shall have the right to life and physical integrity. Freedom of the person shall be inviolable. These rights may be interfered with only pursuant to a law.

Article 3

(1) All persons shall be equal before the law.
(2) Men and women shall have equal rights. The state shall promote the actual implementation of equal rights for women and men and take steps to eliminate disadvantages that now exist.

Article 6

(1) Marriage and the family shall enjoy the special protection of the state.
(2) The care and upbringing of children is the natural right of parents and a duty primarily incumbent upon them. The state shall watch over them in the performance of this duty.
(3) Children may be separated from their families against the will of their parents or guardians only pursuant to a law, and only if the parents or guardians fail in their duties or the children are otherwise in danger of serious neglect.
(4) Every mother shall be entitled to the protection and care of the community.
(5) Children born outside of marriage shall be provided by legislation with the same opportunities for physical and mental development and for their position in society as are enjoyed by those born within marriage.

1.2 *BGB*

§ 1626

(1) The parents have the duty and the right to care for the minor child (parental custody). The parental custody includes the care for the person of the child (care for the person of the child) and the property of the child (care for the property of the child).
(2) In the care and upbringing of the child, the parents take account of the growing ability and the growing need of the child for independent responsible action. They discuss questions of parental custody with the child to the extent that, in accordance with the stage of development of the child, it is advisable, and they seek agreement.
(3) The best interests of the child as a general rule include contact with both parents. The same applies to contact with other persons to whom the child has ties, if maintaining these ties is beneficial for its development.

§ 1626a

(1) Where the parents, at the date of the birth of the child, are not married to one another, they have joint parental custody:
    1. if they declare that they wish to take on parental custody jointly (declarations of parental custody),
    2. if they marry one another or
    3. if the family court transfers joint parental custody to them.
(2) On application by a parent, the family court is to transfer parental custody or a part of parental custody to both parents jointly in accordance with subsection (1) no. 3 if the transfer is not inconsistent with the best interests of the child. If the other parent fails to submit any reasons which might be inconsistent with the transfer of joint parental custody, and if no such reasons are otherwise manifest, it is to be presumed that joint parental custody is not inconsistent with the best interests of the child.
(3) Apart from this, the mother has parental custody.

§ 1666

(1) Where the physical, mental or psychological best interests of the child or its property are endangered and the parents do not wish or are not able to avert the danger, the family court must take the measures necessary to avert the danger.

(2) In general, it is to be presumed that the property of the child is endangered if the person with care for the property of the child violates his maintenance obligation towards the child or his duties connected with the care for the property of the child or fails to comply with orders of the court that relate to the care for the property of the child.

(3) The court measures in accordance with subsection (1) include in particular:
1. instructions to seek public assistance, such as benefits of child and youth welfare and healthcare,
2. instructions to ensure that the obligation to attend school is complied with,
3. prohibitions to use the family home or another dwelling temporarily or for an indefinite period, to be within a certain radius of the home or to visit certain other places where the child regularly spends time,
4. prohibitions to establish contact with the child or to bring about a meeting with the child,
5. substitution of declarations of the person with parental custody,
6. part or complete removal of parental custody.

(4) In matters of care for the person of the child, the court may also undertake measures with effect against a third party.

§ 1671

(1) If parents live apart for a period that is not merely temporary, and if they have joint parental custody, each parent may apply to the family court to transfer parental custody or part of parental custody to him alone. The application is to be granted to the extent that:
1. the other parent consents, unless the child has reached the age of 14 and objects to the transfer, or
2. it is to be expected that the termination of the joint parental custody and the transfer to the applicant is most conducive to the best interests of the child.

(2) If parents live apart for a period that is not merely temporary and if, under section 1626a (3), the mother has parental custody, the father may apply to the family court to transfer parental custody or part of the parental custody to him alone. The application is to be granted if:

1. the mother consents, unless the transfer is inconsistent with the best interests of the child or the child has reached the age of 14 and objects to the transfer, or

2. joint custody cannot be considered, and it is to be expected that the transfer to the father is most conducive to the best interests of the child.

§ 1684

(1) The child has the right to contact with each parent; each parent has a duty and a right of contact with the child.
(2) The parents must refrain from everything that renders more difficult the relationship of the child to the other parent or the upbringing. Similar provisions apply if the child is in the charge of another person.
(3) The family court may decide on the scope of the right of contact and make more detailed provisions on its exercise, including provisions affecting third parties. It may enjoin the parties by orders to fulfil the duty defined in subsection (2). If the obligation in accordance with subsection (2) is considerably violated permanently or repeatedly, the family court may also order custodianship for the implementation of access (access custodianship). Access custodianship includes the right to demand surrender of the child to implement access and to determine where the child is to be for the duration of access. The order is to be time-limited. Section 277 of the Act on the Procedure in Family Matters and in Matters of Non-contentious Jurisdiction applies with the necessary modifications to compensation for expenditure and remuneration of the access custodian.
(4) The family court may restrict or exclude the right of contact or the enforcement of earlier decisions on the right of contact, to the extent that this is necessary for the best interests of the child. A decision that restricts the right of contact or its enforcement for a long period or permanently may only be made if otherwise the best interests of the child would be endangered. The family court may in particular order that contact may take place only if a third party who is prepared to cooperate is present. The third party may also be an agency of the youth welfare service or an association; the latter then determines in each case which individual carries out the task.

§ 1685 II

The same applies to persons to whom the child relates closely if these take or have taken actual responsibility for the child (social family relationship). It is in general to be assumed that actual responsibility has been taken on if the person has been living for a long period in domestic community with the child.

§ 1687

(1) If parents who have joint parental custody live apart not merely temporarily, then in the case of decisions in matters the arrangement of which is of substantial significance for the child their mutual agreement is necessary. The parent with whom the child, with the consent of the other parent or on the basis of a court decision, customarily resides has the authority to decide alone in matters of everyday life. Decisions in matters of everyday life generally occur frequently occur and that have no effects that are difficult to alter on the development of the child. As long as the child, with the consent of this parent or on the basis of a court decision, resides with the other parent, the latter has the authority to decide alone in matters of actual care. § 1629 I 4 and § 1684 II 1 apply with the necessary modifications.
(2) The family court may restrict or exclude the powers under subsection (1) sentences 2 and 4 if this is necessary for the best interests of the child.

§1697a

To the extent not provided otherwise, the court, in proceedings on the matters provided for in this title, makes the decision that, taking into account the actual circumstances and possibilities and the justified interests of those involved, is most conducive to the best interests of the child.

2. Extracts of Relevant Provisions in Chinese Law

2.1 Constitution

Article 46

The State promotes the all-round development of children and young people, morally, intellectually and physically.

Article 49

Marriage, the family and mother and child are protected by the State (I). Parents have the duty to rear and educate their children who are minors, and children who have come of age have the duty to support and assist their parents. Violation of the freedom of marriage is prohibited. Maltreatment of old people, women and children is prohibited (III).

2.2 General Rules of Civil Law

Article 20

A minor under the age of 8 is a person without capacity for civil conduct, who shall be represented in performing civil juridical acts by his or her statutory agent.

Article 23

The guardian of a person without capacity for civil conduct or with limited capacity for civil conduct shall be the statutory agent of the person.

Article 26

Parents have the obligation to raise, educate and protect their minor children.

Article 27

The parents of a minor are his or her guardians.

Where both parents of a minor are dead or incapable of acting as a guardian, one of the following persons capable of acting as a guardian shall act as the guardian of the minor in the following order:

(1) Paternal or maternal grandparents of the minor;
(2) Elder brothers or sisters of the minor;
(3) Other individuals or organisations willing to act as the guardian, provided that it is approved by the urban residents' committee, villagers' committee or civil affairs department of the place of the minor's domicile.

Article 29

Where the parents of a ward are his or her guardians, they may designate the guardian by will.

Article 30

Persons legally qualified for guardianship may, by agreement, determine the guardian. The true will of the ward shall be respected in the determination of guardian by agreement.

Article 34

The duties of a guardian include but are not limited to representing the ward in performing juridical acts and protecting the personal rights, property rights, and other lawful rights and interests of the ward.

The guardian's rights arising from performance of the duty of guardianship in accordance with the law shall be protected by law.

A guardian failing to perform the duty of guardianship or infringing upon the ward's lawful rights and interests shall assume legal liability.

Article 35

A guardian shall perform the duty of guardianship under the principle of most benefiting the ward. The guardian shall not dispose of the ward's property unless for safeguarding the ward's interests.

The guardian of a minor shall, in the performance of the duty of guardianship, respect the ward's true will when making decisions related to the ward's interests according to the ward's age and intelligence.

Article 36

Where a guardian falls under any of the following circumstances, the People's Court shall, upon application of the relevant individual or organisation, disqualify the guardian, arrange necessary provisional guardianship measures, and designate another guardian in accordance with the law under the principle of most benefiting the ward:

(1) Acting seriously to the detriment of the ward's physical and mental health;
(2) Being slack in performing the duty of guardianship or being incapable of performing the duty of guardianship but refusing to delegate part or all of the duty of guardianship to another person, which causes distress to the ward;
(3) Otherwise seriously infringing upon the ward's lawful rights and interests.

For the purposes of this article, the relevant individuals and organisations include but are not limited to: any other person legally qualified for guardianship, an urban residents' committee, a villagers' committee, a school, a medical institution, a women's federation, a disabled persons' federation, an organisation for the protection of minors, an organisation legally formed for seniors and a civil affairs department.

Where the individuals and organisations except the civil affairs department as prescribed in the preceding paragraph fail to apply for the disqualification of the guardian to the People's Court in a timely manner, the civil affairs department shall file such an application with the People's Court.

Article 37

Parents, children, and spouses who support the wards in the form of child support, support for elderly parents, or spousal support in accordance with the law shall continue to perform such obligations after they are disqualified by the People's Courts as guardians.

Article 38

Where the ward's parent or child shows true repentance after being disqualified from guardianship by the People's Court, except one having committed an intentional crime on the ward, the People's Court may, by respecting the ward's true will and according to the circumstances, reinstate his or her guardianship upon his or her application; and the guardianship between the guardian designated by the People's Court and the ward shall terminate concurrently.

Article 39

Under any of the following circumstances, the guardianship shall terminate:

(1) The ward obtains or regains full capacity for civil conduct;
(2) The guardian becomes incapable of guardianship;
(3) The ward or the guardian dies;
(4) The guardian relationship otherwise terminates as determined by a People's Court.

If the ward still needs guardianship after the guardianship terminates, another guardian shall be determined in accordance with the law.

2.3 Marriage Law

Article 3 II

Family violence shall be prohibited.

Maltreatment and desertion of one family member by another shall be prohibited.

Article 21

Parents shall have the duty to bring up and educate their children, and children shall have the duty to support and assist their parents.

If parents fail to perform their duty, children who are minors or are not capable of living on their own shall have the right to demand the costs of upbringing from their parents.

If children fail to perform their duty, parents who are unable to work or have difficulty in providing for themselves shall have the right to demand support payments from their children.

Infanticide by drowning, abandonment of infants and all other acts causing serious harm to infants shall be prohibited.

Article 22

Children may adopt either their father's or their mother's surname.

Article 23

Parents shall have the right and duty to protect and educate their children who are minors. If children who are minors cause damage to the State, the collective or individuals, their parents shall have the duty to bear civil liability.

Article 25

Children born out of wedlock shall enjoy the same rights as children born in wedlock. No one may harm or discriminate against them.

The natural father or mother who does not directly bring up a child born out of wedlock shall bear the child's living and educational expenses until the child can live on its own.

Article 26

The State shall protect lawful adoption. The relevant provisions of this Law governing the relationship between parents and children shall apply to the rights and duties in the relationship between foster-parents and foster-children.

The rights and duties in the relationship between a foster-child and its natural parents shall terminate with the establishment of its adoption.

Article 27

Maltreatment and discrimination shall not be allowed between step-parents and step-children.

The relevant provisions of this Law governing the relationship between parents and children shall apply to the rights and duties in the relationship between step-fathers or step-mothers and their step-children who receive care and education from them.

Article 28

Grandparents and maternal grandparents who can afford it shall have the duty to bring up their grandchildren and maternal grandchildren who are minors and whose parents are dead or have no means to bring them up. Grandchildren and maternal grandchildren who can afford it shall have the duty to support their grandparents and maternal grandparents whose children are dead or have no means to support them.

Article 36

The relationship between parents and children shall not come to an end with the parents' divorce. After divorce, whether the children are directly put under the care of the father or the mother, they shall remain the children of both parents.

After divorce, both parents shall still retain the right and duty to bring up and educate their children.

In principle, the mother shall exercise the parental custody towards a breast-fed infant after divorce. If a dispute arises between the two parents over the parental custody of their child who has been weaned and they fail to reach an agreement, the People's Court shall make a judgement in accordance with the rights and interests of the child and the actual conditions of both parents.

Article 37

If, after divorce, one parent exercises direct parental custody to the child, the other parent shall bear part or whole of the child's necessary living and educational expenses. The two parents shall seek agreement regarding the amount and duration of such payment. If they fail to reach an agreement, the People's Court shall make a judgement.

The agreement or court judgement on the payment of a child's living and educational expenses shall not prevent the child from making a reasonable request, when necessary, to either parent for an amount exceeding what is decided upon in the said agreement or judgement.

Article 38

After divorce, the father or the mother who does not directly bring up the child shall have the right to visit his or her child, and the other party shall have the duty to co-operate.

The manner and time for exercising the right to visit a child shall be decided by the parties through consultation; if they fail to reach an agreement in this regard, the People's Court shall make a judgement.

Where visits to a child by the father or the mother is not conducive to the physical and mental health of the child, the People's Court shall terminate their contact rights; after the cause of such termination disappears, the contact right to the child shall be resumed.

Article 48

Where a person refuses to abide by the judgement or ruling on the costs of maintenance, upbringing or support payments, or on the partitioning or inheritance of property, or visit to a child, the People's Court shall enforce the execution of the judgement or ruling in accordance with law. The individuals and unit concerned shall have the duty to assist such execution.

2.4 Interpretations of the Supreme People's Court to the Marriage Law

2.4.1 Interpretation I

Article 9

When the People's Court tries a case of declaring a marriage invalid, if mediation is not applicable to the trial of the validity of the marriage, it shall make a judgement under the law. Once a judgement on the validity of marriage is made, it shall have legal force.

Where a case involves property partition and child fostering, it may be mediated. Where an agreement is reached upon mediation, a mediation document shall be created. If either party refuses to accept the judgement on property partition and children fostering, the party may appeal.

Article 21

The term 'child support' as mentioned in Article 21 of the *Marriage Law* includes the expenses for life sustention, education, medical care, etc.

Article 24

If a valid judgement of divorce made by the People's Court does not involve contact rights and if the parties concerned bring a separate lawsuit over the contact right, the People's Court shall hear the case.

Article 25

During the course when the parties perform the valid judgement, ruling or mediation document, if a party concerned requests for suspending contact rights, the People's Court shall make a ruling if it believes it is necessary to suspend the contact right after it seeks the opinions of both parties. After the circumstance for the suspension of the visit right disappears, the People's Court shall, upon application of the party concerned, inform them that they may resume contact rights.

Article 26
Concerning underage children, the father or mother who directly brings up the children, or any other legal custodian who bears the obligation of upbringing and educating the underage children shall have the right to request the People's Court for suspending the contact right.

Article 32

Provision in Article 48 of the *Marriage Law* concerning mandatory enforcement by the People's Court in accordance with the law in case any person refuses to execute the judgement or decision on the visit of children refers to the taking of mandatory measures such as detaining and fining the relevant individuals and entities that refuse to help the other party to exercise the right of contact, and does not refer to the enforcement against the body of the children or act of visit.

2.4.2 Interpretation II

Article 4

Where the People's Court hears an invalid marriage suit in which the partitioning of property and upbringing of children are involved, the People's Court shall, in respect of the determination of the validity of the marriage and the handling of other disputes, respectively make judicial documents.

2.4.3 Interpretation III

Article 2

Where one party of a couple files an action before a People's Court for verification of no parenthood and provides necessary evidence, the People's Court may presume that the claim filed by the party for verification of no parenthood stands if the other party fails to provide evidence to the contrary and refuses paternity test.

Where one party of a couple files an action before a People's Court for verification of parenthood and provides necessary evidence, the People's Court may presume that the claim filed by the party for verification of parenthood stands if the other party fails to provide evidence to the contrary and refuses paternity test.

Article 3

During duration of marriage, if one or both parents refuse performing obligations of raising children, the People's Court shall support claims for payment of maintenance costs filed by minor children or those unable to live on their own.

2.5 Opinions of the Supreme People' Court on the Matter of Parental Custody in Divorce Proceedings

Opinions of the Supreme People' Court on the matter of parental custody in divorce proceedings shall be taken into account by the People's Courts of all the levels, according to which:

Article 1
Children under the age of 2 shall live with mother generally unless (1) the mother suffers contagious diseases which cannot be cured, or other diseases and it is not advisable for the children to live with her; or (2) the mother does not fulfil her obligation of parenting, but the father submits the application to live with the children; or (3) the other reasons make it impossible for children to live with the mother.

Article 2

If parents have made an agreement that the children under the age of 2 live with the father and such an agreement will not be detrimental to the growth of the children, the court shall approve this agreement.

Article 3

If both of the parents apply to live with the minor children above the age of 2, application of the parent shall be considered with priority if: (1) he or she has lost fertility; (2) the children have lived such a long time with him or her that changing the living environment would be detrimental to the healthy development of the children; (3) he or she does not have other children, while the other parent does; (4) it would be beneficial for the development of the child to live with him or her, rather than with the other parent who suffers a contagious or other serious illness that cannot be cured.

Article 4

If both parents who are equally suitable to raise the child apply to live with the child, application of the parent whose parents (grandparents of the child) having lived with the child for many years request to and are capable to care for the child might be considered with priority.

Article 5

Opinions of the children above the age of 10 shall be taken into account in the case that parents cannot reach an agreement on the habitual residence of the children after divorce.

Article 6

The agreement of the parents to switch to care for the child can be approved on the condition that the interests of the children are guaranteed.

Article 7

The sum of the child support paid for the child shall be determined after taking the actual needs, the ability of the parents and local living standards into consideration. For the parent who has a fixed income, the sum of child support shall be 20–30 % of his or her monthly income. The sum of child support for two or more than two children can be raised but shall not exceed 50 % of the monthly income; for the parent who does not have fixed income, the sum of child support for the child shall be determined according to the annual income of that year or the average income of the same industry.

Article 8

Child support shall be paid regularly. If possible, such payment can be paid in a single payment.

Article 9

The properties of one party who does not have economic income or is missing can be sold to provide child support.

Article 10

Parents can make the agreement that one of them lives with the child and the other one need not to pay child support. However, such an agreement will not be approved if the parent with whom the child lives cannot afford the costs needed to raise the child, and it is detrimental to the healthy development of the child.

Article 11

Child support shall be paid until the child reaches the age of 18.

For the child between the age of 16 and 18 who has income to maintain a living which is not below the local average standard of living, such payment can be terminated.

Article 12

Parents able to pay shall pay necessary child support to their adult child who cannot live independently in the following circumstances:

(1) losing capacity to work or losing partial capacity to work but with income insufficient to make a living;
(2) still attending school;
(3) having no capacity to live independently.

Article 15

Either of the parents applying to change the status of parental custody or a child applying for an increase of child support shall file another suit.

Article 16

Application of one parent for transfer of parental custody should be granted in the following situations:

(1) if the other parent with whom the child lives suffers from such a serious illness or injury that he or she is not able to continue caring for the child, or
(2) if the other parent does not fulfil his or her obligation to care for the child or abuses the child, or living with this parent would impose negative influence on physical or mental development of the child, or
(3) the child above the age of 10 is willing to live with the applying parent who has the ability to care for this child, or
(4) in other situations with suitable reasons.

Article 17
The agreement made by the parents on change of parental custody shall be approved.

Article 18

Application of the child for increase of child support should be granted in the following situations if the parent has the ability to make the payment:

(1) if the previous sum of child support toward children is not enough to maintain a living according to the local living standard, or
(2) the expenditure of children rises because of treatment of the illness, schooling or the other real needs,
(3) or in other situations with suitable reason.

Article 19

Parents shall not refuse to pay child support because the child changes its family name. The court shall restore the family name of a child if there is a dispute because one parent changes the original family name of the child to the family name of his step-parent without consent of the other parent.

Article 20

During the divorce litigation, the court may designate one parent to temporarily care for the child whom neither of the parents refuses to care for.

Article 21

The People's Court may, according to Article 102 of *Civil Procedure law*, take coercive measures against parties or other persons who refuse to fulfil or interfere with fulfilling obligations to raise the child brought about from effective judgements, adjudications and conciliations.

3. Statistic

3.1 Percentage of the Child Born out of Wedlock in Germany

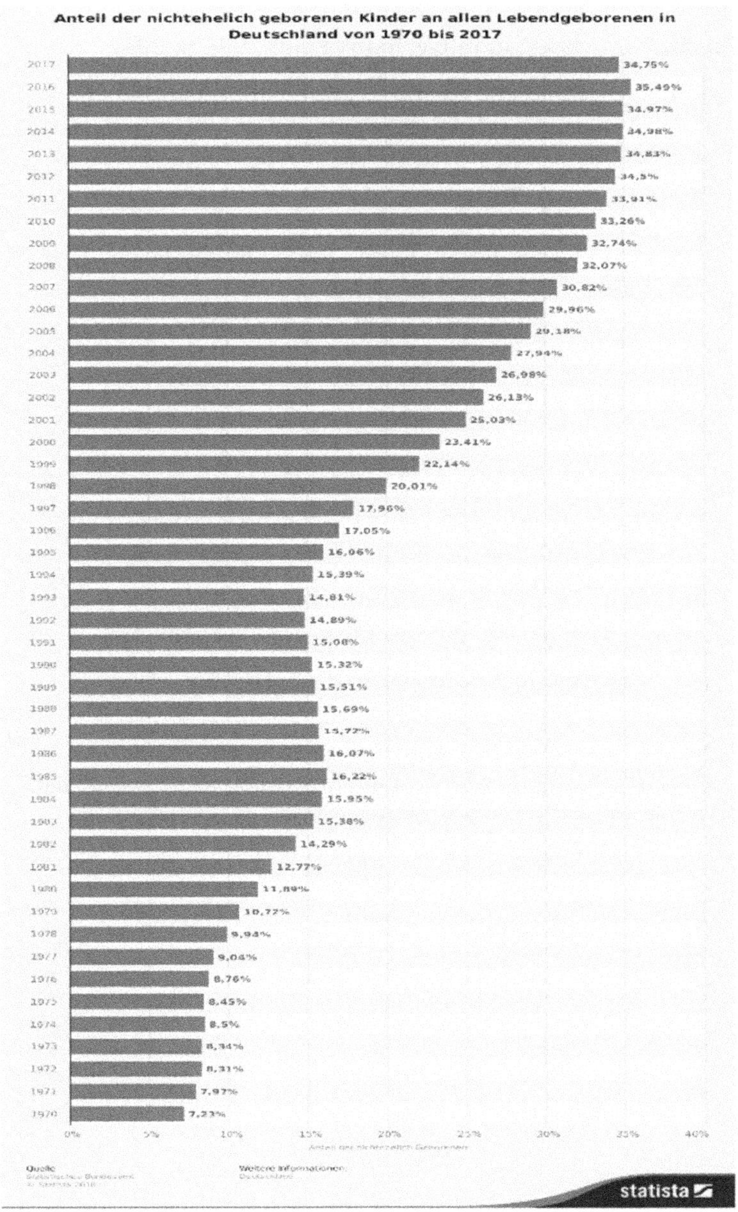

Tab. I : Percentage of the child born out of wedlock from 1970 to 2017

Retrieved from https://de.statista.com/statistik/daten/studie/1324/umfrage/uneheliche-kinder-anteil-an-allen-geburten/ on 12 September 2018.

3.2 Statistic of Abortion in Germany from 1996 to 2017

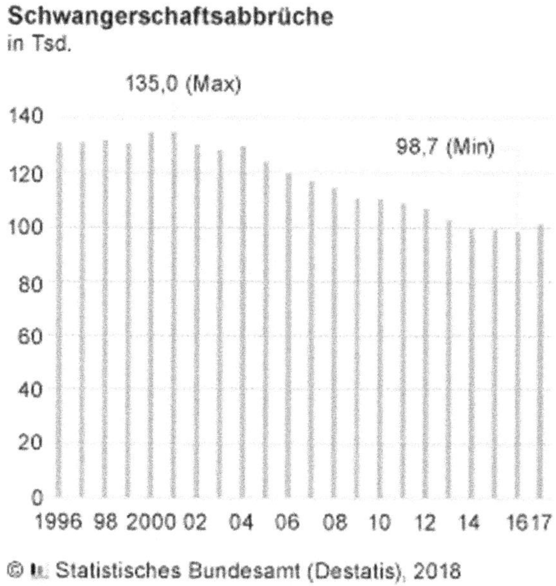

Tab. II : Number of Abortions in Germany from 1996 to 2017

Retrieved from https://www.destatis.de/DE/ZahlenFakten/GesellschaftStaat/Gesundheit/Schwangerschaftsabbrueche/Schwangerschaftsabbrueche.html on 12 September 2018.

Bibliography

Altrogge, Alexandra: Diskriminierung eines nichtehelichen Vaters mangels gesetzlicher Regelung zur gerichtlichen Prüfung eines gemeinsamen Sorgerechts? FamFR 2010, 73

Amend-Traut, Anja/Bongartz, Josef: Der Schwangerschaftsabbruch bei Minderjährigen – rechtliche Perspektiven zwischen Selbststimmung und elterlicher Verantwortung, FamRZ 2016, 5

Arbeitsgruppe Familienrechtliche Gutachten 2015: Mindestanforderungen an die Qualität von Sachverständigengutachten im Kindschaftsrecht, FamRZ 2015, 2027

Arntzen, Friedrich: Elterliche Sorge und Umgang mit Kindern: ein Grundriss der forensischen Familienpsychologie, 2. Auflage, C.H.BECK, München 1994

Balloff, Rainer: Die Beauftragung des Sachverständigen in Kindschaftssachen, FPR 2011, 12

Ballof, Rainer: Das *KJHG* - Noch einmal: Zum Spannungsverhältnis von Beratung und Familiengerichtshilfe nach §§ 17 und 50 *KJHG*, ZfJ 1992, 455

Balloff, Rainer: Alleinerziehung & gemeinsame elterliche Sorge nach Trennung und Scheidung – Eine theoretische und empirische Vergleichsstudie, 1990

Bamberger, Heinz Georg/Roth, Herbert: Beck'scher Online-Kommentar *BGB*, 36. Auflage 2015; Cited as *Bamberger/Roth/Author* (Year), § XXX Rn.

Belling, Detlev W./Eberl, Christina: Der Schwangerschaftsabbruch bei Minderjährigen, FuR 1995, 287

Berg, Tatjana: Die Entwicklung des Sorgerechts der Mütter nichtehelicher Kinder in Deutschland vom Inkrafttreten des *BGB* bis heute 2012, Dekan Fachbereich Rechtspflege, 2012

Bergmann, Alexander/Ferid, Murad/Henrich, Dieter: Internationales Ehe- und Kindschaftsrecht, 2019

Bergmann, Margarethe: Verfahrensbeistand – Ein Beitrag zum Kindeswohl, ZKJ 2016, 288

Bernd von Hoffmann: European private international law, Ars Aequi Libri 1998

Boele-Woelki, Katharina/Ferrand, Frédérique/González Beilfuss, Cristina et al.: Principles of European family law regarding parental responsibilities, Intersentia Publishers 2007

Borkowski, Andrew: Textbook on Roman law, Oxford University Press 2015

Britz, Gabriele: Kinderschutz – aktuelle verfassungsrechtliche Leitlinien, NZFam 2016, 1113

Brokamp, Iris: Die Verrechtlichung der Eltern-Kind-Beziehung in hundert Jahren *BGB*, Verlag Ernst und Werner Gieseking, Bielefeld 2002

Büchner, Brigit/Mach-Hour, Elisabeth: Verfahrensbeistandschaft bei Kindeswohlgefährdung, NZFam 2016, 597

Burschel, Hans-Otto: Anforderungen an die Arbeit eines Verfahrensbeistandes, NZFam 2014, 565

Buxbaum, David C. (editor): Chinese family law and social change in historical and comparative perspective, University of Washington Press, Hongkong 1978

Chen, Siqin: Study of legal system on kinship after divorce, China Social Science Publishing House, 2011

Ch'u, T'ung-tsu: Law and society in traditional China, Hyperion Press, Paris 1961

Clausius, Monika: Prüfungsmaßstab für Sorgerechtsentscheidung bei nicht miteinander verheirateten Eltern, jurisPR FamR 5/2015 Anm. 3

Coester, Michael: Sorgerecht nicht miteinander verheirateter Eltern, FamRZ 2012, 1337

Coester, Michael: Kindesschutz – Übersicht zu den typischen Gefährdungslagen und aktuellen Problemen, FPR 2009, 549

Coester, Michael: Verfassungsrechtliche Vorgaben für die gesetzliche Ausgestaltung des Sorgerechts nicht miteinander verheirateter Eltern, FPR 2005, 60

Coester, Michael: Elternautonomie und Staatsverantwortung bei der Pflege und Erziehung von Kindern, FamRZ 1996, 1181

Coester, Michael: Das Kindeswohl als Rechtsbegriff, Alfred Metzner Verlag, Frankfurt am Main 1983

Coester-Waltjen, Dagmar: Statusrechtliche Folgen der Stärkung der Rechte der nichtehelichen Väter, FamRZ 2013, 1693

Coester-Waltjen, Dagmar/Lipp, Volker/Schumann, Eva: Reformbedarf im nichtehelichen Eltern-Kind-Verhältnis, 10. Göttinger Workshop zum Familienrecht 2011, Universitätsverlag Göttingen 2012

Coester-Waltjen, Dagmar: Der Schwangerschaftsabbruch und die Rolle des künftigen Vaters, NJW 1985, 2175

Cretney, Stephen Michael/Masson, Judith M/Bailey-Harris, Rebecca J: Principles of the family law, Sweet & Maxwell, London 2003

Dethloff, Nina: Familienrecht, 32. Auflage, C.H.BECK, München 2018

Dethloff, Nina/Kaesling, Katharina: Kindesunterhalt und Wechselmodell – Eine vergleichende Perspektive, FamRZ 2018, 73

Dethloff, Nina/Timmermann, Anja: Multiple Elternschaft – Familienrecht und Familienleben im Spannungsverhältnis, P. 173–194 in "Familien mit multipler Elternschaft: Entstehungszusammenhänge, Herausforderungen und Potenziale", Verlag Barbara Budrich, Opladen Berlin Toronto 2017

Dethloff, Nina: Kindeswohl und Väterrechte, BRJ 2010

Dettenborn, Harry: Kindeswohl und Kindeswille, Psychologische und rechtliche Aspekte, 5. Auflage, Ernst Reinhardt Verlag, München 2017

Dickens, B: The modern function and limits of parental rights, Law Quarterly Review 97: 462, 1981

Douglas, Gillian: The family and the state under European Convention on Human Rights, International Journal of Law and the Family 2: 76, 1998

Doukkani-Bördner, Astrid: Kindesmisshandlungen im Haushalt der Eltern und elterliche Sorge, FamRZ 2016, 13

Ebrey, Patricia Buckley: Confucianism and family rituals in imperial China, Princeton University Press, Oxford 1991

Eckert-Schirmer, Jutta: Gemeinsames Sorgerecht nach Scheidung: Leitbild oder soziale Realität? FuR 1996, 206

Ehinger, Uta: Die Regelung der elterlichen Sorge bei psychischer Erkrankung eines Elternteils oder beider Eltern im Überblick, FPR 2005, 253

Elden, Erkan: Der Umgang eines Elternteils mit den Kindern – eine in der Praxis oft schwierige Angelegenheit, NZFam 2017, 8

Ernst, Rüdiger: Gemeinsame Elternverantwortung nach Trennung und Scheidung, DRiZ 2018, 302

Fahl, Holger: Die Verantwortungsgemeinschaft von Familiengerichten und Jugendämtern in Kindschaftsverfahren, NZFam 2015, 247

Fahl, Holger: § 1626a *BGB* und das Kindeswohl – Reformbedarf wegen Verstoßes gegen die UN-Kinderrechtskonvention, NZFam 2014, 155

Feßmann,Thilo: Das Personensorgerecht für Kinder nicht verheirateter Eltern in Deutschland und Italien, Dissertation, Regensburg 2000

Fichtner, Jörg/Salzgeber, Joseph: Die Kommunikation des Sachverständigen mit den Verfahrensbeteiligten und dem Familiengericht, FPR 2013, 478

Fink, Sandra/Bitter, Stephan: Eine unendliche Geschichte – kommt endlich die verfassungsgemäße Reform des Sorgerechts für nichteheliche Kinder? ZKJ 2012, 172

Finke, Fritz: Rechtliche Grundlagen und Ausgestaltung der Kindesbetreuung durch Eltern und Dritte, NZFam 2014, 865

Frier, Bruch W/McGinn, Thomas A.J.: A casebook on Roman family law, Oxford University Press 2004

Fröschle, Tobias: Sorge und Umgang in der Rechtspraxis, 2. Auflage, Verlag Ernst und Werner Gieseking, Bielefeld 2018

Gardner, Daniel K: Chu His and the Ta-hsüeh, Neo-Confucian reflection on the Confucian canon, Harvard University Press 1986

Gernhuber, Joachim/Coester-Waltjen, Dagmar: Familienrecht, C.H.Beck, München 2010

Glosser, Susan L.: Chinese visions of family and state, 1915–1953, University of California Press, California 2003

Gottwald, Peter/Schwab, Dieter/Büttner, Eva: Family & succession law in Germany, C.H.Beck, München 2001

Grandel, Mathias/Stockmann Roland (publisher): Stichwortkommentar Familienrecht, 3. Auflage, Nomos 2014; Cited as *StichwortKo/Author* (Year), § XXX Rn.

Häfele, Günter: Seelische erkrankte Eltern und Kindeswohlgefährdung, FPR 2003, 307

Hammer, Stephan: Anmerkung zum OLG Hamburg, Beschluss v. 17.12.2015 – 2 UF 106/14 –, FamRZ 2016, 916

Hammer, Stephan: Die gerichtliche Anordnung des Wechselmodells, FamRZ 2015, 1433

Hähnchen, Susanne: Vergangenheit und Zukunft der Rechte des nichtehelichen Vaters, JZ 2015, 708

Harris-Short, Sonja/Miles, Joanna/Rob, George: Family law: text, cases and materials, 3. Edition, Oxford University Press 2015

Hau, Wolfgang: Europäische und autonome Zuständigkeitsgründe in Ehesachen mit Auslandsbezug, FPR 2002, 616

Hauck, Ronny: Der Schutz von Minderjährigen bei Eingriffen in höchstpersönliche Rechte und Rechtsgüter, NJW 2012, 2398

Heiderhoff, Bettina: Herausforderungen durch neue Familienformen – Zeit für ein Umdenken, NJW 2016, 2629

Heiderhoff, Bettina: Anspruch des Kindes auf Klärung der genetischen Vaterschaft? NJW 2016, 1918

Heilmann, Stefan: Kindeswohl und Wechselmodell, NJW 2015, 3346

Heilmann, Stefan: Praxiskommentar Kindschaftsrecht, Bundesanzeiger Verlag 2015

Heilmann, Stefan: Schützt das Grundgesetz die Kinder nicht? Eine Betrachtung der bisherigen Kammerrechtsprechung des BVerfG im Jahr 2014, NJW 2014, 2909

Heilmann, Stefan: Die Reform des Sorgerechts nicht miteinander verheirateter Eltern – Das Ende eines Irrwegs? NJW 2013, 1473

Heiß, Hans/Castellanos, Helen: Gemeinsame Sorge und Kindeswohl nach neuem Recht, 1. Auflage, Nomos 2013

Heiß, Thomas A: Höchste Anforderungen an Feststellungen zur Kindeswohlgefährdung bei Sorgerechtsentziehung, NZFam 2015, 86

Helms, Tobias: Rechtliche, biologische und soziale Elternschaft – Herausforderungen durch neue Familienformen, NJW-Beil 2016, 49

Helms, Tobias: Die Einführung der sogenannten vertraulichen Geburt, FamRZ 2014, 609

Henrich, Dieter: Anmerkung zum EGMR Urteil v. 25.9.2012 – 33783/09, FamRZ 2012, 1935

Herring, Jonathan: Relational autonomy and family law, Springer Press 2014

Hoffmann, Birgit: Das Gesetz zur Stärkung der Rechte des leiblichen, nicht rechtlichen Vaters, FamRZ 2013, 1077

Hohm, Karl-Heinz: Grundrechtsträgerschaft und "Grundrechtsmündigkeit" Minderjähriger am Beispiel öffentlicher Heimerziehung, NJW 1986, 3107

Honsell, Heinrich: Römisches Recht, Springer Verlag, 8. Auflage 2015

Huang, Philip C. C.: Code, Custom, and legal practice in China, Stanford University Press, California 2001

Huber, Peter/Antomo, Jennifer: Die Neuregelung der elterlichen Sorge nicht miteinander verheirateter Eltern, FamRZ 2012, 1257

Jagert, Uwe: Zur Frage der elterlichen Sorge über ein noch nicht geborenes Kind bei einem Elternstreit über einen zulässigen Schwangerschaftsabbruch, FamRZ 1985, 1173

Jin, Mei: Modern and contemporary transition of Chinese law of domestic relation, Law Press 2010

Johannsen, Kurt H./Henrich, Dieter: Familienrecht, Kommentar, 6. Auflage, C.H.BECK, München 2015; Cited as *Johannsen/Henrich//Author* (Year), § XXX Rn.

Jokisch, Beate: Das Wechselmodell – Grundlagen und Probleme (Teil 1), FuR 2013, 679

Jopt, Uwe-Jörg: Nacheheliche Elternschaft und Kindeswohl – Plädoyer für das gemeinsame Sorgerecht als anzustrebenden Regelfall, FamRZ 1987, 875

Kaser, Max/Knütel, Rolf/Lohsser, Sebastian: Römisches Privatrecht, C.H.BECK, München 2017

Katz, Sanford: Family law in America, Oxford University Press 2015

Kaufmann, Ferdinand: Eltern, Kinder und Fachkräfte der Jugendämter im familiengerichtlichen Verfahren zur Regelung der elterlichen Sorge bei Trennung und Scheidung, FamRZ 2001, 7.

Keuter, Wolfgang: Vereinfachtes Verfahren zur Übertragung der gemeinsamen elterlichen Sorge – ein Fremdkörper in Kindschaftssachen, FamRZ 2015, 825

Kindler, Heinz/Walper, Sabine: Das Wechselmodell im Kontext elterlicher Konflikte, NZFam 2016, 820

Kindler, Heinz: Kinderschutz im *BGB*, FPR 2012, 426

Kindler, Heinz: Folgewirkungen schwerer psychischer Erkrankungen mindestens eines Elternteils auf die Entwicklung von Kindern, FPR 2005, 227

Kirsten-Pia, Hansen: Das Recht der elterlichen Sorge nach Trennung und Scheidung, Luchterhand 1993

Klinkhammer, Frank: Beschneidung männlicher Kleinkinder und gesetzliche Vertretung durch die Eltern, FamRZ 2012, 1913

Kohler, Mathias: Vom Umgang mit der Umgangspflegschaft, JAmt 2010, 226

Kostka, Kerima: Neue Erkenntnisse zum Wechselmodell, ZKJ 2014, 54

Kostka, Kerima: Elterliche Sorge und Umgang bei Trennung und Scheidung – unter besonderer Berücksichtigung der Perspektive des Kindes, FPR 2005, 89

Kruk, Edward: Child custody – access and parental responsibilities, The University of British Columbia 2008

Krumm, Carsten: Die wichtigsten Praxisprobleme der persönlichen Kindesanhörung nach § 159 FamFG, FamFR 2013, 265–268

Lack, Katrin: Anmerkung zum BGH Beschluss v. 15.6.2016 – XII ZB 419/15, FamRZ 2016, 1446

Lambrecht, Christine: Neuregelung der Sorge für nicht verheiratete Eltern, DRiZ 2010, 318

Lang, Christiane A.: Entwurf eines Gesetzes zur Stärkung der Rechte des leiblichen, nicht rechtlichen Vaters, FPR 2013, 233

Lenz, Albert: Kinder psychisch kranker Eltern – interinstitutionelle Kooperation als Voraussetzung für wirksame Hilfeleistungen, FPR 2005, 246

Lipp, Martin: Das elterliche Sorgerecht für das nichteheliche Kind nach dem Kindschaftsreformgesetz (*KindRG*), FamRZ 1998, 65

Löhnig, Martin: Pendelkinder – Kindeswohl und gleichberechtigte, geteilte elterliche Verantwortung, NZFam 2016, 817

Löhnig, Martin: Lösungsmodelle für das Sorgerecht nicht miteinander verheirateter Eltern – Plädoyer für einen Perspektivenwechsel, in Reformbedarf im nichtehelichen Eltern-Kind-Verhältnis, 10. Göttinger Workshop zum Familienrecht 2011

Luthin, Horst: Übertragung des Entscheidungsrechts betreffend Schutzimpfungen auf einen Elternteil, NZFam 2016, 431

Luthin, Horst: Gemeinsames Sorgerecht nach der Scheidung, Bielefeld 1987

Luthin, Horst: Zur Neuregelung des elterlichen Sorgerechts, FamRZ 1979, 986

Lüblinghoff, Joachim: Das Gesetz zur Änderung des Sachverständigenrechts, NJW 2016, 3329

Lüblinghoff, Joachim: Gutachten in Kindschaftssachen, NZFam 2015, 579

Lüderitz, Alexander: Die Rechtsstellung ehelicher Kinder nach Trennung ihrer Eltern im künftigen Recht der Bundesrepublik Deutschland, FamRZ 1975, 606

Lüderitz, Alexander: Übertragung der elterlichen Gewalt an beide Elternteile nach Scheidung, FamRZ 1971, 625

Maaß, Martin: Wechselmodell ohne Barunterhaltspflicht! – Erwiderung auf die Stellungnahmen von Spangenberg (FamRZ 2016, 1426) und Wohlgemuth (FamRZ 2016, 1427), FamRZ 2016, 1428

Maaß, Martin: Keine Barunterhaltspflicht im echten Wechselmodell, FamRZ 2016, 603

MacCormack, Geoffrey: The spirit of traditional Chinese law, University of Georgia Press, Athens 1996

Mandla, Christoph: Gesetz über den Umfang der Personensorge bei einer Beschneidung des männlichen Kindes, FPR 2013, 244

Manthe, Ulrich: Geschichte des römischen Rechts, C.H.BECK, München 2000

Mayer, Thomas: Der Kindesverbund – Ein Plädoyer, FamRZ 2016, 430

Mayer, Simone: Die Bestellung eines Verfahrensbeistands, jM 2016, 272

Meder, Stephan: Rechtsgeschichte, 4. Auflage, Köln, Weimar, Wien 2011

Menne, Martin: Aktuelle Praxisfragen grenzüberschreitender Kindschaftssachen, FamRB 2015, 359

Mortsiefer, Melanie C.: Die Gefährdungsmitteilung des Jugendamts an das Familiengericht, NJW 2014, 3543

Motzer, Stephan: Neue Tendenzen beim Umgangsrecht, FPR 2007, 275

Mousourakis, George: Roman law and the origins of the civil law traditions, Springer Press, Auckland 2015

Muscheler, Karlheinz: Familienrecht, 4. Auflage, Vahlen Verlag, München 2017

Münchner Kommentar zum *BGB*: Band 8 Familienrecht (§§ 1589–1921), 3. Auflage, C.H.BECK, München 1992; Band 9 Familienrecht II, 7. Auflage, C.H. BECK, München 2017. Cited as *MüKo/Author* (Year), § XXX Rn.

Obermann, Torsten: Normative Strukturen des Umgangs, FamRZ 2016, 1033

Ossenbühl, Fritz: Die Interpretation der Grundrechte in der Rechtsprechung des Bundesverfassungsgerichts, NJW 1976, 2100

Palandt Kommentar zum *BGB*: 77. Auflage, C.H.BECK, München 2018; Cited as *Palandt/Author* (Year), § XXX Rn.

Pätzhorn, Birgitta: Das gemeinsame Sorgerecht der Eltern nach Scheidung in Kalifornien und Deutschland Ein Rechtsvergleich, EMF Bürotechnik GmbH, 2000

Peschel-Gutzeit, Lore Maria: Die neue Regelung zur Beschneidung des männlichen Kindes, NJW 2013, 3617

Peschel-Gutzeit, Lore Maria: Der doppelte Vater – Kritische Überlegung zum Gesetz zur Stärkung der Rechte des leiblichen, nicht rechtlichen Vaters, NJW 2013, 2465

Peschel-Gutzeit, Lore Maria: Die geschichtliche Entwicklung der Vaterstellung im deutschen Recht seit 1900, FPR 2005, 167

Pietzker, Adolf: Häufig vorkommende psychiatrische Erkrankungen im Sorge- und Umgangsverfahren – Beschreibung der Krankheitsbilder, FPR 2005, 222

Plettenberg, Ina: Vater, Vater, Mutter, Kind – Ein Plädoyer für die rechtliche Mehrvaterschaft, Mohr Siebeck Verlag, Tübingen 2016

Raumer, Stefan: Wozu braucht man Deutschland einen EGMR – wenn es ein BVerfG hat? AnwBl. 2011, 195

Rauscher, Thomas: Familienrecht, C.F.Müller Verlag, 2008

Rist, Tobias: Gleichberechtigung und Sorgerecht – Die Stärkung der Rechte der Väter uneheliche Kinder durch den Entwurf zur Reform des Sorgerechts nicht miteinander verheirateter Eltern, in Jura Studium & Examen, Ausgabe 4, 2012

Rixen, Stephan: Das Gesetz über den Umfang der Personensorge bei einer Beschneidung des männlichen Kindes, NJW 2013, 257

Rohmann, Josef: Billigung nach § 156 FamFG, Kindeswohlprüfung und Grenzen der Billigung, FPR 2013, 307

Rotax, Horst-Heiner: Elterliche Sorge und Tod, FPR 2008, 151

Roth-Stielow, Klaus: Nochmals: Der Schwangerschaftsabbruch und die Rolle des künftigen Vaters, NJW 1985, 2746

Röthel, Anne: Autonomie im Familienrecht der Gegenwart, JZ 2017, 117

Rummel, Carsten: Die Freiheit, die Reform des Kindschaftsrechts und das "ganz normale Chaos der Liebe", ZfJ 1997, 202

Salgo, Ludwig: Aktuelle Tendenzen der Verfahrensbeistandschaft, ZKJ 2013, 349

Salzgeber, Joseph: Das Wechselmodell, NZFam 2014, 921

Santos Pais, Marta: 'General introduction to the Convention on the Rights of the Child: from its origin to its implementation', Defence for Children International, Selected essays on international children's rights (1993), Vol. 1

Scharl, Petra/Schmid, Jürgen: Sucht und Persönlichkeitsstörung in Kindschaftssachen, FamRB 2013, 224

Scherer, Inge: Schwangerschaftsabbruch bei Minderjährigen und elterliche Zustimmung, FamRZ 1997, 589

Scherpe, Jens M.: European family law volume I – The impact of institutions and organisations on European family law, Edward Elgar Pub, Cheltenham 2016

Schilling, Roger: Rechtliche Probleme bei der gemeinsamen Sorge nach Trennung bzw. Scheidung, NJW 2007, 3233

Schleicher, Hans: Jugend- und Familienrecht, C.H.BECK, München 2014

Schmid, Jürgen: Juristische Grundsätze zu Umgangsmodellen, NZFam 2014, 881

Schmitt, Stefanie: Das Sorgerecht nichtverheirateter Väter, Nomos & Stämpfli Verlag 2017

Schumann, Eva: Gutachten B zum 72. Deutschen Juristentag, Gemeinsam getragene Elternverantwortung nach Trennung und Scheidung – Reformbedarf im Sorge-, Umgangs- und Unterhaltsrecht? C.H.BECK, München 2018 = NJW-Beil 2018 33

Schwab, Dieter: Familienrecht, 26. Auflage, C.H.BECK, München 2018

Schwab, Dieter/Gottwald, Peter/Lettmaier, Saskia: Family and succession law in Germany, Wolters Kluwer 2017

Schwab, Dieter: Elterliche Sorge und Religion, FamRZ 2014, 1

Schwab, Dieter: Handbuch des Scheidungsrechts, München 1977; 3. Auflage, München 1995; 7. Auflage, Vahlen Verlag, München 2013

Schwab, Dieter: Familie und Staat, FamRZ 2007, 1

Schwab, Dieter: Elterliche Sorge bei Trennung und Scheidung der Eltern, FamRZ 1998, 457

Schwedler, Anna: Die vertrauliche Geburt – Ein Meilenstein für Schwangere in Not? NZFam 2014, 193

Seibert, Helga: Verfassung und Kindschaftsrecht – Neue Entwicklungen und offene Fragen, FamRZ 1995, 1457

Siedhoff, Eckhardt: Schwangerschaftsabbruch bei Minderjährigen und elterliche Zustimmung, FamRZ 1998, 8

Sommer, Anja: Die Rechtsstellung des Kindes im familiengerichtlichen Verfahren, FPR 2012, 376

Söpper, Silvia: Handy und Umgangsrecht, FamRZ 2002, 7

Spangenberg, Ernst: Wechselmodell ohne Barunterhaltspflicht? – Stellungnahme zu Maaß FamRZ 2016, 603, FamRZ 2016, 1426

Spickhoff, Andreas: Grund, Voraussetzungen und Grenzen des Sorgerechts bei Beschneidung männlicher Kinder, FamRZ 2013, 337

Staudinger Kommentar zu *BGB*: Cited as *Staudinger/Author* (Year), § XXX Rn.

Sünderhauf, Hildegund: Vorurteile gegen das Wechselmodell: Was stimmt, was nicht? Argumente in der Rechtsprechung und Erkenntnisse aus der psychologischen Forschung, FamRB 2013, 333

Sünderhauf, Hildegund: Wechselmodell: Psychologie-Recht-Praxis, Springer VS, Wiesbaden 2013

Vogel, Harald: Die Untätigkeitsbeschwerde im Familienrecht, FPR 2009, 165

Wabnitz, Reinhard Joachim: Mitwirkung der Jugendhilfe in familiengerichtlichen Verfahren – Rechtsgrundlagen, Aufgaben, Selbstverständnis, ZfJ 2000, 336

Walter, Tonio: Der Gesetzesentwurf zur Beschneidung – Kritik und strafrechtliche Alternative, JZ 2012, 1110

Weber, Albrecht: Die Entwicklung des Familienrechts seit Mitte 2015, NJW 2016, 3076

Weber, Albrecht: Die Entwicklung des Familienrechts seit Mitte 2014, NJW 2015, 3068

Weber, Albrecht: Die Entwicklung des Familienrechts seit Mitte 2013, NJW 2014, 3072

Willutzki, Siegfried: Der Schutzauftrag des Jugendamtes im neuen Recht, FPR 2008, 488

Willutzki, Siegfried: Familiengericht und Jugendamt – neue Formen der Zusammenarbeit, ZfJ 1994, 202

Winkel, Georg: Grenzüberschreitendes Sorge- und Umgangsrecht und dessen Vollstreckung, Gieseking 2001

Wohlgemuth, Gisela: Zum Vorschlag von Maaß FamRZ 2016, 603, FamRZ 2016, 1427

Won, Tayy-Yih: Das taiwanesische Sorgerecht der Eltern nach der Ehescheidung im Vergleich mit dem deutschen Recht, Köln 2001

Yang, Bojun: Interpretation of the analects of Confucius, Zhonghua Book Company, Beijing 1980

Zekoll, Joachim/Reimann, Matthias: Introduction to German law, Wolters Kluwer Law & Business, München 2005

Zhang, Jinfan: The tradition and modern transition of Chinese law, Springer Verlag, Berlin Heidelberg 2014

Zivier, Ezra: Die neuen gesetzlichen Regelungen zur Umgangspflegschaft, ZKJ 2010, 306

Zorn, Dagmar: Das Recht der elterlichen Sorge, 3. Auflage, Walter de Gruyter 2016

www.ingramcontent.com/pod-product-compliance
Ingram Content Group UK Ltd.
Pitfield, Milton Keynes, MK11 3LW, UK
UKHW021014120926
8556IPUK00040B/1126

9 783631 838372